THE
BIG BOOK
OF
Small
HOUSEHOLD
REPAIRS

THE BIG BOOK OF
Small
HOUSEHOLD REPAIRS

YOUR GOOF-PROOF GUIDE TO FIXING OVER 200 ANNOYING BREAKDOWNS

Charlie Wing

Rodale Press, Inc.
Emmaus, Pennsylvania

OUR MISSION

We publish books that empower people's lives.

RODALE BOOKS

Printed in the United States of America on acid-free ∞, recycled ♻ paper

The Big Book of Small Household Repairs
Editorial Staff
Editor: **Robert A. Yoder**
Interior Book Designer: **Frank M. Milloni**
Cover Designer (hardcover): **Jerry O'Brien**
Cover Designer (paperback):
    Randall Sauchuck
Cover and Interior Illustrator: **Charlie Wing**
Copy Editor: **Nancy N. Bailey**
Manufacturing Coordinator: **Patrick T. Smith**
Indexer: **Nan N. Badgett**

Rodale Books
Editorial Director, Home and Garden:
    Margaret Lydic Balitas
Managing Editor, Woodworking and DIY
    Books: **Kevin Ireland**
Art Director, Home and Garden:
    Michael Mandarano
Associate Art Director, Home and Garden:
    Mary Ellen Fanelli
Copy Director, Home and Garden:
    Dolores Plikaitis
Office Manager, Home and Garden:
    Karen Earl-Braymer
Editor-in-Chief: **William Gottlieb**

If you have any questions or comments concerning this book, please write to:

Rodale Press, Inc.
Book Readers' Service
33 East Minor Street
Emmaus, PA 18098

Library of Congress Cataloging-in-Publication Data
Wing, Charlie, date.
    The big book of small household repairs : your goof-proof guide to fixing over 200 annoying breakdowns / Charlie Wing.
        p.   cm.
    Includes index.
    ISBN 0–87596–649–7 hardcover
    ISBN 0–87596–752–3 paperback
    1. Dwellings—Maintenance and repair—Amateurs' manuals. 2. Household appliances—Maintenance and repair—Amateurs' manuals.
I. Title.
TH4817.3.W56   1995
643'.7—dc20   95–7408

Distributed in the book trade by St. Martin's Press

2 4 6 8 10 9 7 5 3   hardcover
2 4 6 8 10 9 7 5 3   paperback

To John Totman of the Sebasco Lodge Repairatorium,
Master of Zen and the art of repair

Contents

ELECTRICAL

FLOORS

FURNISHINGS

HEATING & COOLING

INSULATION

LAWN & GARDEN

MASONRY

PLUMBING

ROOFING & SIDING

WALLS & CEILINGS

WINDOWS

INTRODUCTION

I have been writing books on home building and home repair for 20 years. With the courage and naïveté that bless the inexperienced, I first coauthored *From the Ground Up*—a book that promised to answer not only questions of home building but also some of the thornier issues of human existence. In succeeding books, my focus has narrowed but with increased detail. This effort, number ten, is the logical conclusion to that process. *The Big Book of Small Household Repairs* is designed to provide detailed solutions to all of the annoying little problems homeowners suffer.

Isn't this the opposite of progress? I think not. I have come to realize that a majority of homeowners live lives of quiet resignation, hostage in their own homes to a myriad of minor, yet aggravating, defects. These defects are too small to warrant the attention of $50-an-hour professionals (or the homeowners' wallets are too slim), so the defects persist, like pebbles in a shoe.

Why do homeowners tolerate these pebbles? Visit any bookstore and you will see that there are dozens of books containing the solutions. Some of these books are virtual encyclopedias of home building and repair. A Martian, new to our planet, given these books and access to the local home center, could build himself (or herself) the American Dream. In the same bookstore, however, you will find shelves full of cookbooks—ten times as many cookbooks as home repair books. Cookbooks are used day in and day out; home repair books are not.

Why are cookbooks so often used while home repair books gather dust? Why do

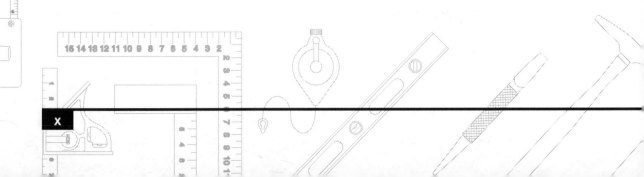

my wife and millions of other home-makers think nothing of tackling a new recipe, with dozens of ingredients and steps, while the bathroom door still won't latch? It's because cookbooks do not intimidate their readers; cookbooks do not require that you understand the chemistry of foods and possess every kitchen implement ever invented. On a single page they list the quantities of ingredients, the basic utensils, and simple step-by-step directions guaranteed to result in the mouth-watering four-color concoction "shown in the photo at right."

I will tell you a secret. *The Big Book of Small Household Repairs* is my cookbook. I wanted to call the materials "ingredients," the tools "utensils," and the step-by-step directions "recipes," but the publishers wouldn't let me. They said book buyers and readers would be confused; they would not know whether it was a cookbook or a home repair book. But it doesn't matter what the publishers call it—in my mind, it is a cookbook of home repair. Keep it in your workshop or keep it in your kitchen, but start cooking up repairs today.

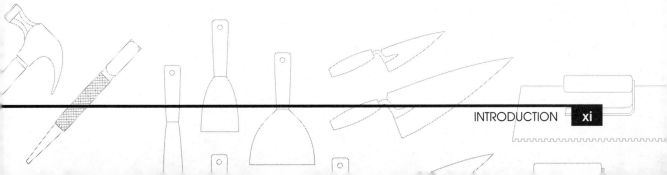

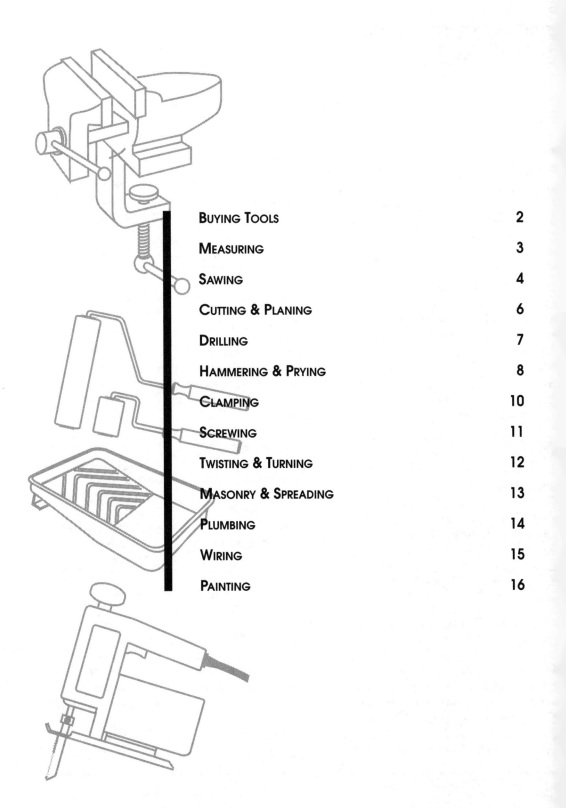

Nothing is more discouraging to a person doing home repairs than using inferior tools. Driving a difficult screw with a toy screwdriver is like trying to play a horn concerto on a kazoo. Well, things are looking up in the tool department.

Remember when "Made in Japan" was synonymous with shoddy? Japanese automobiles sure changed that attitude. And can you find a single electronic item that is not made offshore today? While a brand name is still an indication of quality, it is now possible to get a serviceable substitute for one-third the price. Even the big chain stores are importing tools—increasingly from China—under their own names. Top-of-the-line Craftsman tools are still guaranteed for life, but notice that Sears now carries a second line of tools under the Sears brand. Least expensive of all are imported product lines with American-sounding names, such as "Central Forge" and "Pittsburgh."

How can you tell if a tool is good? First read the following discussion of tools to get a sense of how the tool is used and which characteristics are critical. Then handle the tool. Does it look good, or is it rough around the edges? Does it feel good? Do moving parts operate smoothly, or do they bind? If the tool has a warranty, will the retailer you bought it from replace it, or do you have to send the tool to a location across the country for postage exceeding the original purchase price?

Toolbox or Bag? I'll never forget how I learned to carry my tools in a bag. Through ignorance and laziness, I had managed to ruin my boat's diesel engine. I had built and rebuilt half a dozen houses, but rebuilding a diesel engine was definitely beyond my capability, so I called a certified diesel mechanic. When he arrived, I was speechless. He arrived in the requisite pickup truck and was wearing the ex-

pected coveralls, but he was carrying his tools in a lady's leather handbag. "I'm paying this guy $45 an hour?" I thought to myself, but I bit my lip. In an hour he had muscled the 400-pound engine into his pickup, and two days later he was back with the good-as-new engine. I was impressed, so I asked why he carried his tools in a lady's handbag.

"This bag doesn't rust, it doesn't scratch floors, and it's easy to carry up ladders. Got it at Goodwill for 50 cents."

You can buy a canvas tool bag with 24 pockets for $15. My present bag is a nifty Liz Claiborne model I got down at Goodwill for a buck.

What to Buy. The kit below was determined by counting the number of repairs in which each tool appears in this book. Each list can be purchased without breaking the bank by watching sales.

Starter Kit

Screwdriver set	Slip-joint pliers
Utility knife	Wood chisel
Hammer	Carpenter's square
Drill and bits	Nail set
Putty knife	Receptacle tester
Adjustable wrench	Wire brush
Tape measure	Cold chisel
Long-nose pliers	Crosscut saw
Paintbrushes	Hacksaw
Pry bar	Plastic goggles

Wish List for Next Christmas

Diagonal-cutting pliers	Staple gun
Groove-joint pliers	Wire stripper
Neon circuit tester	Block plane
Triangular trowel	Combination square
Caulking gun	Flat file
Metal snips	Keyhole saw
Multitester	Locking pliers

MEASURING

Tape Measure. The tape measure is used to measure length, width, height, and inside, outside, and around distances. To measure inside distances—such as between window casings—add the width shown on the tape case to the tape reading. To measure the diameter of a cylinder, measure the circumference and divide by 3.14. *Recommendation:* Buy a brand-name, 16-foot tape measure with a lock.

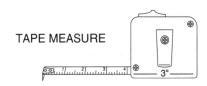

TAPE MEASURE

Carpenter's Square. The 18 × 24-inch carpenter's square is used more for drawing lines for sawing and establishing 90-degree angles than for measuring. The long, metal blades also serve as straightedges for guiding a utility knife blade. *Recommendation:* Buy an inexpensive, steel carpenter's square with deeply stamped markings.

CARPENTER'S SQUARE

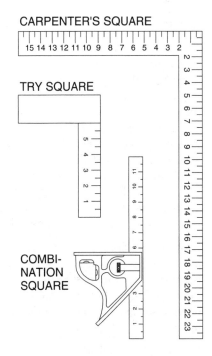

TRY SQUARE

Try Square. A smaller version of the carpenter's square is the 6 × 8-inch try square, used to establish 90-degree cuts on framing material and other narrow boards. Although the carpenter's square can be used for the same purpose, it is unwieldy. *Recommendation:* Buy an inexpensive, flat blade, steel try square with deeply stamped markings.

Combination Square. Marking cuts at both 90 and 45 degrees, measuring depth, drawing straight lines, marking parallel lines, and establishing both level and vertical—the combination square does everything the try square does and more, so purchase the combination square first. *Recommendation:* Look for the model that has the best protection for the level bubbles.

COMBI-NATION SQUARE

Carpenter's Level. Levels range in length from 2 inches (a line level that hangs from a string) to 4-foot professional models. A good compromise is a 2-foot model with horizontal, vertical, and 45-degree level bubbles. Make sure the one you purchase has either excellent bubble protection or replaceable levels. *Recommendation:* Buy an inexpensive, plastic 2-foot level with three bubbles.

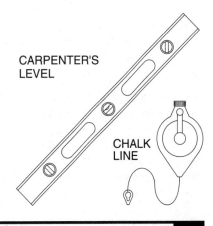

CARPENTER'S LEVEL

CHALK LINE

Chalk Line. If you coat a string with powdered chalk, stretch it tightly, and pluck it, the string will deposit a straight line of chalk. The modern chalk line is a reel within a refillable container of chalk dust. A hook at the end of the string allows the line to be stretched and plucked by one person. *Recommendation:* Buy an extra container of chalk.

SAWING

Saws come in many different shapes and sizes, but good technique for all hand saws is the same. Follow these tips:

- Cut on the waste side of the line.

- Start the cut on a pull stroke.

- Take long, light strokes.

- Resharpen or replace the blade when the cut wanders.

Crosscut Saw. The name comes from the fact that it is designed to cut across wood grain. It will also cut in the direction of the grain, but the ripsaw is faster. The crosscut saw is also the saw of choice for plywood that has grain in both directions. The teeth are fine, ranging from 8 to 14 per inch. To cut a board, rest or clamp the board in a horizontal position, place one hand on the board, and cut downward at a 45-degree angle with the other hand. If the saw binds, wedge the blade of a screwdriver in the cut to spread the wood. Hold the end of the board toward the end of the cut to prevent splintering. *Recommendation:* Buy a brand-name saw with a 26-inch blade and 9 teeth per inch.

Ripsaw. Designed to rip in the direction of the grain—along the length of a board—the ripsaw has five to six coarse teeth per inch. Ripping should be done on the downstroke, angled at 60 degrees. *Recommendation:* If you need to saw a lot of boards lengthwise, buy a circular saw instead.

Backsaw. The backsaw gets its name from the rigid spline that stiffens its back. Its purpose is to make very accurate, fine, straight cuts across the grain. It is often used in a miter box that has slots to hold the saw at precise angles of 45 and 90 degrees. *Recommendation:* Buy a 12-inch saw with 12 teeth per inch and an inexpensive wood miter box.

Keyhole Saw. The blade of a keyhole saw is less than 1 inch wide and 10 inches long with ten teeth per inch. The blade tapers to a point, allowing the start of a cut from a small predrilled hole. The keyhole saw's narrow blade allows it to cut tight curves. *Recommendation:* Buy an inexpensive keyhole saw with pistol grip.

CROSSCUT SAW AND RIPSAW

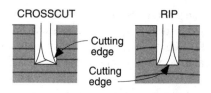

CROSSCUT · RIP

Cutting edge

Cutting edge

BACK SAW IN A MITER BOX

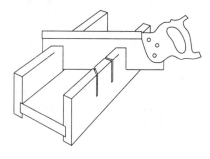

KEYHOLE SAW

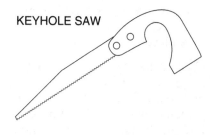

Coping Saw. The blade of a coping saw is extremely thin, allowing the blade to follow very sharp curves. The flexible blade is strung under tension in a C-shaped frame. Because the frame is on both sides of the material being cut, the depth of the frame—the throat—should be deep. The blade can also be rotated 360 degrees within the frame. Flat blades are about 5 inches long with 15 to 20 teeth per inch. Round blades cut in any direction without rotating the blade. *Recommendation:* Buy a selection of blades for cutting wood, plastic, and metal.

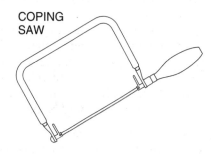

COPING SAW

Hacksaw. The hacksaw is a versatile saw for cutting almost any material but it is used primarily for metal. Blades are available in lengths of 8, 10, and 12 inches, with 14 to 32 teeth per inch. The frame can be adjusted to accommodate different length blades and rotated in increments of 90 degrees. Cut on the down stroke using both hands to apply steady moderate pressure. *Recommendation:* Buy a hacksaw with a heavy frame, a rubber handle, and an assortment of 12-inch blades.

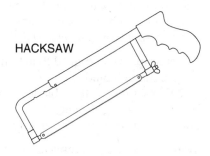

HACKSAW

Saber Saw. Don't throw your other saws away, but if you get into home repair, you'll soon want a saber saw. With the proper blades, the electric saber saw can do everything the crosscut, keyhole, coping, and hacksaws can—and without the expenditure of elbow grease. The better saws have variable speed and rotating—scrolling—heads. *Recommendation:* Buy a variable-speed, scrolling saw with a variety of blades.

SABER SAW

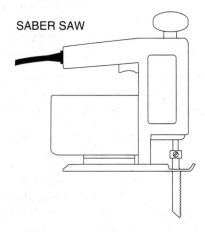

Cutting & Planing

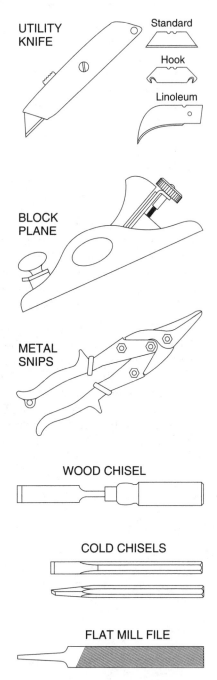

UTILITY KNIFE

Standard

Hook

Linoleum

BLOCK PLANE

METAL SNIPS

WOOD CHISEL

COLD CHISELS

FLAT MILL FILE

Utility Knife. The usefulness of a utility knife is due to the retractable, replaceable, incredibly strong, and razor-sharp blade. Blades are available in several shapes, including standard straight, hook, and linoleum. Nonretractable versions are less expensive, but the danger of having a razor-sharp blade in a pocket or tool bag outweighs the savings.
Recommendation: Buy a brand-name, retractable version with at least ten extra standard blades.

Block Plane. Planes are wood chisels set into bodies to control the depth of cut. A short body allows the blade to follow curves, while a long body evens irregular surfaces. The block plane is the shortest of the planes and is designed to cut across end grain, such as the end of a board. Always set the blade for minimum depth, and plane from the edge toward the center to avoid splintering. *Recommendation:* Buy a block plane first.

Metal Snips. More rugged than household shears, metal snips can cut through mild steel sheet metal up to 0.05 inches thick. Aviation snips have three blade designs, indicated by handle color, to cut straight (yellow), right curves (green), and left curves (red). *Recommendation:* Buy yellow aviation snips.

Wood Chisels. If you can learn to use wood chisels only for their intended use—slicing clean wood—you will develop a love for these ancient tools. Use one just once as a screwdriver or pry bar, however, and you'll have to sharpen it—no easy task for a novice. Plastic and steel-capped chisels can be struck lightly with a hammer. *Recommendation:* Buy a four-piece set, 1/4 inch to 1 inch, with steel-capped handles.

Cold Chisel. Less sharp but tougher than wood chisels, a cold chisel is designed to cut through metal and masonry. A cold chisel's hard temper makes it susceptible to chipping, so wear plastic goggles when striking one with a hammer. *Recommendation:* Buy a 1/2-inch flat cold chisel.

Flat Mill File. Metal files are like a series of closely spaced planes, hard tempered to smooth and remove metal. The mill file, with parallel teeth in one direction, is best at smoothing steel and sharpening blades. The bastard file, with teeth in two directions, is better and faster at smoothing nonferrous metals. File teeth require frequent cleaning with a wire brush. *Recommendation:* Buy an 8-inch, flat mill file.

DRILLING

A drill is a mechanical device for holding and twisting a bit—the tool that does the cutting. For very light jobs, nothing beats a small manual drill. For heavy jobs, such as drilling large holes or driving many screws, an electric drill is indispensable. The cordless electric drill combines the best features of the manual and the electric.

Manual Drill. The drill shown comes with a selection of wood bits, but other bits can be used. Most manual drills can handle bits up to $1/4$ inch but are useless for either spade or masonry bits or for driving screws. *Recommendation:* Buy a small, plastic, ergonomic drill.

Electric Drill. These drills come in different sizes that can hold bits with shanks up to $1/4$, $3/8$, or $1/2$ inch. Better drills have variable-speed triggers and are reversible in direction. Cordless drills are usually $3/8$-inch, variable speed, and reversible since they are used for driving screws more often than for drilling holes. *Recommendation:* Buy a $3/8$-inch, variable speed drill if you will be using the drill rarely; a $3/8$-inch, variable speed, reversible, cordless drill if you plan to use it at least once a month.

Twist Bits. The best general-purpose bits for occasional drilling in both wood and metal are standard twist bits, available in sizes from $1/16$ inch to $1/2$ inch in $1/64$-inch increments. Materials to consider, in order of increasing life and cost, are high-speed steel, titanium-coated high-speed steel, and cobalt. *Recommendation:* Buy a 13-piece, $1/16$-inch to $1/4$-inch, titanium-coated set.

Spade Bits. Also known as woodboring bits, spade bits work well boring holes up to 1 inch in diameter. They are available in sizes from $1/4$ inch to 1 inch in $1/16$-inch increments. Do not even think about using these bits in metal, no matter how soft. They are easily dulled, but they can be sharpened with a small flat file. *Recommendation:* Buy a five-piece set, from $1/4$ inch to 1 inch in $1/8$-inch increments, with a shank extension.

Masonry Bits. Using either twist bits or spade bits on masonry will rapidly dull their cutting edges. The carbide tips of masonry bits will not dull, although the bits are next to useless for drilling other types of material. *Recommendation:* Buy a small set, including at least $1/4$-inch, $3/8$-inch, and $1/2$-inch bits.

MANUAL DRILL

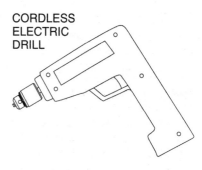

CORDLESS ELECTRIC DRILL

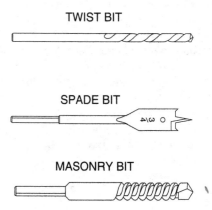

TWIST BIT

SPADE BIT

MASONRY BIT

Hammering & Prying

Hammer. Although it is designed specifically for hammering and removing nails, the curved-claw hammer can perform most hammering tasks. In fact, the curved-claw hammer is so common that we even refer to it simply as a hammer. A good hammer is a thing of beauty—it looks good, it feels good, and it works well. Look for a name-brand model with a smoothly machined head, precisely beveled claw, and wood, cushioned-metal, or fiberglass handle. If you are not very strong, consider a 10-ounce version for small household repairs. For general carpentry, a standard 13- or 16-ounce model is better. Wear safety glasses when hammering any hardened metal such as concrete nails and cold chisels. *Recommendation:* Buy a 13-ounce, curved-claw hammer with a fiberglass handle.

Tack Hammer. For driving brads and tacks, the 13-ounce hammer is awkward. Enter the tack hammer, weighing in at a mere 5 ounces with a magnetic head for starting tacks without smashing your fingers. Tip: If you don't have a tack hammer, hold the tack with long-nose pliers instead of your fingers. For nonmagnetic fasteners, pass the tip of the fastener through a piece of masking tape, then stick the masking tape to the hammer head. The masking tape is easily removed just before the fastener is driven home. *Recommendation:* Buy any model with a magnetic head.

Nail Sets. All nail heads are smaller than the face of the smallest hammer. So how do you hammer a nail flush or below the surface? You use a nail set with a tip just smaller than the nail head. Do not confuse the nail set, which has a cupped head, with a center punch, which looks the same but has a pointed tip. Center punches are used to start holes and will slip off a nail head and make an ugly hole if used as a nail set. With tiny finish nails, it is permissible to use a nail set that is larger than the nail head since the dent made by the nail set will be tiny in any case. *Recommendation:* Buy two nail sets, including one set with the smallest head you can find.

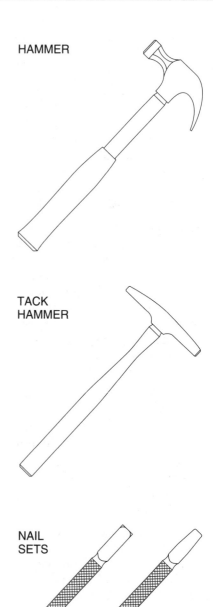

HAMMER

TACK HAMMER

NAIL SETS

Sledge Hammer. Sledges, ranging in weight from 2 pounds to 20 pounds, are for when you really need to pound. The lighter sledges—also known as baby sledges or X-pound hammers—have hammer-length handles. The big sledges have axe-length handles for swinging over your head. Except for breaking up large concrete slabs, a baby sledge will accomplish all of your household tasks. *Recommendation:* Buy a 3-pound sledge with a wood handle.

Mallet. A mallet should be used when hitting wood parts. It is less likely to mar the wood than a metal hammer. If all of the tools you plan to hammer have metal or metal-capped handles, you can dispense with the mallet. For hammering wood objects together—such as chair legs and rungs—keep a wood block scrap in your tool kit to place between the object and your hammer. *Recommendation:* Unless you are a cabinetmaker, you don't need a mallet.

Staple Gun. In the good old days staples were a sign of shoddy construction, but staples are now the accepted method for light fastening as well as for roofing and siding. The most common construction staples are $1/2$ inch wide and range in length from $1/4$ inch to $9/16$ inch in $1/16$-inch increments. For most applications, standard steel staples are acceptable. For outdoor or wet applications, choose stainless-steel staples. *Recommendation:* Buy a name-brand model taking T-50 staples.

Pry Bar. There are many tools designed for prying. Mechanics' pry bars are used to move heavy objects; wrecking or ripping bars are used for demolishing buildings; cat's paws are used to remove recessed nails. The flat pry bar shown is designed for nondestructive nail pulling and wedging. All varieties of pry bars are available in a range of sizes. *Recommendation:* Buy a 12- to 15-inch flat pry bar.

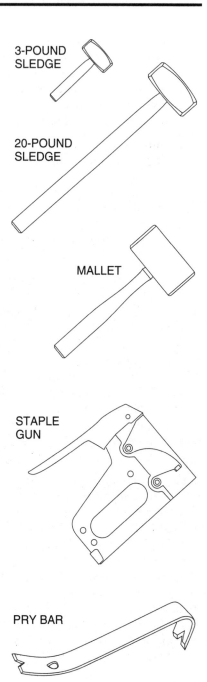

3-POUND SLEDGE

20-POUND SLEDGE

MALLET

STAPLE GUN

PRY BAR

CLAMPING

You will, on occasion, want to clamp an object down while you work on it, sometimes for control, sometimes for safety. With ingenuity and a sturdy table, bench, or countertop you can get by at first with humble C-clamps. Later, with all the money you've saved by doing your own repairs, you can afford more specialized clamps.

C-Clamps. Aptly named, C-clamps can be used to clamp objects together for gluing or assembling or to clamp them to a secure base while you perform shaping operations. The size of a C-clamp refers to the maximum opening. Use scraps of wood between the clamped piece and the jaws to prevent marring. Since C-clamps are not precise instruments, it is better to purchase more rather than better clamps. *Recommendation:* Start with two inexpensive 4-inch clamps.

Locking C-Clamp. Adapting the jaws of regular locking pliers turns them into a quick-clamp version of the C-clamp. Like regular locking pliers, this clamp requires precision forming and machining and is thus expensive. Try the adjusting screw over its full range before buying one since the quality of the screw threads is the chief difference between a high-quality clamp and a cheap knock-off. *Recommendation:* Buy one or more 11-inch swivel-pad clamps—to minimize marring—but only if you do a lot of repetitive assembly operations.

Bench Vise. The bench vise with flat or curved jaws and an anvil for shaping metal is designed for mechanics. It can be used for woodworking projects by slipping thin scraps of wood between the jaws and the work piece. More specialized than the bench vise, a woodworking vise has large, flat, smooth jaws that are designed to grip wood without marring. It mounts flush with the top of the work surface and is suitable only for mounting permanently on a workbench. *Recommendation:* Buy an inexpensive bench vise with 4-inch jaws. If your workbench is the kitchen table or countertop, consider the clamp-on version shown in the illustration at right.

C-CLAMP

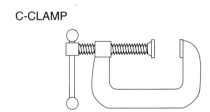

LOCKING
C-CLAMP

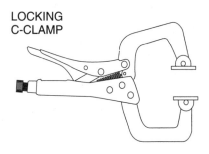

BENCH
VISE

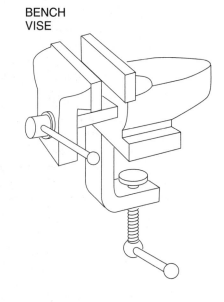

SCREWING

Slotted Screwdrivers. You will come to hate the slotted screw. Unless the screwdriver tip fits the slot exactly in both thickness and width, the tip will often damage the screw head to the point that it can neither be driven further nor removed. This is why the quality and size of screwdriver tip is so important. *Recommendation:* Buy a set of standard screwdrivers with $1/4$-inch, $5/16$-inch, and $3/8$-inch tips, or a driver with replaceable tips. In addition, buy a stubby version with a $1/4$-inch tip.

Phillips Screwdrivers. A Phillips screw offers the advantage that the crossed-slot design keeps the tip of the screwdriver centered. Two sizes of heads predominate: one-point and two-point. *Recommendation:* Buy two Phillips screwdrivers with one-point and two-point tips, or a driver with those insert tips.

Offset Screwdriver. Sometimes there is not room even for the $1^{1}/2$-inch stubby screwdriver to work. Enter the offset screwdriver. *Recommendation:* Buy either one with slotted and Phillips heads at opposite ends or a ratcheting model that accepts insert tips.

Insert Tips. With insert tips, the reversible, variable-speed electric drill becomes a power screwdriver at no additional cost. If a tip breaks, you need only replace the inexpensive tip rather than the whole screwdriver. And, when you are on a ladder, you need only one screwdriver instead of a set. *Recommendation:* Buy a magnetic insert tip holder and several different sizes of slotted and Phillips insert tips.

Nutdrivers. Nutdrivers are like screwdrivers, except that they drive nuts. You can purchase nutdriver tips to fit your insert screwdriver or electric drill. *Recommendation:* Buy five drivers, either as insert tips or with handles, from $1/4$ inch to $1/2$ inch.

Allen Wrenches. Those little screws with no heads and hexagonal holes in place of slots are called setscrews. The tools for driving and removing them are Allen wrenches—also known as hex keys. *Recommendation:* Buy a "jackknife" set of eight, from 0.05 inch to $15/32$ inch. Larger sizes and metric versions can be bought individually as the need arises.

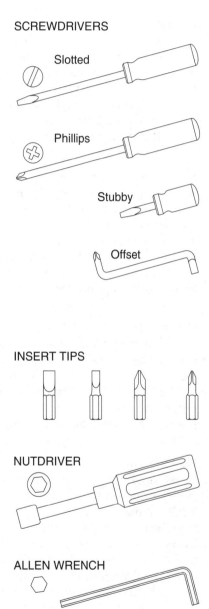

SCREWDRIVERS

Slotted

Phillips

Stubby

Offset

INSERT TIPS

NUTDRIVER

ALLEN WRENCH

Adjustable Wrenches. With both English and metric open-end wrenches, you would end up with a 50-pound tool bag. Several good adjustable wrenches replace the need for both sets in normal home maintenance. Before purchasing low-cost adjustable wrenches, try adjusting the jaws. The jaws of high-quality wrenches open and close smoothly without hanging up. *Recommendation:* Buy either a single 8-inch wrench or a set of 6-, 8-, and 10-inch wrenches.

ADJUSTABLE WRENCH

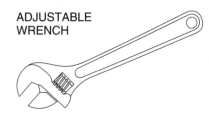

Slip-Joint Pliers. As useful as the adjustable wrench, slip-joint pliers have deep teeth and adjustable jaws to grip odd-shaped objects, as well as square and hexagonal nuts and bolts. Use adjustable wrenches to turn nuts and bolts; use slip-joint pliers to turn round and odd-shaped items as well as loosely fastened nuts and bolts. *Recommendation:* There is nothing very precise about the tool, so buy an inexpensive single 8-inch pliers or a set of 6-, 8-, and 10-inch pliers.

SLIP-JOINT PLIERS

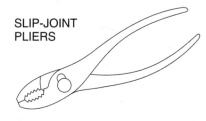

Groove-Joint Pliers. The logical extension of slip-joint pliers are groove-joint pliers. Instead of two positions, the jaws can be set to slide in any one of five grooves so that the jaws are effective over a considerable range of openings. The long handles nearly touch when the jaws are set in the proper groove so that you can grip them with maximum pressure. *Recommendation:* As with slip-joint pliers, this is not a precision tool, so buy an inexpensive 10-inch model.

GROOVE-JOINT PLIERS

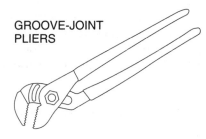

Locking Pliers. Also known by the original trade name, Vise-Grips, locking pliers are the ultimate pliers. The jaws are opened with a knob until they fit around an object, then the compound-leverage handles are squeezed shut, resulting in a veritable death grip on the object. Every time I use locking pliers, I think of how lucky I am not to be the object in the jaws. In fact, the only drawback is that they often leave a lasting impression, even on metal objects. The compound-leverage handle mechanism has been adapted to a wide variety of jaws, from needle-nose to C-clamp. *Recommendation:* Buy a brand-name, curved claw, 10-inch model with the standard jaws shown in the illustration at right.

LOCKING PLIERS

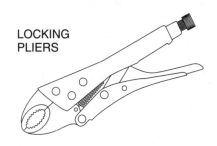

MASONRY & SPREADING

Triangular Trowel. The tool most associated with masonry is the triangular bricklayer's trowel. With this one tool, the mason can scoop up, spread, and smooth mortar. A smaller version is the pointing trowel. *Recommendation:* You will be using a trowel for minor repairs, so buy the pointing trowel.

Steel Trowel. The steel trowel has a very smooth, flat, rectangular blade and is used to apply the final finish to concrete surfaces. *Recommendation:* Purchase a steel trowel only if you need to smooth a large concrete surface.

Rubber-Edged Grout Float (not illustrated). Whether you are merely regrouting tile joints or tiling a new floor or wall, you will want the rubber-edged grout float for filling the joints with grout. The rubber edge acts like a squeegee in wiping the tile surface and depositing the grout in the joints. *Recommendation:* Buy one if you are going to work on more than a single tile.

Pointing Tool. A pointing tool forms the final shape of the mortar joint between masonry units. Various mortar joints are possible—concave, flush, raked, struck, V-shaped, and weathered. *Recommendation:* Buy the concave pointing tool.

Putty Knives. Developed for the purpose of applying window putty, putty knives are the tools to use for spreading materials having the consistency of peanut butter. Since it is impossible to achieve a perfectly smooth surface unless the blade is wider than the area being covered, the wide putty knife is twice as wide as the standard putty knife. It is often used after the standard putty knife to apply a wider second coat. As part of a geometric series, the 6-inch drywall knife is twice as wide as the wide putty knife. The width of putty knives increases geometrically so that successive coats of drywall compound can taper to a flatter finish. *Recommendation:* Buy one of each width.

Notched Spreader. The notched spreader is nothing more than a flat blade with square notches. As the toothed edge of the spreader is dragged across the floor, adhesive flows from the notches, resulting in a perfectly uniform distribution of adhesive. *Recommendation:* For small areas, buy a throwaway plastic spreader; buy a steel spreader only if installing a whole floor.

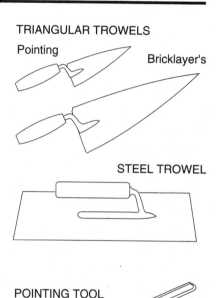

TRIANGULAR TROWELS

Pointing

Bricklayer's

STEEL TROWEL

POINTING TOOL

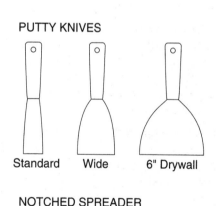

PUTTY KNIVES

Standard   Wide   6" Drywall

NOTCHED SPREADER

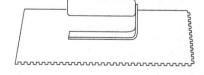

Plunger. If the water won't move, we'll plunge it until it does! The plunger and good old elbow grease work most of the time. *Recommendation:* Buy a funnel-cup plunger.

Hand Auger. In the old days, one had to coil a dripping, offensive snake by hand after each use. Luckily, some genius invented the spooling mechanism shown in the illustration at right. To use the hand auger, push the flexible snake into the drain until resistance is met, tighten the locknut, and turn the handle clockwise while pushing on the body. The spiral hook at the end will either bore through a soap or grease blockage or snag fibrous material so that it can be retrieved. *Recommendation:* Buy this tool only if the need arises.

Closet Auger. Specially adapted to the toilet, the closet auger is short and stiff because nine times in ten the blockage is just beyond the first bend and is formidable. Unfortunately, many objects flushed down a toilet are not susceptible to being snagged by the tip of an auger. Tip: If the toilet drains at all, flush one end of a hand towel down the toilet while holding on to the other end. When the towel has nearly disappeared, yank on it and—voilà!—out comes the comb, toothbrush, aerosol cap, or whatever was too hard to be snagged by the auger. *Recommendation:* Buy an inexpensive closet auger.

Pipe Wrenches. Pipe wrenches resemble bench vises on long handles. They are often used in pairs—one to grip the pipe, the other to grip the fitting. Otherwise you may find that, by allowing the pipe to turn, you have loosened a connection inside the wall or floor instead of the one intended. *Recommendation:* Buy low-cost 10-inch and 18-inch wrenches.

Basin Wrench. This is a wrench you may never need, but if you do, there will be no other solution. It has spring-loaded jaws on a swivel and a long handle so that you can reach up behind a sink to turn the faucet supply slip nuts. *Recommendation:* Since there is usually room for locking pliers, don't buy one until you need it.

Spud Wrench. There are two plumbing nuts that are very large, yet do not require much torque—the locknut securing a sink drain and the spud nut securing a toilet tank drain. The spud wrench is perfect for both. It is available fixed and adjustable. *Recommendation:* Buy the adjustable version.

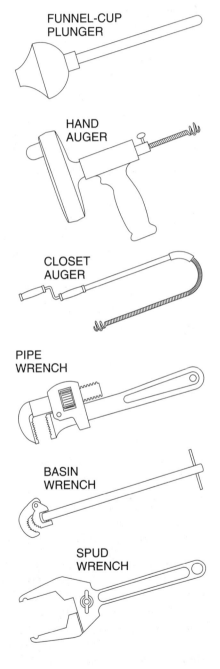

FUNNEL-CUP PLUNGER

HAND AUGER

CLOSET AUGER

PIPE WRENCH

BASIN WRENCH

SPUD WRENCH

Diagonal-Cutting Pliers. Anyone doing electrical repairs should have a good pair of diagonal-cutting pliers. You will soon find that they are useful for a variety of other tasks as well. *Recommendation:* Buy a 7-inch, brand-name model.

Long-Nose Pliers. Nothing beats long-nose pliers in reaching into small spaces and for forming loops in the ends of wire. The jaws are subject to high stress, so quality is important. *Recommendation:* Buy a 7- to 8-inch, brand-name model.

Wire Stripper. A variety of tools are called wire strippers. Most perform only that task. Also known as the electrician's multipurpose tool, the wire stripper shown in the illustration at right strips insulation, cuts wire, measures the size of wire, cuts small bolts, and crimps terminals and wires. *Recommendation:* Buy a brand-name kit that includes an assortment of insulated wires and terminals.

Receptacle Tester. Plug a receptacle tester into a receptacle and the three little lights will tell you exactly what is ailing the circuit—whether it be alive, dead, or potentially deadly! *Recommendation:* Get one at any hardware store or Radio Shack and test all of your receptacles today.

Neon Circuit Tester. For less than the price of a quarter-pound burger, the neon circuit tester will tell you whether it is safe to touch a wire. Unclip it from your shirt pocket, hold one probe to the metallic box or bare wire, touch the other probe to the wire in question, and you'll have your answer: If the neon bulb glows, the wire is "hot." *Recommendation:* Buy one at any hardware store or Radio Shack.

Multitester. Also known as a multimeter and a VOM (volt ohm meter), the multitester will measure voltage, current, or resistance—in any circuit—whether AC or DC. You may associate multitesters with electronic technicians. Do you also think that only French chefs are qualified to use French whips? All that is required to measure volts, amps, and ohms is to turn the selector switch to the appropriate position and place the color-coded insulated probes on the wires or terminals. Multitesters can be purchased for as little as $10. Even super accurate digital models are available for less than $20. *Recommendation:* Buy a low-cost, digital pocket multitester at Radio Shack.

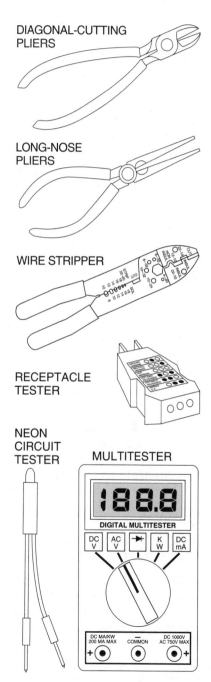

DIAGONAL-CUTTING PLIERS

LONG-NOSE PLIERS

WIRE STRIPPER

RECEPTACLE TESTER

NEON CIRCUIT TESTER

MULTITESTER

Paintbrushes. The big question regarding paintbrushes is not the size—the job usually makes that obvious—but the type to use. Years ago, natural bristle brushes were regarded as the best. All of that has changed. In fact, natural bristle brushes are the only type you cannot use with latex paint. There are also inexpensive, throwaway bristle and foam brushes on the market, so you have to decide whether to buy ten throwaways or a single high-quality brush for the same money and then clean and store it after each use. *Recommendation:* Buy several of each size of foam brush for jobs such as trim and window sashes, and use pads and rollers for big jobs.

If you don't follow our recommendation, you need to know how to clean your expensive brush. For a lunch break, or even overnight, don't clean it. Place the brush in a plastic resealable bag and zip it tightly. Lay the brush flat or suspend it from the hole in the handle. If the job is over, wash latex paint from the brush in warm, soapy water. Work the bristles between your fingers and rinse until you can no longer see any traces of paint. For other paints, stains, and varnishes, do the same in paint thinner. Hang a clean brush from its handle.

Paint Pads. Foam-backed paint pads carry a large amount of paint so that large areas can be covered at one time. The large pad keeps the pressure low, resulting in a very smooth application. Interchangeable pads are available in a variety of naps to suit the roughness of the surface. Like paint rollers, most pad handles are threaded and accept standard mop handles so that you can paint as high as the ceiling without a stepladder and the floor without getting on your knees. *Recommendation:* Buy pad refills so you won't have to clean them, and buy at least a short extension handle.

Wheeled Edger Pad. If you have steady hands, skip this tool. Otherwise, the wheeled edger pad—a small paint pad with wheels set into its edge—is just the thing for painting the margins between ceiling and wall or wall and trim. *Recommendation:* Buy one to see if you like using it.

PAINTBRUSHES

Flat

Sash

Foam

Artist's

PAINT PAD

WHEELED EDGER PAD

Paint Roller. Nothing beats a paint roller—especially one on a long extension handle—for painting walls and ceilings. Rollers come in a variety of naps to suit the roughness of the surface—even that of concrete block. They also come in a variety of widths, the most common being 9 inches, 7 inches, and 3 inches. In addition to eliminating the need for a stepladder, extension handles keep the roller from splattering paint on you. *Recommendation:* Buy a 9-inch roller with ⅜-inch nap.

Paint Tray. The paint tray is a prerequisite for using a paint roller. The tray has a deep reservoir at one end and a washboard slope at the other end. You first dip the roller in the deep end, then roll it several times over the washboard to distribute the paint. Clean the tray immediately after use with warm soapy water and a coarse scrub pad. *Recommendation:* Buy a tray packaged with a roller.

Paint Scraper. The key to successful painting is surface preparation—washing to remove chalk, dirt, and grease and scraping to remove loose paint. Effective scraping requires force and a very sharp scraper. If dull, the scraper merely bounces over the paint. *Recommendation:* Buy a hook-type scraper with extra blades and use a small flat mill file to sharpen the blades every five minutes.

Wire Brushes. With the ability to reach crevices, stiff wire brushes are necessary for the preparation of irregular surfaces. Wire brushes are also good at removing paint from rungs and banisters. They are available with plain steel, stainless steel, and nonscratching brass bristles. *Recommendation:* Buy a large, coarse steel brush plus a small, nonscratch brass brush.

Caulking Gun. Many caulks and sealants come only in standard-size, economical cartridges designed to fit the caulking gun. If you use cartridges, you must have a caulking gun. *Recommendation:* The caulking gun is a simple device, so buy an inexpensive model.

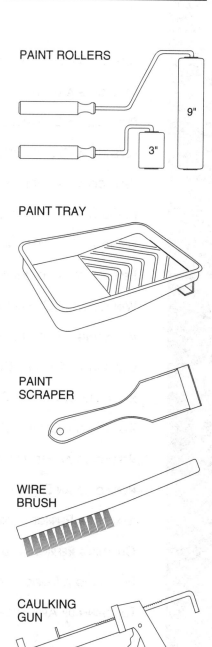

PAINT ROLLERS

9"

3"

PAINT TRAY

PAINT SCRAPER

WIRE BRUSH

CAULKING GUN

FIXING A SLOW-FILLING DISHWASHER

If your automatic dishwasher fills more slowly than it did when first installed, it probably has a clogged inlet screen. Cleaning this tiny screen should speed things up.

MATERIALS
- **Masking tape**
- **Vinegar**

TOOLS
Screwdriver • Slip-joint pliers
• Long-nose pliers • Toothbrush

1. Turn off the power to the dishwasher at the main panel or, if you have a portable dishwasher, unplug it.

2. Turn off the hot water supply valve to the dishwasher under the sink.

3. Remove the access panel (Figure A). It may rotate down, or you may have to remove several screws.

4. Using slip-joint pliers, unscrew the hot-water-hose couplings at the inlet valve and at the water supply valve under the sink.

5. Look for an inlet screen in either end of the hot water hose. If it's there, go to Step 7. If it's not there, it will be just inside the inlet (Figure B); go to Step 6.

6. Label the wires on the inlet valve with masking tape to indicate their position. Then, pull the wires off the terminals with long-nose pliers.

7. Carefully pry out the inlet screen with a small screwdriver.

8. Clean the screen with a toothbrush and running water. If it is coated with mineral deposits, soak it in vinegar overnight and clean it again.

9. Pop the screen back in and reconnect the hoses. Reattach the wires to the inlet valve and restore the power. Turn on the supply valve and check for leaks. Tighten the hose couplings as necessary.

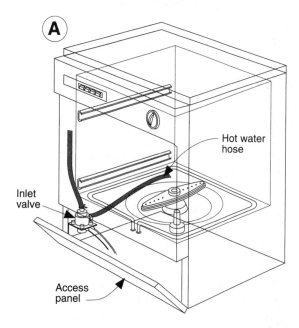

Hot water hose

Inlet valve

Access panel

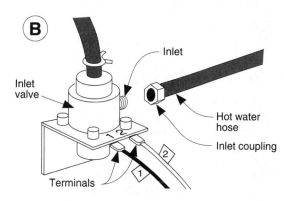

Inlet valve

Inlet

Hot water hose

Inlet coupling

Terminals

REPLACING A DISHWASHER INLET VALVE

If your dishwasher fills too slowly, the problem is probably a clogged inlet screen. (See "Fixing a Slow-Filling Dishwasher" on page 19.) If it won't fill at all or it makes funny noises while filling, the dishwasher probably has a defective inlet valve. Luckily, this is a part you can buy and replace.

MATERIALS
- Masking tape
- Replacement inlet valve

TOOLS
Screwdriver • Slip-joint pliers • Long-nose pliers • Adjustable wrench

1. Turn off the power to the dishwasher at the main panel or, if it is a portable dishwasher, unplug it.

2. Turn off the hot water supply valve to the dishwasher under the sink.

3. Remove the access panel. It may rotate down, or you may have to remove several screws (Figure A).

4. Using slip-joint pliers, unscrew the hot-water-hose couplings at the inlet valve (Figure B) and the water supply valve under the sink.

5. Using the slip-joint pliers, squeeze together the ends of the fill hose clamp and slide it up the hose. Then, pull the fill hose off the inlet valve (Figure B).

6. Label the wires on the inlet valve with masking tape to indicate their position (Figure B). Then, pull the wires off the terminals with long-nose pliers.

7. Using an adjustable wrench, remove the inlet valve mounting bolts and remove the inlet valve. Take it to an appliance service center and buy a replacement.

8. To install the new inlet valve, bolt it in place. Reattach the wires, the fill hose, and the hot-water hose.

9. Restore the power, turn on the supply valve, and check for leaks. Tighten the hose couplings as necessary.

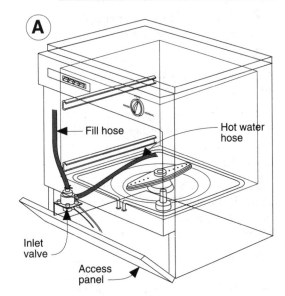

A

Fill hose

Hot water hose

Inlet valve

Access panel

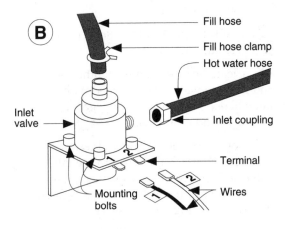

B

Fill hose

Fill hose clamp

Hot water hose

Inlet valve

Inlet coupling

Terminal

Mounting bolts

Wires

REPLACING A DISHWASHER FLOAT SWITCH

The float switch—located at the bottom of the dish compartment—tells the dishwasher when the compartment is empty and when it is full. If the float switch is defective or jammed, the dishwasher may either not fill or—your worst nightmare—never stop filling! Once you've cleaned up the mess, the switch is easy to check and replace.

MATERIALS
- Masking tape
- Replacement float switch

TOOLS
Toothbrush • Screwdriver
• Long-nose pliers • Multitester

1. Locate the float inside the dishwasher (Figure A). Check that the float moves freely by lifting it and letting it fall. If it sticks, pull the float off the stem and clean the stem with a toothbrush. Replace the float and check the operation.

2. If the dishwasher still fills incorrectly, turn off the power at the main panel. If the dishwasher is portable, unplug it.

3. Remove the access panel to expose the float switch housing (Figure B). It may rotate down or you may have to remove several screws.

4. Label the float switch wires with masking tape to indicate their position. Then pull the wires off the terminals with long-nose pliers.

5. Set a multitester to *R* or *OHMS* and hold its probes against the switch terminals while a helper lifts the float. With the float up, the multitester should read over 1,000 ohms; with the float down, it should read under 10 ohms.

6. If the switch fails the test, remove its mounting screws, take it to an appliance service center, and buy a replacement.

7. Mount the new switch, reattach the wires, and replace the access panel.

8. Restore the power.

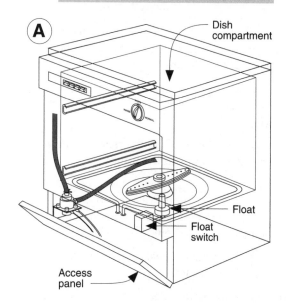

A — Dish compartment, Float, Float switch, Access panel

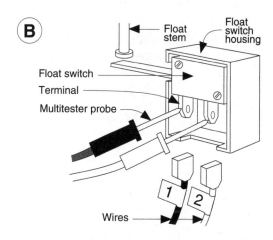

B — Float stem, Float switch housing, Float switch, Terminal, Multitester probe, Wires, 1, 2

LEVELING A CLOTHES WASHER

Does your clothes washer do the fandango? If it does hop around, the first thing to check is whether all of its feet are in contact with the floor. A clothes washer balancing on two feet is akin to a person on one foot—you wouldn't expect either to stand still for long. If shimming all the feet to touch the floor doesn't do the job, level it as described below.

MATERIALS
None

TOOLS
Carpenter's level • Adjustable wrench

1. Place a carpenter's level on the front edge of the top of the washer and check the bubble (Figure A).

2. Using an adjustable wrench, loosen the locknuts on the front leveling feet (Figure B).

3. Use the adjustable wrench to turn the front feet until the bubble is centered.

4. Tilt the clothes washer forward slightly to let the self-adjusting rear feet adjust.

5. Turn the level 90 degrees so it is parallel with the sides.

6. Making identical adjustments to both front feet, turn them to center the bubble again.

7. When the washer is level in both directions—side to side and front to back—tighten the front locknuts against the bottom of the washer to prevent the feet from moving.

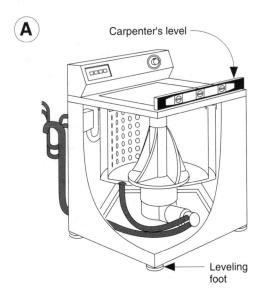

A Carpenter's level

Leveling foot

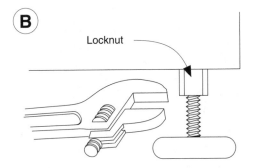

B Locknut

REPLACING A CLOTHES WASHER SNUBBER

If your clothes washer sounds like someone is banging an oil drum with a baseball bat, it may need a new shock absorber, known as a snubber. But try lighter loads and adjusting the feet first. You can quickly see if your machine has a snubber by following Steps 1 through 4; some new models don't.

1. Unplug the clothes washer.

2. Tape the lid shut with duct tape.

3. Insert a putty knife under the top, 2 inches or so from a corner, push the putty knife in to release the clip, and lift the corner (Figure B). Repeat at the other corner, and swing the top up.

4. Draw a sketch to record exactly how the snubber spring rod is installed (Figure A).

5. Lift the looped end of the spring rod off the snubber.

6. Using an adjustable wrench, remove the nut and bolt that fasten the end of the snubber spring rod to the washer frame (Figure B).

7. Using slip-joint pliers, unscrew the old snubber.

8. Remove the snubber spring rod. Take the rod and the snubber to an appliance service center and purchase replacements.

9. Screw the new snubber in, install the new snubber spring rod, and snap the spring rod over the snubber.

10. Close the lid, remove the duct tape, and plug the clothes washer back in.

MATERIALS
- Duct tape
- Replacement snubber and spring rod

TOOLS
Putty knife • Adjustable wrench • Slip-joint pliers

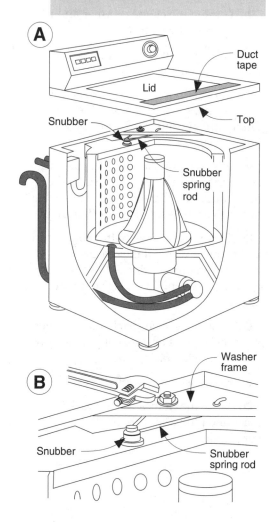

FIXING A SLOW-FILLING CLOTHES WASHER

If your clothes washer fills more slowly than it did when new, something may be clogged. If all of your faucets run slowly, the problem could be in the water pipes. However, if just the clothes washer is slow, the problem is probably nothing more complicated than clogged inlet screens.

MATERIALS

Vinegar

TOOLS

Slip-joint pliers • Screwdriver • Toothbrush

1. Unplug the clothes washer and pull it away from the wall.

2. Turn off both water supply valves, which are on the wall behind the washer.

3. Using slip-joint pliers, loosen the hose couplings in the back of the washer. Then unscrew and remove the hoses (Figure A).

4. Inlet screens should be visible inside either the inlet valve hose ports or the hose couplings. Carefully pry the screens out with a small screwdriver (Figure B).

5. Clean the screens with a toothbrush and running water. If the screens are coated with mineral deposits, soak them in vinegar overnight and clean them again.

6. Push the screens back into the inlet valve hose ports or hose couplings with the convex side facing out.

7. Reconnect the supply hoses.

8. Move the clothes washer back into place and plug it in. Turn on the water supply valves.

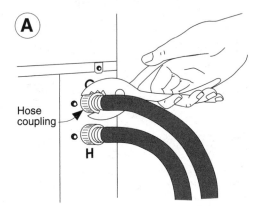

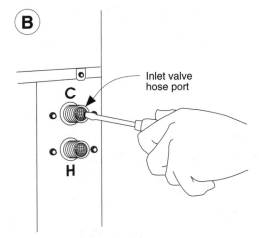

FIXING AN OVERFLOWING CLOTHES WASHER

If your clothes washer fills and fills and fills to overflowing—quickly turn off the water supply valves! After you have cleaned up the mess, check the level switch, which is designed to tell the machine when it's full enough. Either the plastic pressure hose has fallen off, or you need to replace the switch.

MATERIALS

- Masking tape
- 2' length of ¼" plastic tubing
- Replacement level switch

TOOLS

Screwdriver • Long-nose pliers
• Multitester

1. If there is still water in the clothes washer tub, empty it either by hand or electrically. Unplug the clothes washer.

2. Remove the screws that fasten the console. Pull the console up and back, and let it rest on its hinges (Figure A).

3. Label the three wires of the level switch with masking tape. Using long-nose pliers, pull the wires off the terminals (Figure B).

4. Remove the pressure hose from the level switch and slip a 2-foot length of ¼-inch plastic tubing over the port.

5. Set a multitester to *R* or *OHMS* and place the two probes on the two outside terminals of the level switch (Figure C). With the probes in place, have a helper blow on the end of the tubing. If the multitester reading doesn't drop to less than 10 ohms, unscrew the level switch and take it to an appliance service center and purchase a replacement.

6. Fasten the new switch in place, and connect the pressure hose and wires.

7. Lower the console into position and refasten it.

8. Plug in the washer.

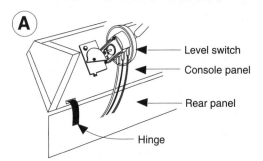

Level switch
Console panel
Rear panel
Hinge

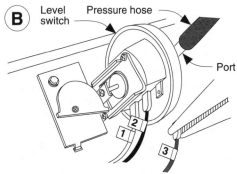

Level switch   Pressure hose
Port

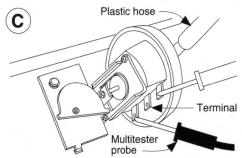

Plastic hose
Terminal
Multitester probe

REPLACING A CLOTHES WASHER INLET VALVE

If your clothes washer fills too slowly, the problem is probably a clogged inlet screen. (See "Fixing a Slow-Filling Clothes Washer" on page 24.) If it won't fill at all or if it makes funny noises while filling, the problem may be a defective inlet valve, which you can easily replace.

MATERIALS
- Duct tape
- Masking tape
- Replacement inlet valve

TOOLS
Slip joint pliers • Putty knife
• Nutdriver• Multitester

1. Unplug the clothes washer and pull it away from the wall.

2. Turn off both water supply valves, which are the on the wall behind the washer.

3. Using slip-joint pliers, loosen the hose couplings in the back of the washer, which lead to the inlet valve. Then unscrew and remove the supply hoses (Figure A).

4. Tape the washer's lid shut with duct tape.

5. Insert a putty knife under the top, 2 inches or so from a corner, push the putty knife in to release the clip, and lift the corner (Figure B). Repeat at the other corner, and swing the top up.

6. Using a nutdriver, remove the screws fastening the inlet valve to the rear panel and remove the valve (Figure C).

7. The valve will have one, two, or three pairs of wires. Label each wire and corresponding terminal with masking tape, then pull the wires off the terminals with long-nose pliers.

8. Set a multitester to *R* or *OHMS* and place the probes on each pair of terminals (Figure D). If the tester reads less than 10 or more than 1,000 ohms on any pair of terminals, the inlet valve must be replaced.

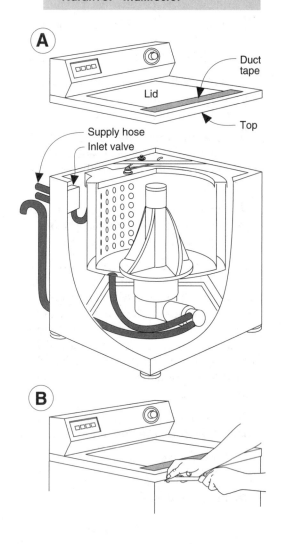

9. Using the slip-joint pliers, pinch the hose clamp holding the inlet hose on the inlet valve, slide the clamp down the hose, and work the hose off the valve.

10. Take the inlet valve to an appliance service center and purchase a replacement.

11. Work the end of the inlet hose over the outlet port of the new inlet valve. Squeeze the ends of the hose clamp with the slip-joint pliers and work the clamp up over the outlet port to clamp the hose back in place.

12. Connect the wires to the terminals of the new inlet valve.

13. Insert the inlet valve hose ports through the holes in the rear panel of the washer and refasten the inlet valve.

14. Swing the washer top down and remove the duct tape from the lid.

15. Connect the water supply hoses to the inlet valve hose ports.

16. Plug in the washer and move it back in place.

17. Turn on the water supply valves and check for leaks. Tighten the supply hose couplings as necessary.

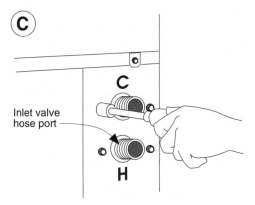

C

Inlet valve hose port

C

H

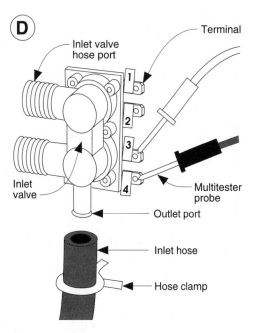

D

Terminal

Inlet valve hose port

Inlet valve

1

2

3

4

Multitester probe

Outlet port

Inlet hose

Hose clamp

WINTERIZING A CLOTHES WASHER

Do you have a clothes washer at a summer camp? If so, don't just lock the doors and leave it for the winter. Water in the inlet valve and pump can freeze and crack the valve and pump bodies. All you need to protect the machine is a ½ gallon of nontoxic antifreeze, often labeled RV. Jack Daniels works just as well but costs four times as much.

MATERIALS
- ½ gallon nontoxic antifreeze (propylene glycol)
- 1 cup liquid clothes detergent

TOOLS
Slip-joint pliers

1. Turn off both water supply valves.

2. Pull the washer away from the wall to gain access to the back.

3. Using slip-joint pliers, loosen the hose couplings at the washer, then unscrew and remove the supply hoses (Figure B).

4. Turn the washer timer control knob to *FILL* and the temperature selection controls to *WARM WASH* (Figure A).

5. Turn on the washer for ten seconds.

6. Lift the lid and pour ½ gallon of *nontoxic* antifreeze—propylene glycol—into the washer.

7. Plug in the clothes washer.

8. Turn the washer timer control to *DRAIN AND SPIN* and let the washer run for ten seconds.

9. The washer is now freeze-proof. To use it again, reconnect the supply hoses, pour 1 cup of liquid clothes detergent into the washer, and run the empty machine through a complete cycle.

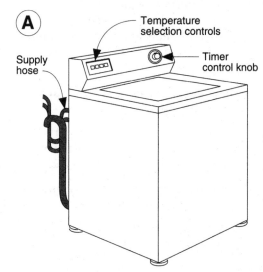

A — Temperature selection controls / Timer control knob / Supply hose

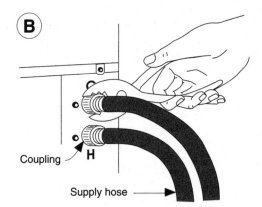

B — Coupling / H / Supply hose

REPLACING A CLOTHES DRYER LIGHT BULB

Do you need a flashlight to see what is in your clothes dryer? If so, it may be because the drum light has burned out. If your dryer has a drum light and it's broken, it's easy to replace. The bulb is an ordinary household bulb of 25 to 40 watts.

MATERIALS
Replacement light bulb

TOOLS
None

1. Unplug the dryer.

2. Open the loading door and locate the white plastic light cover at the back of the drum (Figure A).

3. Twist the plastic cover counter-clockwise to remove it (Figure B). If the cover will not turn, try twisting it clockwise.

4. Remove the old light bulb.

5. Replace the bulb with one of the same or lower wattage. In any case, do not exceed 40 watts.

6. Line up the tabs on the light cover with the slots in the back of the drum, and twist the light cover clockwise to engage the tabs.

7. Restore the power.

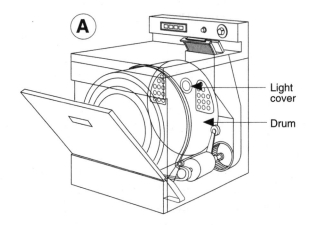

Light cover

Drum

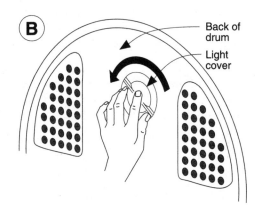

Back of drum

Light cover

CLEANING A CLOTHES DRYER VENT

Residential energy audits have shown that more than 90 percent of the clothes dryer exhaust ducts and hoods have significant deposits of lint. The lint restricts the exhaust air flow and makes the dryer work less efficiently than it should. You should clean your dryer's vent and ducting twice a year.

MATERIALS
Duct tape

TOOLS
Screwdriver • Toothbrush • Heavy twine • Hand towel

1. Unplug the dryer. If it's a gas dryer, turn off the gas supply valve as well.

2. Pull the dryer out to gain access to the rear panel (Figure A). If you have a gas dryer, do not kink the gas supply tubing.

3. Remove the duct from the outlet at the bottom of the rear panel and from the exhaust hood where it exits the building. If the duct is a plastic hose, loosen the hose clamps at each end with a screwdriver first. If the duct is metal, you may have to remove duct tape from the joints.

4. Use a toothbrush to remove lint from the dryer outlet and the flapper of the exhaust hood outside (Figure B).

5. Feed heavy twine through the entire length of the duct. You may have to remove duct tape from the joints and separate the duct into shorter sections.

6. Using the twine, tie a knot around the middle of a hand towel (Figure C).

7. Pull the towel back and forth through the duct to remove the lint.

8. Retape any joints you disconnected. Reconnect the duct ends to the dryer outlet and the exhaust hood.

9. Restore the power and turn the gas supply back on if necessary. Carefully move the dryer back in place.

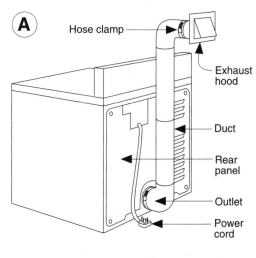

A Hose clamp — Exhaust hood — Duct — Rear panel — Outlet — Power cord

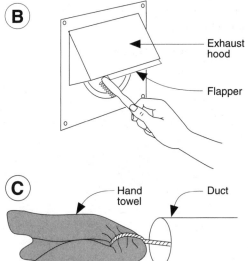

B Exhaust hood — Flapper

C Hand towel — Duct

REPLACING A CLOTHES DRYER TIMER

Symptoms of a defective clothes dryer timer are a dryer that will not start or one that stops in the middle of a cycle. If the timer is working, the timer control knob should move—although watching it is somewhat like watching grass grow.

MATERIALS
- Masking tape
- Replacement timer

TOOLS
Screwdriver • Long-nose pliers • Nutdriver

1. Unplug the dryer.

2. Remove the timer control knob by pulling it toward you (Figure A).

3. Using a screwdriver, remove the screws that fasten the console to the end caps. The screws may be either in the sides or the front of the end cap. Lay the console down on the top of the dryer.

4. If they are not already marked, label the wires in the back of the timer with masking tape to avoid confusion when reconnecting them.

5. Using long-nose plier, pull the wires off the terminals (Figure B).

6. Using a nutdriver, remove the screws that fasten the timer (Figure C).

7. Take the timer to an appliance service center and purchase an replacement.

8. Using the nutdriver, secure the new timer to the console with screws.

9. Connect the wires to the terminals.

10. Refasten the console to the end caps, push the timer control knob back on, and restore the power.

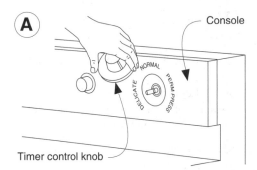

A

Console

Timer control knob

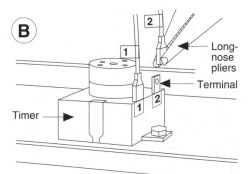

B

Long-nose pliers

Terminal

Timer

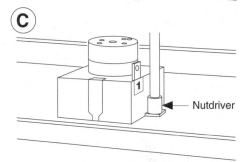

C

Nutdriver

REPLACING A CLOTHES DRYER BELT

The belt that turns the drum is usually the first thing to go on a clothes dryer. The clue to a broken belt is that the dryer will make all of its normal noises, but the drum will not turn. It may seem that you have totally disassembled the dryer by the time you get to the belt, but the procedure for replacing it is really straightforward.

MATERIALS
- Duct tape
- Masking tape
- Replacement belt

TOOLS
Screwdriver • Putty knife
• Long-nose pliers • Nutdriver

1. Unplug the dryer. If it is a gas dryer, turn off the gas supply valve as well.

2. If your dryer has its lint filter slot on top, pull the lint filter out of its slot in the top of the dryer (Figure A). Using a screwdriver, remove the two screws in front of the filter slot (Figure B).

3. Tape the loading door closed with duct tape.

4. Slip the blade of a putty knife between the top and front of the dryer, 2 inches or so in from a corner (Figure C). Push in on the putty knife to release the clip. Repeat at the other front corner and swing the top up.

5. Slip the putty knife between the access panel and the bottom of the loading door at the midpoint. Push in on the putty knife to release the clip while pulling one of the top corners of the acccess panel toward you until the access panel opens.

6. If there are wires connected to a door switch on the inside of the front panel, label the wires and the terminals with masking tape, then remove the wires with long-nose pliers. Remove any clips that secure the wires to the front panel.

7. Using either a screwdriver or a nutdriver, loosen but do not remove the two screws at the bottom of the front panel.

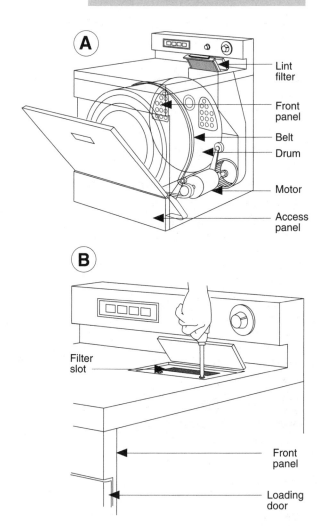

A — Lint filter / Front panel / Belt / Drum / Motor / Access panel

B — Filter slot / Front panel / Loading door

8. Have a helper hold up the front of the dryer drum by its flange while you remove the two screws inside the top of the front panel (Figure D).

9. Remove the two bottom screws you previously loosened and remove the front panel. Lower the drum.

10. Note how the old belt loops around the drum, the motor pulley, and the idler pulley so you won't be confused when you install the new belt.

11. Push the idler pulley toward the motor pulley (Figure E) and remove the belt from the motor pulley and drum.

12. Take the old belt to an appliance service center and purchase a replacement.

13. Place the new belt around the drum with the ribbed surface on the drum.

14. Feed the belt under the idler pulley and, while pushing the idler pulley toward the motor pulley, slip the belt around the motor pulley.

15. With a helper holding the front of the drum up, replace the front panel.

16. Reconnect the front panel wires. Replace the access panel and swing the top down.

17. If necessary, replace the screws in front of the lint filter slot and put the lint filter back in its slot.

18. Restore the power and turn the gas supply on, if necessary.

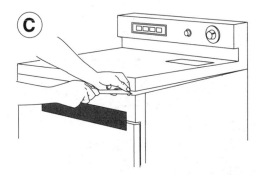

C

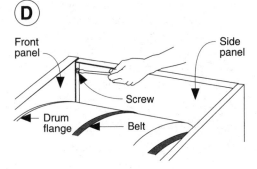

D

Front panel

Side panel

Screw

Drum flange

Belt

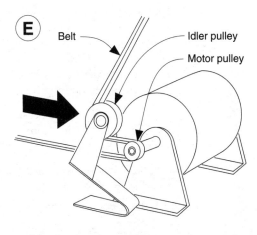

E

Belt

Idler pulley

Motor pulley

REPLACING AN ELECTRIC SURFACE ELEMENT

There is no reason to suffer the inconvenience of a cold or lukewarm electric range surface element. You can tell if one is broken by simply switching it with a working element.

1. Turn on the range's surface elements to determine which do not work (Figure A).

2. Turn off the surface elements. Unplug the range or turn off the power at the main panel. Let the elements cool.

3. Switch the element you suspect is defective with a working element. The elements sit on supports and are plugged into two-prong receptacles. To remove an element, lift the element from its support and pull its prongs straight out of the receptacle (Figure B).

4. Restore the power and turn on the two switched elements.

5. If the suspect element does not work in the second receptacle either, the element is bad and must be replaced; go to Step 6. However, if it now works, the problem is either dirty prongs or defective wiring in the range or element control. Turn off the power. Clean the prongs and push them into their original slot. If the element now works, your problem is solved, but if it doesn't work, the wiring is defective. Call an appliance repair service.

6. If the element is bad, take it to an appliance service center or hardware store and purchase a replacement.

7. Plug the replacement element into the receptacle and lower the element onto its support. Restore the power.

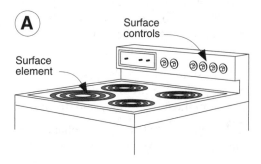

A

Surface controls

Surface element

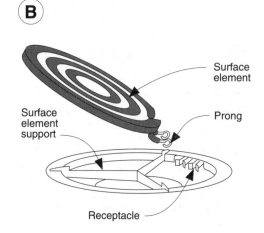

B

Surface element

Surface element support

Prong

Receptacle

REPLACING AN ELECTRIC OVEN ELEMENT

Have you been living without home-baked cookies because your oven doesn't work? You can tell if one of your oven elements is defective by switching them. If one proves defective, you can easily obtain a replacement either at your appliance dealer or an appliance service center.

MATERIALS
Replacement oven element

TOOLS
Screwdriver • Nutdriver

1. Turn the oven control to *BAKE* to see if the lower element is working. Likewise, turn the oven control to *BROIL* to see if the upper element is working.

2. If neither element is working, the problem is most likely in the range wiring or oven control; call an appliance repair service. If one is working, but not the other, continue to Step 3.

3. If the elements are identical, you can switch them. Unplug the range or turn off the power at the main panel, remove the screws from the element support brackets (Figure B), and pull the elements out to expose the wires. Using a screwdriver or nutdriver, remove the wires from the element terminals (Figure C). Switch the elements and reinstall them.

4. Restore the power and repeat Step 1. If the suspect element now works and the formerly working element doesn't, the problem is in the range wiring or oven control; call an appliance repair service. If the suspect element is still not working, the element must be replaced.

5. Turn the power off and remove the bad element. Take it to an appliance service center, and purchase a replacement.

6. Reattach the two element terminals to the supply wires and remount the element support bracket. Restore the power.

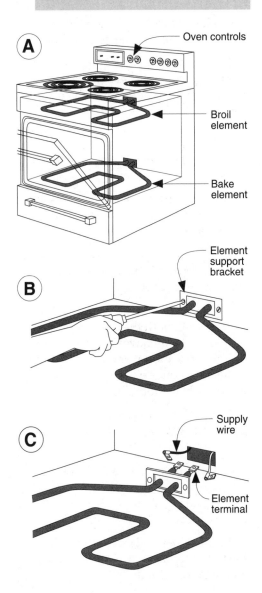

A — Oven controls / Broil element / Bake element

B — Element support bracket

C — Supply wire / Element terminal

MAKING A REFRIGERATOR DOOR STAY CLOSED

Refrigerator and freezer doors are designed to close automatically, mainly to deal with absent-minded teenagers. If you often find your refrigerator door open, here's what you can do about it—other than giving the kids away.

MATERIALS
None

TOOLS
Carpenter's level • Adjustable wrench • Slip-joint pliers • Nutdriver • Screwdriver

1. Place a carpenter's level on top of the refrigerator, parallel to the door.

2. Using an adjustable wrench or slip-joint pliers, turn the leveling feet at the front corners to center the bubble.

3. Adjust the rear feet until both touch the floor.

4. Turn the level 90 degrees so that it lines up with a side of the refrigerator.

5. Making identical adjustments to both, turn the front feet to center the bubble again.

6. Open the door slightly. If it closes, you are done. If it stays open or opens further, go on to Step 7.

7. Using a nutdriver, slightly loosen the screws of both the top and middle hinges. You may have to use a screwdriver to pry the cover off the top hinge. If the refrigerator has a single door, loosen only the top hinge screws.

8. With the doors closed, shift the doors sideways to line them up with the sides of the refrigerator.

9. Tighten the screws and close the doors to check the alignment. If necessary, repeat Steps 7 through 9. Replace the hinge cover.

10. If the door still stays open, adjust the front leveling feet so that the refrigerator leans back slightly.

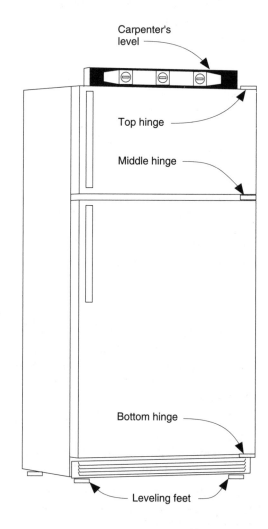

Carpenter's level

Top hinge

Middle hinge

Bottom hinge

Leveling feet

CLEANING REFRIGERATOR COILS

If your refrigerator seems to be laboring, the problem may be dusty condenser coils. The condenser dissipates the heat pumped out of the refrigerator box. Dust on the coils and fins acts as insulation, preventing the heat from dissipating efficiently. Clean the coils once every year.

MATERIALS
None

TOOLS
Vacuum cleaner with brush attachment • Toothbrush

If your refrigerator has a condenser coil on the back, follow these steps:

1. Pull the refrigerator away from the wall so you can gain access to the back. You may have to unplug it.

2. Using a vacuum cleaner with a brush attachment, loosen and vacuum up the lint and dirt from the coil and fins.

3. Restore the power and move the refrigerator back to its original position.

If there is no coil on the back of your refrigerator, follow these steps:

1. Unplug the refrigerator.

2. Open the lower refrigerator door and prop it open.

3. Hold the motor compartment grille at both ends, push it down, and rotate the top toward you. If the top does not release, look for projecting tabs that will release the grille. Lift the grille off its bottom supports and set it aside.

4. While a helper shines a light into the motor compartment, vacuum the condenser coil.

5. Clean any dust off the condenser fan blades with an old toothbrush.

6. Replace the motor compartment grille and restore the power.

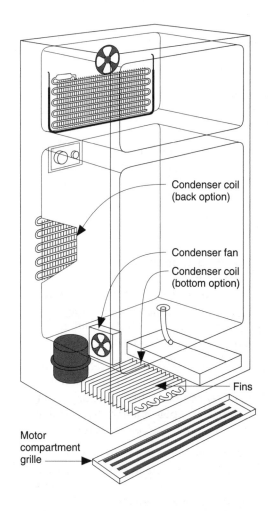

Condenser coil (back option)

Condenser fan

Condenser coil (bottom option)

Fins

Motor compartment grille

REPLACING A REFRIGERATOR DEFROST HEATER

Does your automatic-defrost freezer resemble a glacier? If so, your freezer may have a burned-out defrost heater. Using a multitester, you can easily determine whether the defrost heater needs replacing. If you don't have a multitester, call an appliance repair service.

MATERIALS
Replacement defrost heater

TOOLS
Screwdriver • Multitester

1. Unplug the refrigerator.

2. Clean out the freezer compartment. Place frozen food in a cooler.

3. Using a screwdriver, remove the screws securing the evaporator cover (Figure A). You may have to remove shelves and shelf supports to gain access to the cover.

4. Remove the evaporator cover, exposing the evaporator coil and the U-shaped defrost heater that wraps around the perimeter of the coil.

5. Pull apart the ends of the defrost heater from their supply wires.

6. Set a multitester to *R* or *OHMS*. Touch the two multitester probes to the two ends of the defrost heater element (Figure B). The meter should read between 10 and 1,000 ohms. If not, the heater is bad and must be replaced.

7. From the back of the refrigerator, record the manufacturer and model of the refrigerator. With that information, purchase a replacement defrost heater from an appliance service center.

8. Remove the old defrost heater and install the new one in the same way. Connect the wires, and replace the evaporator cover. Restore the power.

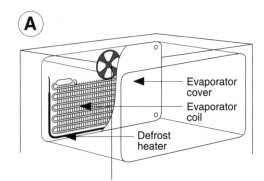

A

Evaporator cover
Evaporator coil
Defrost heater

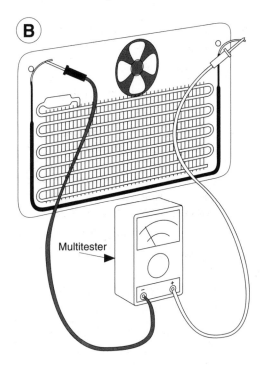

B

Multitester

TOUCHING UP APPLIANCE SCRATCHES

A scratched or scuffed paint finish on an appliance will not affect the performance of the appliance, but it may detract from the appearance of the kitchen you just spent $10,000 remodeling. A can of touch-up paint will cost no more than $5. If the appliance is white, you can obtain "appliance white" gloss enamel at any hardware store.

MATERIALS

- Household cleaner
- Matching touch-up paint
- 600-grit sandpaper

TOOLS

Kitchen scrub pad

Wash the surface to be painted with a kitchen scrub pad and household cleaner, rinse with fresh water, and dry.

If the scratch is small, follow these steps (Figure A):

1. Purchase a 1/2-ounce bottle of touch-up paint at an appliance service center.

2. Brush the smallest amount of paint possible into the scratch, and let it dry.

If the scratched area is large, follow these steps (Figure B):

1. Purchase a 15-ounce spray can of matching paint at an appliance service center.

2. Using 600-grit sandpaper, lightly sand the area to be painted.

3. Wipe the area with a damp cloth and let it dry.

4. Shake the spray can according to the directions on the can.

5. Spray the entire area *very lightly* and let it dry.

6. Repeat Step 5 until the sprayed area looks the same as the surrounding area. This will require several applications. Resist the urge to spray thick coats. Heavy applications will result in a wavy appearance.

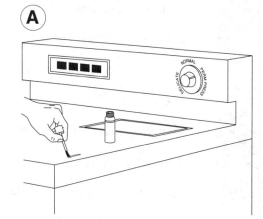

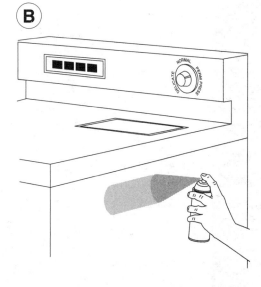

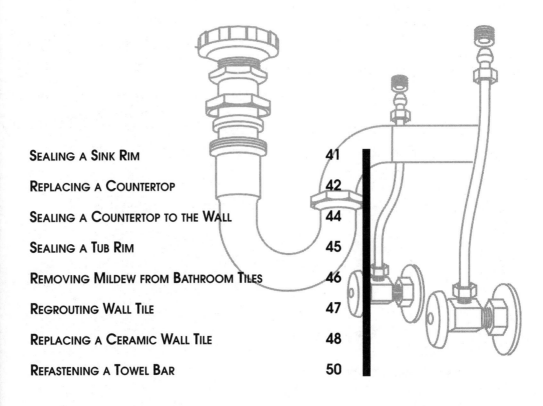

B A T H S & K I T C H E N S

SEALING A SINK RIM

If you find water inside a vanity cabinet but no drips on either the drain or supply pipes, chances are good that water spilled on the countertop is leaking under the rim of the sink. The cure for this leak is to seal the rim of the sink to the countertop with silicone sealant.

MATERIALS
- 3 wood matches
- Tube of clear silicone sealant

TOOLS
Screwdriver • Groove-joint pliers
• Adjustable wrench • Sponge

1. Look under the sink to see how it is attached to the countertop. If there are no sink clips (Figure A), go to Step 3.

2. Loosen the sink clips by turning the screws counterclockwise.

3. Push the sink up and insert three wood matches to hold the sink about 1/8 inch above the countertop.

4. If the sink is held too tightly by its attached pipes, turn off the water supply valves and open both faucets. Loosen the drain slip nut with groove-joint pliers and both supply slip nuts with an adjustable wrench (Figure B).

5. Squeeze a bead of silicone sealant under the sink rim (Figure C). Use your forefinger moistened with water to spread the sealant so there are no gaps except at the matches.

6. Remove the matches and press the sink down. The sealant will fill the holes left by the matches. Tighten the sink clips, if applicable.

7. Wipe up any sealant that has squeezed out with a wet sponge.

8. Tighten the slip nuts you may have previously loosened, then turn the water back on. If the supply lines leak, tighten the slip nuts further, as required.

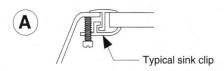

A — Typical sink clip

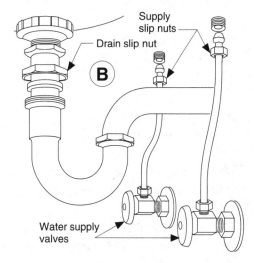

B — Supply slip nuts — Drain slip nut — Water supply valves

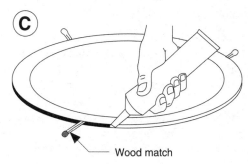

C — Wood match

REPLACING A COUNTERTOP

Replacing a countertop is not hard, but you must work carefully so that the new countertop will fit exactly as the old one did. The key is taking exact measurements so that you don't have to add or modify plumbing or wiring.

1. Measure the existing countertop with a tape measure and make a simple sketch of it, showing the countertop's shape and dimensions.

2. Take your sketches to a home center, and order a replacement countertop.

3. After the new countertop arrives, confirm that it has the exact dimensions you asked for. If not, return it for replacement or modification.

4. Shut off the water supply valves under the sink (Figure A).

5. Disconnect the drain slip nut with groove-joint pliers and the two supply slip nuts with an adjustable wrench (Figure A).

6. Remove the sink clips under the rim of the sink with a screwdriver (Figure B).

7. If there is a garbage disposal, turn off its circuit breaker or remove its fuse in the service panel. Flip the disposal switch to make sure the electricity has been disconnected.

8. Remove the access panel at the bottom or side of the garbage disposal. Pull out the wires, and twist off the wire nuts that connect the white and black wires. Loosen the screw, and remove the green or copper ground wire from the disposal housing (Figure C).

MATERIALS

- Replacement countertop
- Scotch tape
- Kraft paper
- Tube of clear silicone sealant

TOOLS

Tape measure • Groove-joint pliers
• Adjustable wrench • Screwdriver
• Utility knife • Drill and $1/2$" spade bit
• Keyhole or saber saw • Putty knife

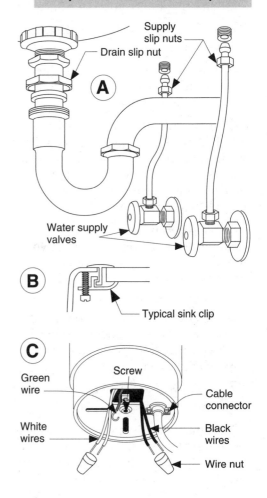

Supply slip nuts
Drain slip nut
A
Water supply valves

B
Typical sink clip

C
Screw
Green wire
White wires
Cable connector
Black wires
Wire nut

9. Loosen the cable connector, and pull the cable out of the disposal (Figure C).

10. Lift the sink and garbage disposal assembly out of the countertop.

11. Remove the screws that attach the countertop to the base cabinet (Figure D).

12. Cover the old countertop with kraft paper, and tape the paper in place. Using a utility knife, trim the paper to exactly match the edges of the countertop. Carefully cut the paper to match the sink cutout (Figure E).

13. Tape the paper pattern to the new countertop and trace the cutout on to the new countertop.

14. With a 1/2-inch spade bit, drill holes in the four corners of the cutout. Complete the cutout with a keyhole or saber saw (Figure F).

15. Place the countertop on the base cabinet, and then drill screw pilot holes, using the old screw holes as guides. Screw down the countertop to the base cabinet.

16. Remove any old caulk under the sink rim with a putty or utility knife. Then lay a 1/4-inch bead of clear silicone sealant around the rim of the cutout.

17. Drop the sink assembly down into the cutout, while a helper guides the supply and drain pipes into their fittings.

18. Reattach supply and drain slip nuts, garbage disposal wiring, and sink clips. Check for water leaks and tighten the slip nuts as necessary.

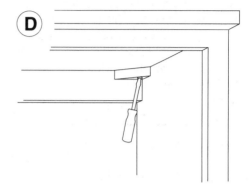

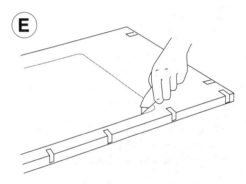

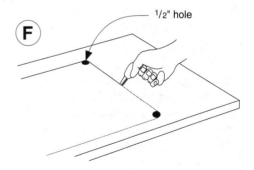

1/2" hole

SEALING A COUNTERTOP TO THE WALL

As with a tub or shower, water allowed to regularly penetrate the joint between a kitchen or bath countertop and the wall behind it may damage the wall or the floor. Note that Figures B and C show two options for the sealing material. The silicone sealant should last longer but is more difficult to apply than the tape.

1. Remove all old caulk with a screwdriver or small chisel (Figure A).

2. Remove all grease, oil, and dirt with household cleaner and a scrub pad.

3. Rinse the area thoroughly with water, and allow it to dry overnight.

4. Using a utility knife, cut the tip of a tube of silicone sealant at about a 30-degree angle until the hole in the tip has an inside diameter of 3/16 inch.

5. Puncture the inner seal of the sealant tube, if there is one, by inserting the tip of the screwdriver or a long nail.

6. Apply a 3/16-inch bead of sealant to the joint, pushing the tip ahead (Figure B). As an alternative, press self-adhesive tub-sealer tape into the joint (Figure C). Run a forefinger over the tape several times, increasing the pressure each time.

7. If you used silicone sealant, moisten your forefinger with water, and smooth the silicone bead with just enough pressure to spread the material but not extrude it beyond your fingertip. Fight the impulse to smooth it a second time—the sealant will probably drag and end up looking worse!

8. Quickly wash your hands with soap and water.

MATERIALS

- Household cleaner
- Tube of clear silicone sealant or roll of self-adhesive tub-sealer tape

TOOLS

Screwdriver or chisel • Scrub pad
• Utility knife

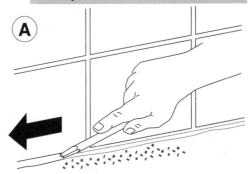

A

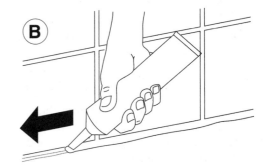

B

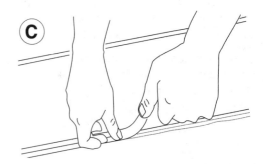

C

SEALING A TUB RIM

When you shower, water collects at the tub/tile joint. If water is allowed to penetrate the joint, it may damage the wall or the floor beneath the tub. Note that Figures B and C show two options for the sealing material. The silicone sealant should last longer but is more difficult to apply than the tape.

MATERIALS

Tube of clear silicone sealant or roll of self-adhesive tub-sealer tape

TOOLS

Screwdriver • Utility knife • Long nail

1. Remove the old caulk from the tub/tile joint with a small screwdriver (Figure A). Use the plain blade from a utility knife to scrape the flat surfaces of the tub and tile, taking care not to scratch areas that will show.

2. Using a utility knife, cut the tip of a tube of silicone sealant at about a 30-degree angle until the hole in the tip has an inside diameter of 3/16 inch.

3. Puncture the inner seal of the sealant tube, if there is one, by inserting the tip of the screwdriver or a long nail.

4. Apply a 3/16-inch bead of sealant to the joint, pushing the tip ahead (Figure B). As an alternative, press self-adhesive tub-sealer tape into the joint (Figure C). Run a forefinger over the tape several times, increasing the pressure each time.

5. If you used silicone sealant, wet your forefinger and smooth the sealant in a continuous motion. Apply only enough pressure to smooth the sealant but not extrude it beyond your fingertip.

6. Avoid the impulse to smooth the joint a second time. The sealant will probably drag and end up looking worse. You can trim messy spots with the utility knife after the sealant cures.

7. Quickly wash your hands with soap and water.

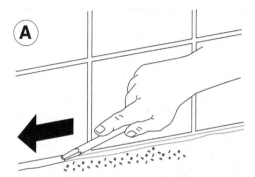

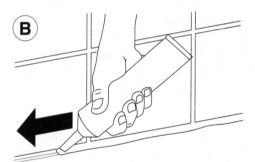

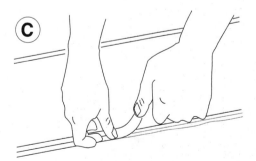

REMOVING MILDEW FROM BATHROOM TILES

When the joints between your bathroom tiles turn black and splotchy, do not despair. You probably do not have to replace the grout. Mildew fungus has found the damp grout a nice place to live. Getting rid of mildew is nearly as simple as claimed on television, but don't wear clothes that might be damaged by chlorine bleach. Increase ventilation and natural sunlight to prevent its reoccurrence.

MATERIALS
- 1 cup of chlorine bleach
- Penetrating grout sealer

TOOLS
Sponge with handle • Stiff-bristled toothbrush • Paintbrush

1. Mix 1 cup of chlorine bleach in 1 quart of water.

2. Apply the bleaching liquid to several feet of grouted joint using a sponge with a handle (Figure A).

3. Scrub the wet grouted joint with a stiff-bristled toothbrush (Figure B).

4. Repeat Steps 2 and 3 until all of the mildewed joints have been scrubbed.

5. If, after 15 minutes, the mildew has not disappeared from the area first scrubbed, repeat the wetting and scrubbing process until it does.

6. Rinse the entire work area with fresh water.

7. After the grout has dried, apply penetrating grout sealer to the joints with a paintbrush (Figure C).

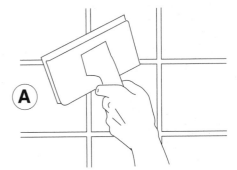

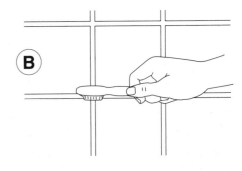

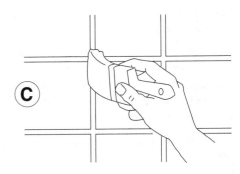

REGROUTING WALL TILE

If the grout between your bathroom tiles begins to fall out, take early preventive action. Otherwise, you will find yourself replacing the tiles instead of just the grout. You don't have to be a professional mason to work with grout. Next to replacing faucet washers, regrouting is one of the most common bathroom repairs.

MATERIALS

- 1 cup of phosphoric acid
- Box of powdered grout

TOOLS

Beer-can opener • Grout saw
• Rubber gloves • Sponge
• Rubber-edged grout float

1. Remove all loose grout using a beer-can opener (Figure A). If the grout is too hard for the beer-can opener or if you have a lot of joint to regrout, you can purchase a special grout saw at a tile store. If the grout is tinted, you may want to regrout the whole wall rather than try to match the original color.

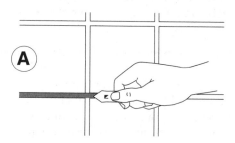

2. Mix 1 cup of phosphoric acid (available at a hardware store) into 1 quart of water.

3. Using rubber gloves and a sponge, wash all of the affected area with the diluted acid (Figure B). Rinse all surfaces with fresh water.

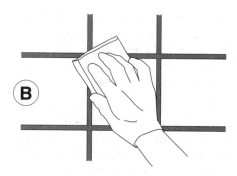

4. Mix the powdered grout, following the manufacturer's directions.

5. Apply the grout to the tile joints with your bare forefinger (Figure C). If you are doing a large surface, apply the grout by wiping diagonally across the entire wall surface with a rubber-edged grout float. Wipe the grout in several directions to fill the joints.

6. Wipe off the excess grout with a damp, but not saturated, sponge. Be careful not to remove too much grout from the joints.

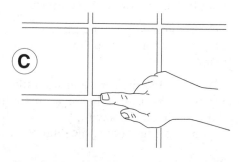

7. After the grout dries, wipe the tiles again to remove any residue.

REPLACING A CERAMIC WALL TILE

Replacing one or more ceramic wall tiles is more complicated than replacing just the grout, but the individual steps are no more difficult. The only difficult step may be one we have not listed—finding a replacement tile that matches the color of the original. If you are lucky, prescient, or a pack rat, you may have a few extras in the basement or garage. If not, take a large piece of the damaged tile to a professional tile installer, who probably has a large assortment of leftovers from hundreds of previous jobs. This may be your only source for discontinued colors.

MATERIALS

- Patching plaster
- Latex primer paint
- Waterproof tile mastic
- Replacement ceramic tile
- Block of wood
- Box of powdered grout

TOOLS

Beer-can opener • Grout saw
• Goggles • Cold chisel • Hammer
• Paint brush • Putty knife • Sponge
• Rubber-edged grout float

1. Remove the grout from around the damaged or missing tile, using a beer-can opener (Figure A). If the grout is too hard for the beer-can opener or if you are replacing a large number of tiles, you can purchase a grout saw at a tile store.

2. Wearing goggles to protect your eyes from flying debris, gently chip away the damaged tile with a cold chisel and a hammer (Figure B). Try not to damage the wall behind the tile.

3. Remove most of the old tile mastic with the cold chisel and hammer and, if necessary, fill any holes with patching plaster. It is not necessary to remove every trace of the old mastic—just enough so that the new tile will lie even with the surface of the existing wall.

4. If you used patching plaster, let it dry for 24 hours, then paint it with latex primer to seal it.

5. Spread ⅛ inch of waterproof tile mastic on the back of the replacement tile with a putty knife, staying ¼ to ½ inch in from the edges of the tile (Figure C).

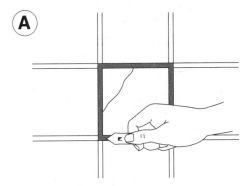

(A)

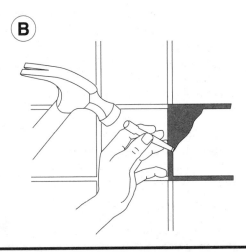

(B)

6. Place the tile and gently tap it level with the original wall surface with a block of wood and hammer (Figure D).

7. Mix the powdered grout, following the manufacturer's directions.

8. Apply the grout to the tile joints with your bare forefinger (Figure E). If you are replacing a large number of tiles, apply the grout by wiping diagonally across the entire surface with a rubber-edged grout float. Wipe the grout in several directions to fill the joints.

9. Wipe off any excess grout with a damp, but not saturated, sponge. Be careful not to remove too much grout from the joints.

10. After the grout dries, wipe the tiles to remove any residue.

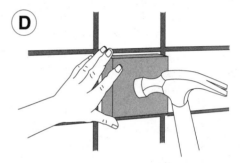

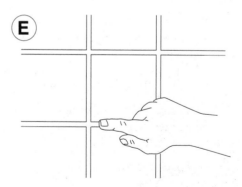

REFASTENING A TOWEL BAR

If a towel bar is attached to plaster or drywall with simple wood screws, it is only a matter of time before the screws pull out of the soft wall material. The cure is to replace the wood screws with toggle bolts—bolts that have large, flat "wings" to grip the back side of the wall.

MATERIALS
4 toggle bolts and wings

TOOLS
Screwdriver • Utility knife

1. Remove the towel bar (Figure A). First, cut around the bracket with a utility knife to break the paint bond, if necessary. Turn the wood screws clockwise to enlarge the holes, and then pull the towel-bar end caps straight back.

2. At a hardware store, purchase toggle bolts and wings to match the diameter of the screw holes in the end caps.

3. Compress the wings of one of the toggle bolts, and use them to determine how much the old holes will have to be enlarged to fit the wings. Mark the outlines of the holes. Enlarge the marked holes with a utility knife or a Phillips screwdriver.

4. Remove the wings from the toggle bolts, push the bolts through the towel-bar end caps, and spin the wings one or two turns onto the bolt (Figure B).

5. Compress the toggle wings, and insert the winged bolt ends through the holes in the wall.

6. Pull back the toggle bolts gently to engage the wings and then tighten them with a screwdriver. Before tightening the toggle bolts completely, insert the towel bar into the end caps.

7. Finish tightening the toggle bolts to secure the towel bar to the wall firmly (Figure C).

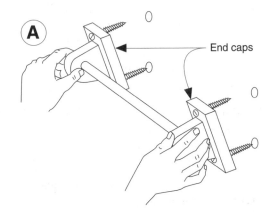

End caps

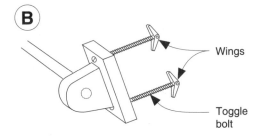

Wings

Toggle bolt

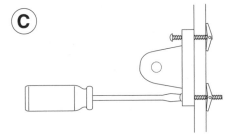

DOORS

TROUBLESHOOTING A BINDING DOOR

Most homes have at least one door that doesn't quite fit. The cure is usually shimming a hinge or removing wood either by sanding or planing. First identify the area of binding, then make the repair following the options in the order listed.

MATERIALS
80-grit sandpaper

TOOLS
Screwdriver • Wood chisel

When binding occurs at area *a* or *c* (Figure A), try these options:

- Tighten the hinge screws. (See "Tightening Hinge Screws" on page 55.)

- Shim the top hinge. (See "Shimming a Hinge on a Sagging Door" on page 56.)

- Sand or plane the door edge at *a* or *c*. (See "Trimming a Binding Door" on page 54.)

When binding occurs at area *b* or *d* (Figure B), first check to see if parts of the door have come unglued. If so, the only simple solution is that described in "Bracing a Sagging Door" on page 57. If the door is not sagging, try these options:

- Tighten the hinge screws. (See "Tightening Hinge Screws" on page 55.)

- Shim the bottom hinge. (See "Shimming a Hinge on a Sagging Door" on page 56.)

- Sand or plane the door edge at *b* or *d*. (See "Trimming a Binding Door" on page 54.)

When binding occurs along the top edge (Figure C), try these options:

- Sand the top edge of the door with 80-grit sandpaper.

- Plane the top edge of the door. (See "Trimming a Binding Door" on page 54.)

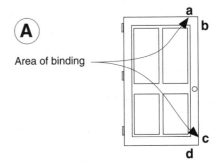

Area of binding

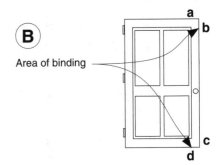

Area of binding

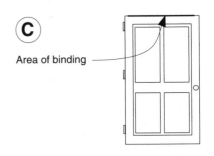

Area of binding

When binding occurs along the bottom edge (Figure D), follow these steps:

1. Take down the door by removing the bottom, middle, and top hinge pins in that order.

2. Plane the bottom edge of the door. (See "Trimming a Binding Door" on page 54.)

When binding occurs along the hinged edge (Figure E), try these options:

• Shim one or both of the hinges. (See "Shimming a Hinge on a Sagging Door" on page 56.)

• If the door now binds along the latch edge, remove the shims, then remove the door from the hinges, and plane the hinge edge. (See "Trimming a Binding Door" on page 54.) Without deepening the hinge mortises, refasten the door to its hinges.

When binding occurs along the latch edge (Figure F), follow these steps:

1. Take down the door by removing the bottom, middle, and top hinge pins in that order. Remove the hinge leaves.

2. Plane the hinge edge. (See "Trimming a Binding Door" on page 54.)

3. With a sharp wood chisel, deepen the hinge mortises until the hinge lies flush with the newly planed edge.

4. Refasten the hinge leaves to the door, and rehang the door by replacing the hinge pins. If you deepened a mortise too much and the hinge side now binds, shim the hinge. (See "Shimming a Hinge on a Sagging Door" on page 56.)

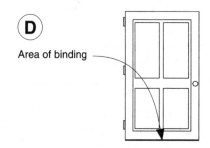

D Area of binding

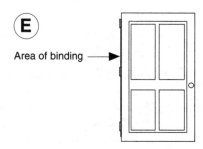

E Area of binding

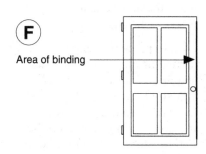

F Area of binding

TRIMMING A BINDING DOOR

Trimming a door that binds can be frustrating for the best handyperson. The trick is deciding when you have removed enough wood. Be careful not to remove too much. Instead, remove a little at a time even if it takes three or four times to get it right.

1. Determine which edge of the door requires planing (Figure A). If the door sticks only at the top or the bottom of the latch side, you may be able to shim a hinge. (See "Shimming a Hinge on a Sagging Door" on page 56.)

2. Carefully mark the amount of wood to be removed on both door faces with a pencil and a carpenter's square.

3. Remove the door by removing the screws from the door side of the hinges.

4. Brace the door so that the edge to be planed is facing up and at waist (or lower) height. If you are planing the top or bottom, you'll need to stand on a stairway, porch, deck, or stepladder. Get a helper to hold the door, if possible.

5. To plane the top or bottom (Figure B), adjust a block plane blade by turning the adjustment knob to remove the thinnest shaving possible. Cut from both ends toward the middle to avoid splintering the wood at the edges.

6. To plane the hinge edge (Figure C), adjust the plane blade to remove a thin shaving. If there is too much resistance, adjust it to remove a thinner shaving. Use continuous strokes for the length of the door, bearing down on the heel as you finish the cut. After planing, you will have to chisel out the hinge mortises to make the hinges fit flush again.

MATERIALS
None

TOOLS
Carpenter's square • Screwdriver • Block plane • Wood chisel

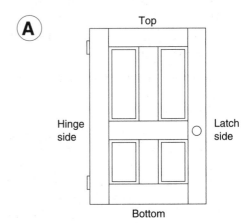

A
Top
Hinge side
Latch side
Bottom

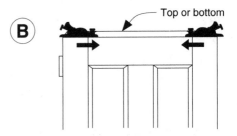

B
Top or bottom

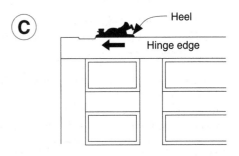

C
Heel
Hinge edge

TIGHTENING HINGE SCREWS

When doors get slammed shut or kids swing on them, the hinge screws eventually work loose. If you catch the problem early, simply tightening the screws will do. If the screws have enlarged their holes, however, the golf-tee trick below will do the job. Consult your favorite golfer for tees.

1. Try tightening the hinge screws.

2. If a screw turns without getting tighter, the wood threads are stripped. The simplest solution is to use longer screws. With one of the old screws as a model, purchase new screws of the same diameter but ¼ inch longer. Since the longer screws will bite into fresh wood, they will probably hold.

3. If the longer screws don't work, you'll need to plug the old holes and start over. Do one hinge at a time so that you don't have to remove the door. Remove the jamb-side hinge leaf. Dip wood golf tees into carpenter's glue, and lightly hammer the tees into each of the loose holes until just snug (Figure A).

4. After 24 hours, cut the tees flush with a utility knife.

5. Unfold the hinge leaf back into place, and lightly punch-drill centering holes with a common nail.

6. Drill pilot holes of a diameter half that of the shank portion of the original screws (Figure B).

7. Replace and tighten the screws. If the screws are too difficult to drive, back them out, lubricate the threads with paste wax or a bar of soap, and try again.

MATERIALS
- **Replacement wood screws**
- **Wood golf tees**
- **Carpenter's glue**
- **Common nail**
- **Paste wax or a bar of soap**

TOOLS
Screwdriver • Hammer • Utility knife • Drill and pilot bit

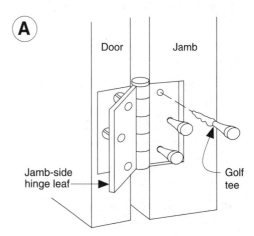

A

Door Jamb

Jamb-side hinge leaf

Golf tee

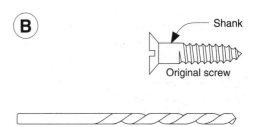

B

Shank

Original screw

Drill bit for pilot hole

SHIMMING A HINGE ON A SAGGING DOOR

Both houses and their doors—at least the wood variety—sag with age. If the door is sufficiently smaller than its opening, shimming just one of the hinges should free a door binding at any of the four spots shown in Figure A. The beauty of shimming is that you don't have to remove the door.

MATERIALS

$1/16$"- to $1/8$"-thick dense cardboard

TOOLS

Screwdriver • Utility knife
• Drill and bit

1. First check to make sure all of the hinge screws are tight. If they spin loosely in their holes, see "Tightening Hinge Screws" on page 55. Using longer screws may solve your problem.

2. Determine which hinge requires shimming (Figure A):

- **If the door binds at either *a* or *c*,** the top hinge needs a shim.

- **If the door binds at either *b* or *d*,** the bottom hinge needs a shim.

3. Open the door and remove the screws from the jamb side of the hinge.

4. Using the hinge leaf as a template, trace the outline of the hinge and screw holes on a piece of dense cardboard to create a shim.

5. Cut out the shim with a utility knife, and mark the screw locations. Drill clearance holes in the shim for the screws.

6. Place the shim in the jamb cutout, and refasten the hinge to the jamb (Figure B). If the screws don't go in tightly, replace them with new screws of the same diameter but $1/4$ inch longer.

7. If the door still sticks, repeat Steps 3 through 6, using additional or thicker shims.

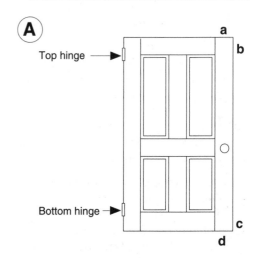

A

Top hinge →

a
b

Bottom hinge →

c
d

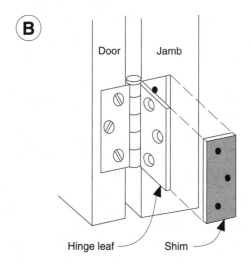

B

Door   Jamb

Hinge leaf   Shim

BRACING A SAGGING DOOR

Wood doors, like people, sag with age. This is particularly true of wood screen doors, which are often flimsy. The cure is a screen door turnbuckle. If you object to its appearance, you can replace it—once you eliminate the sag—with a fixed length of 1 × 3 lumber or fancier wood molding screwed in place.

MATERIALS
• **Screen door turnbuckle**
• **Roundhead wood screws**

TOOLS
Screwdriver • Drill and pilot bit

1. Purchase a screen door turnbuckle at a hardware store or home center. Before installing, adjust it by hand so that only two threads are visible inside each end of the body.

2. Place the turnbuckle in its approximate position, from the top of the hinge side to the bottom of the latch side—both on the room side of the door—and mark the location of the top-most screw (Figure A).

3. Drill a pilot hole for the top screw. The bit diameter should be about half that of the shank—the unthreaded portion—of the screw.

4. Install the top screw through the top end of the turnbuckle.

5. Repeat Steps 2 through 4 for the bottom-most screw at the bottom of the latch side of the door. Don't add the other screws yet as their positions on the door may shift as you tighten the turnbuckle.

6. Turn the turnbuckle body with a screwdriver (Figure B) until the sag is removed and the door closes easily.

7. Drill pilot holes and install the remaining screws.

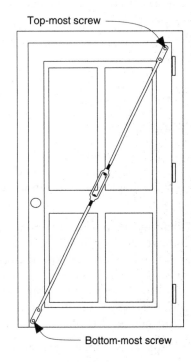

Top-most screw

Bottom-most screw

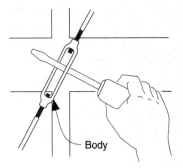

Body

ADJUSTING BIFOLD DOORS

Over time, bifold doors may sag so that they fail to close evenly or drag as they are closed. Fortunately, adjustments are simple. Both top and bottom hinge brackets are designed to slide, once you have loosened their adjusting screws or bolts.

MATERIALS
None

TOOLS
Screwdriver • Book • Adjustable wrench

First determine which of the hinge brackets needs to be adjusted, as follows:

• *If the doors do not meet*, both top and bottom brackets should be moved toward the center.

• *If the doors press too tightly together and will not close*, both top and bottom brackets should be moved away from the center.

• *If the doors sag toward the center*, either the top brackets should be moved further apart, or the bottom brackets should be moved closer together.

To adjust a top hinge bracket (Figure A), remove the door by lifting it up and out of the bottom bracket, and then pull down from the top bracket. Loosen the adjusting screw, slide the bracket in or out, as needed, then tighten the adjusting screw and test the fit.

To adjust a bottom hinge bracket (Figure B), shim the door up with a book, loosen the bracket bolt with an adjustable wrench, and slide the bracket in or out, as needed. When just right, tighten the bolt and remove the book.

To adjust the door height, turn the bottom hinge pin clockwise (to lower the door) or counterclockwise (to raise the door) with the adjustable wrench.

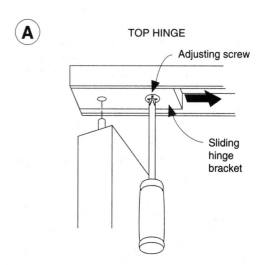

(A) TOP HINGE

Adjusting screw

Sliding hinge bracket

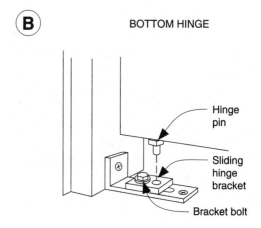

(B) BOTTOM HINGE

Hinge pin

Sliding hinge bracket

Bracket bolt

ADJUSTING A SLIDING CLOSET DOOR

If your sliding closet doors don't hang straight, you can fix them in the same way the contractor did when they were installed by adjusting the roller brackets at the top of the doors.

MATERIALS
None

TOOLS
Screwdriver

From inside the closet, identify the general type of roller bracket from which the door hangs (Figure A or Figure B). Determine whether the door should be raised or lowered at each bracket, and use an arrow to mark the direction it needs to be adjusted correctly.

If the bracket resembles the type shown in Figure A, slightly loosen the two screws, pry the bracket up or down with a screwdriver blade, and retighten the bracket screws.

If the bracket resembles the type shown in Figure B, simply rotate the thumb wheel in the appropriate direction to raise or lower the door.

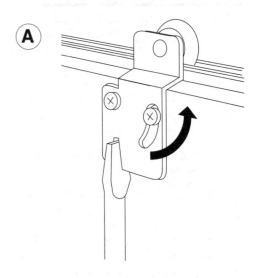

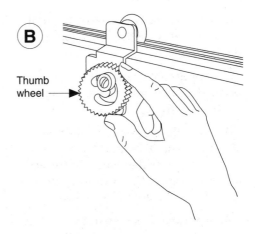

Thumb
wheel →

PATCHING A HOLLOW DOOR

They don't make doors the way they used to. If they did, we couldn't afford them! But even today's low-cost hollow-core doors can be patched. This repair works best if the door is painted rather than naturally finished because the patch won't show once the door is repainted.

MATERIALS
- Scrap of lauan plywood
- Contact cement

TOOLS
Try square • Utility knife

1. Using a try square and a razor-sharp utility knife, lay out and cut a rectangular patch of lauan plywood, just large enough to cover the damaged area (Figure A). The wood grain of the patch should lie in the same direction—up and down—as the grain of the door.

2. Using a sharp pencil, trace the outline of the patch on the door.

3. Using the utility knife, cut out the damaged area of the door using the pencil line as a guide (Figure B). (If the door has cardboard reinforcements inside, repair the hole with auto-body filler. See "Repairing a Dent in Aluminum Siding" on page 252 for how to do this.)

4. Cut two backer strips of lauan plywood half as wide but 1 inch longer than the lauan patch.

5. Apply contact cement to the inside perimeter of the hole and to one side of the backer strips.

6. After the contact cement dries— about 15 minutes—insert the backer strips, and press the cemented surfaces together, using a finger to apply pressure from inside the door (Figure C).

7. Apply contact cement to the back side of the lauan patch and to the front faces of the backer strips. After the cement dries, press the patch into place.

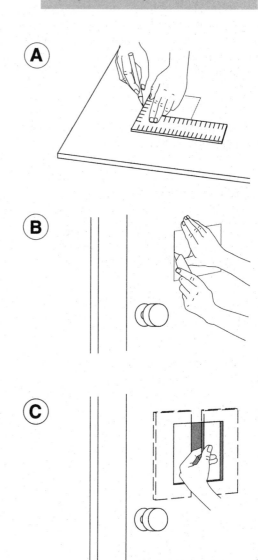

A

B

C

ADJUSTING PATIO DOOR ROLLERS

If your patio door is difficult to open or close, either the track is dirty, the door is dragging on the bottom, or it is off its track. If it's off the track, have a strong person lift it straight up while you guide the bottom rollers onto the track. If it's on the track already, adjusting the clearance may be as simple as turning the bottom adjusting screws.

MATERIALS
Household cleaner

TOOLS
Vacuum cleaner • Toothbrush • Screwdriver

1. Before adjusting the rollers, thoroughly clean the bottom track. Vacuum loose material; use household cleaner and a toothbrush to remove built-up grease.

2. Identify the bottom adjusting screws. On wood patio doors, the screws are usually hidden behind plastic caps (Figures A and B). On aluminum patio doors, the screws are usually on the bottom vertical edge (Figure C).

3. Check to see if the door has top rollers as well (few patio doors do). If your door does have top rollers, lower them by turning their screws counterclockwise one full turn.

4. To raise a corner of the door, turn its bottom adjusting screw clockwise; to lower, turn the screw counterclockwise.

5. Adjust the rollers in both corners until the door rides clear of the floor and closes squarely.

6. If you loosened top rollers in Step 3, retighten them by turning their screws clockwise until the top of the door is snug.

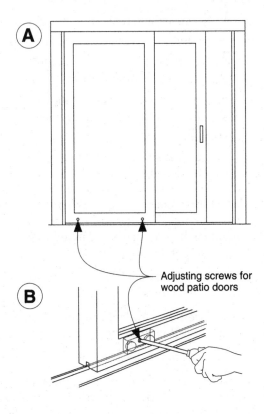

Adjusting screws for wood patio doors

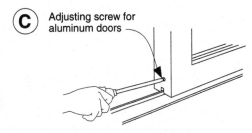

Adjusting screw for aluminum doors

REPLACING A PATIO DOOR LATCH

The only trick to replacing the latch on a patio door is finding an exact or equivalent replacement. Replacement latches can generally be found at either glass dealers or stores that specialize in aluminum storm door and window hardware. It helps to know the brand of the door.

MATERIALS
Replacement patio door latch assembly

TOOLS
Screwdriver

1. Remove the screws from the interior door handle.

2. Remove the interior door handle, along with the spindle (Figure A).

3. Remove the screws from the latch assembly and pull the assembly out (Figure B).

4. Take the latch assembly to a glass dealer or store specializing in storm door and window hardware and purchase an exact replacement. As a last resort, a lumberyard may be able to order a replacement latch, provided you can tell them the brand of the door.

5. Install the new latch assembly and tighten its screws.

6. Insert the new spindle through the hole in the door into the latch assembly.

7. Replace the door handle.

8. If the door will not latch, loosen the screws in the strike plate, which is in the door jamb (Figure C), and slide the strike plate up or down until the latch catches. Tighten the strike plate screws.

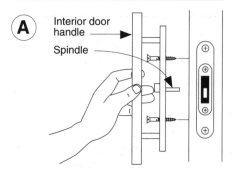

A — Interior door handle / Spindle

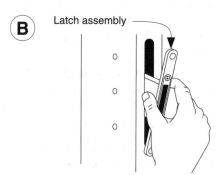

B — Latch assembly

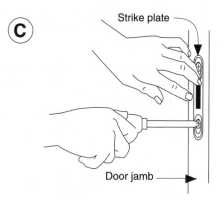

C — Strike plate / Door jamb

REPLACING A PATIO DOOR WEATHER STRIP

When the weather strip on a patio door wears or breaks, the door can become an annoying and expensive source of cold drafts. If you feel a draft around a patio door on windy days, inspect its weather strip. Fortunately, replacing the weather strip is simple once you've removed the door from its track.

MATERIALS
- **Replacement patio door weather strip**
- **Masking tape**

TOOLS
Screwdriver • Putty knife • Long-nose pliers • Utility knife

1. First determine whether the type of weather strip to be replaced is a push-in type or a slide-in type (Figure A). The slide-in type will have a dovetail "tongue."

2. If the weatherstrip is the push-in type, carefully pry it out of its slot using a screwdriver and go to Step 5.

3. If the weather strip is the slide-in type, you'll have to remove the sliding door (Figure B). With a helper, lift the door and swing its bottom edge out and off the track. If the rollers catch on the track, hold them up with your fingers or a putty knife until they clear the track.

4. Slide the old weather strip out of its track with long-nose pliers.

5. Take the old weather strip to a glass dealer to obtain an exact or equivalent replacement.

6. Trim the new weather strip to the required length with a utility knife.

7. Insert the new weather strip.

8. If you had to remove the door, replace it by inserting the top edge into the top track, then seating the bottom rollers on the bottom track. If the rollers hang too low to clear the track, temporarily tape them with masking tape. Remove the tape after the rollers are seated.

A

PUSH-IN WEATHER STRIP   SLIDE-IN WEATHER STRIP

B

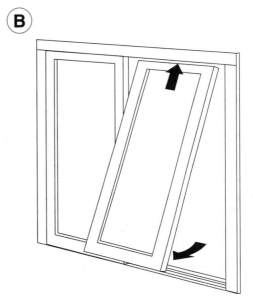

REPLACING AN EXTERIOR THRESHOLD

An exterior threshold may require replacement because it has rotted and is allowing water to penetrate to the sill below. Or, it may have simply worn out from generations of feet. In any case, it is simpler to replace than you might expect. If you haven't any carpentry experience at all, you may want to solicit the help of a handy friend or neighbor. No technique is involved—just the confidence to butcher what appears to be a significant part of your house!

MATERIALS
- **Threshold stock**
- **10d galvanized finish nails**
- **Latex exterior paint or wood stain and varnish**

TOOLS
Backsaw • Screwdriver • Hammer • Wood chisel • Slip-joint pliers • Drill • Paintbrush

1. Using a backsaw, cut the old threshold into three sections. Make the cuts about 4 inches from the door frame on each end (Figure A). If the backsaw blade threatens to damage the interior floor as you approach the end of the cut, have a helper pry up the middle section with a screwdriver while you saw.

2. If it wasn't already done, pry up and remove the middle section with a screwdriver (Figure B).

3. Remove the end pieces by either of the following options:

- Hammer the exterior projecting tongue of the threshold toward the center of the doorway.

- Split the end pieces into small sections with a wood chisel and pull the pieces out with slip-joint pliers.

4. Leaving a saw blade width between the pieces, fit the three pieces you just removed together on the new threshold stock and carefully trace the pattern.

5. Saw out the new threshold with the backsaw.

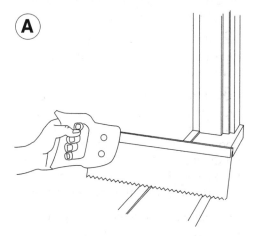

(A)

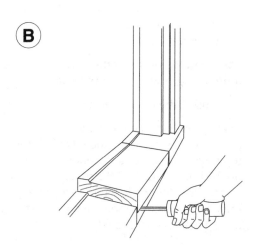

(B)

6. Remove or hammer flush any nails that are projecting from the floor or door frame.

7. Tap the new threshold into place from the outdoor side (Figure C). Don't force the fit; trim the threshold with the backsaw, if necessary.

8. Drill pairs of $\frac{1}{16}$-inch pilot holes at each end of the threshold (Figure D).

9. Hammer 10d galvanized finish nails into the pilot holes.

10. Paint or stain and varnish the new threshold so that it will last longer the next time around.

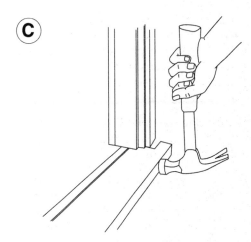

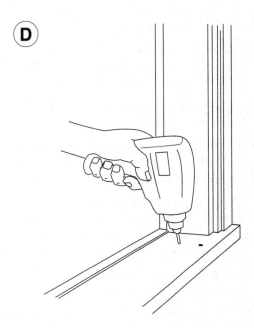

ADJUSTING A GARAGE DOOR

If your garage door raises too easily or too hard or if it fails to seal around the edges, don't contract for a new one. It probably just needs one or more of the three simple adjustments below. First determine what's causing the problem, and then follow the steps to correct it.

If the door jams while moving, the vertical tracks need adjustment (Figure A). With the door down, follow these steps:

1. Using an adjustable wrench, loosen the lag bolts. Tap the brackets with a hammer until the rollers on the door are centered in the tracks. Retighten the lag bolts.

2. Loosen the track bolts with the adjustable wrench. Tap the tracks with the hammer so the exterior face of the door just contacts the door jamb. Retighten the bolts.

If the door lock bar doesn't catch, the bar guides need adjusting (Figure B). With the door down, follow these steps:

1. Loosen the screws holding the bar guides to the door.

2. Tap the guides up or down until the lock bar is centered in the slots in the vertical tracks. Retighten the screws.

If the door is difficult to either raise or lower, the spring tension requires adjustment (Figure C). With the door up, follow these steps:

1. Detach the end of the steel cable from the track or the garage.

2. Retie the knot in the tension adjust clip so there is no slack just when the door is in the fully raised position. Reattach the steel cable.

MATERIALS
None

TOOLS
Adjustable wrench • Hammer • Screwdriver

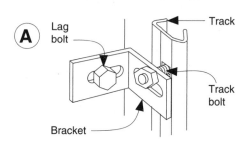

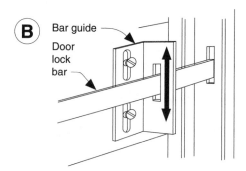

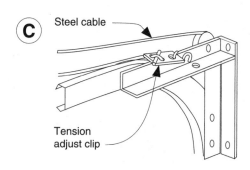

REPLACING A CYLINDER LOCK

Cylinder locks often need replacement. Sometimes they simply wear out. But, more often, if you've moved into a home or apartment, you'll want the security of your own new lock. Don't call the locksmith! Changing the lock will take no more than half an hour. If you have more than one exterior door, purchasing locks that share a common key will make your life easier.

MATERIALS
Replacement cylinder lock

TOOLS
Screwdriver

1. Insert a small screwdriver into the slot in the shank of the interior knob to release the knob (Figure A).

2. Remove the interior knob and rose to expose the mounting plate bolts.

3. Back out the mounting plate bolts, and remove the mounting plate (Figure B).

4. Remove the exterior knob, rose, and cylinder from the exterior side.

5. Remove the screws from the face plate, and pull out the latch assembly (Figure C).

6. Take the parts to a hardware store or home center, and purchase a replacement lock of the same dimensions.

7. Install the new lock in the reverse order, as follows:

   1. Latch assembly and face plate

   2. Cylinder and exterior rose and knob (Verify that the cylinder has engaged the latch by turning the exterior knob.)

   3. Mounting plate (Don't overtighten the mounting plate, or the mechanism may jam.)

   4. Interior rose and knob (The knob should snap into place.)

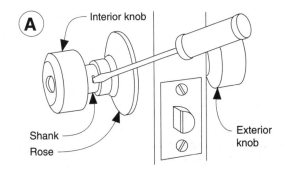

A — Interior knob / Shank / Rose / Exterior knob

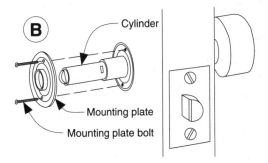

B — Cylinder / Mounting plate / Mounting plate bolt

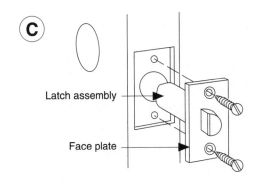

C — Latch assembly / Face plate

REPLACING A MORTISE LOCK

The mortise lock is more complicated than a cylinder lock, so its replacement is a bit more involved. Even so, removing and replacing it requires loosening or removing only five screws—a job that should be within anyone's abilities. Make sure you get a replacement that is exactly the same size.

MATERIALS
Replacement mortise lockset

TOOLS
Screwdriver

1. Remove the deadbolt knob, interior knob, and exterior knob by loosening their setscrews and pulling them out (Figure A).

2. Pull out the spindle, if it didn't come out with the knobs.

3. Loosen the cylinder setscrew, and unscrew the cylinder from the exterior side of the door (Figure B).

4. Remove the screws holding the lock body, and pull the body straight out (Figure C).

5. Take the lock body with you to a hardware store, and purchase a replacement of the same dimensions.

6. Install the new lock components in the reverse order, as follows:

1. Insert the lock body and tighten its screws.

2. Screw in the lock cylinder and tighten its setscrew.

3. Insert the spindle.

4. Replace the interior, exterior, and deadbolt knobs, and tighten their screws.

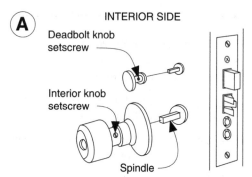

A INTERIOR SIDE
Deadbolt knob setscrew
Interior knob setscrew
Spindle

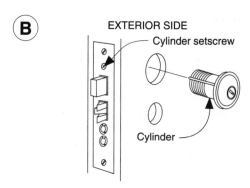

B EXTERIOR SIDE
Cylinder setscrew
Cylinder

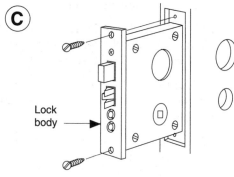

C
Lock body

SHIMMING A STRIKE PLATE

If your door fails to latch, but the striker and the hole in the strike plate are in line, then the striker may simply fail to extend far enough to catch the plate. The answer is not to move the latch but to extend the strike plate by inserting a shim behind it. All you need is some dense cardboard such as posterboard; even shirt cardboard will work.

MATERIALS

- $1/16$"- to $1/8$"-thick dense cardboard
- Wood screws

TOOLS

Screwdriver • Utility knife
• Drill and bit

1. Remove the strike plate screws and gently pry the plate away from the jamb. If the plate resists because it is painted in, break the paint film with a utility knife.

2. Using the strike plate as a template, trace the outline of the plate, its opening, and the two screw holes onto the cardboard (Figure A).

3. Cut out the shim and its large opening with the utility knife (Figure B).

4. Drill clearance holes for the screws in the shim.

5. Refasten the strike plate with the shim beneath it (Figure C), and try the door.

6. If the door still doesn't latch, insert a second shim.

7. Since the shim will prevent the screws from penetrating to their original depth, the screws may now be loose. If so, replace the old screws with new screws of the same diameter but $1/4$ inch longer.

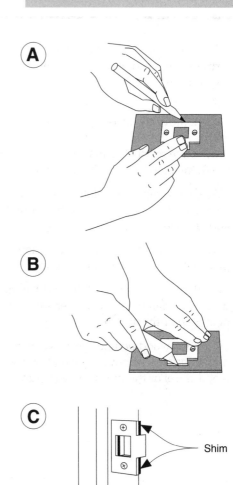

A

B

C

Shim

FILING A STRIKE PLATE

How many doors do you wedge objects into or against to hold them closed? That's the job of the striker and strike plate. If the striker misses the hole in the strike plate by 1/8 inch or less, the simplest solution is filing the opening to make it deeper, as shown below. If the mismatch is more than 1/8 inch, moving the strike plate is the answer. (See "Relocating a Strike Plate" on the opposite page.)

MATERIALS
None

TOOLS
Screwdriver • Utility knife • Bench vise • Flat file • Wood chisel

1. Before removing the strike plate, determine which edge requires filing and the amount to be removed. Mark the edge to be filed accordingly.

2. Remove the strike plate screws, and gently pry the plate away from the jamb. If the plate resists because it is painted in, break the paint film with a utility knife.

3. Clamp the strike plate in a bench vise with the edge to be filed horizontal and close to the vise jaws.

4. Using a flat file, remove the plate material down to the mark (Figure A).

5. Replace the strike plate, and try the door. If the latch still doesn't engage, repeat Steps 1 through 5.

6. If the wood behind the strike plate now interferes, remove the wood with a wood chisel or the utility knife (Figure B).

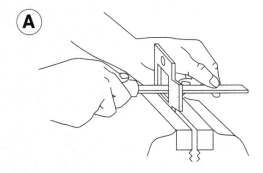

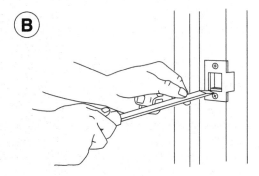

RELOCATING A STRIKE PLATE

If you have a door that refuses to stay latched, measure the amount by which the striker misses the strike plate cutout. If the mismatch is 1/8 inch or less, the simplest solution is filing the opening to make it deeper. (See "Filing a Strike Plate" on the opposite page.) If the mismatch is greater than 1/8 inch, move the strike plate, as shown below.

MATERIALS
Wood putty

TOOLS
Screwdriver • Utility knife • Wood chisel • Drill and pilot bit

1. Remove the strike plate screws, and gently pry the plate away from the jamb. If the plate resists because it is painted in, break the paint film with a utility knife.

2. Hold the strike plate in the desired location, and mark the new top and bottom edges of the strike plate cutout and bolt cutout as well as the screw holes on the jamb (Figure A).

3. Plug the old screw holes with wood putty.

4. Using a wood chisel, extend the strike plate cutout and bolt cutout up or down by chiseling out the wood to the marked lines (Figure B).

5. After the wood putty has dried—24 hours is safe—drill new pilot holes using a bit half the diameter of the shank—the unthreaded portion—of the screws.

6. Install the strike plate in its new location.

7. If you wish, fill the gap between the strike plate and the jamb with wood putty.

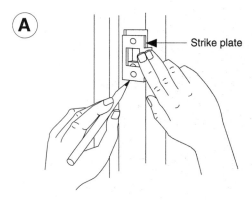

A — Strike plate

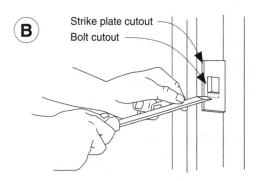

B — Strike plate cutout
Bolt cutout

ADJUSTING A STORM DOOR CLOSER

A storm door closer is designed to pull the door in rapidly, then slow down as it approaches the latch. If your storm door either fails to close or bangs closed, try adjusting the closer adjusting screw, as described below. That usually does the trick. Otherwise, replace the closer, following the manufacturer's directions.

MATERIALS
None

TOOLS
Screwdriver

1. Identify the closer adjusting screw, which is located in the end of the door closer cylinder (Figure A).

2. To make the door close more slowly, turn the adjusting screw one-half turn clockwise (Figure B). To make the door close more quickly, turn the adjusting screw counterclockwise.

3. Open the door fully, then let go and observe how it closes.

4. Repeat Steps 2 and 3 until the door closes quickly but without banging.

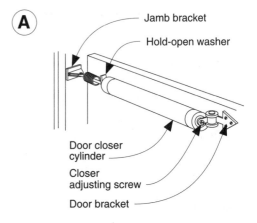

A

Jamb bracket

Hold-open washer

Door closer cylinder

Closer adjusting screw

Door bracket

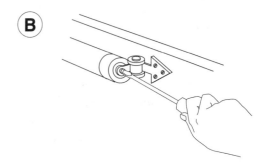

B

PATCHING A SCREEN

Often, all it takes to invite fearsom "no-see-ums" or other ravenous blood suckers into your house is a tiny hole in a screen. Here are three methods for "barring the door."

For tears less than 1 inch long in any screening material (Figure A), follow these steps:

1. Bend the torn screen strands back to their original positions.

2. Apply model cement to the tear, and spread with a cotton swab.

3. Quickly poke clear as many holes as possible with a toothpick.

For large tears in metal screening (Figure B), follow these steps:

1. Cut a patch of similar screening to overlap the damaged area by ¼ inch.

2. Bend the patch strand ends down.

3. Place the patch over the hole so that the ends of the strands fit into the mesh on the screening. Press the patch tightly against the screening, and bend the strand ends around the original screen with your fingers.

For large tears in plastic or fiberglass screening (Figure C), follow these steps:

1. Cut a patch of similar screening to overlap the damaged area by ¼ inch.

2. Place the patch over the hole with the strands lined up.

3. Thread thin nylon fishing line onto a #18 tapestry sewing needle, and lace the patch to the original screen.

MATERIALS

Model cement, matching screening material, or thin nylon fishing line

TOOLS

Toothpick • Cotton swab • Heavy-duty scissors • #18 tapestry sewing needle

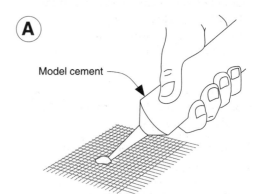

(A) Model cement

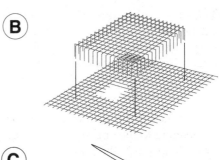

(B)

(C)

REPLACING A WOOD DOOR SCREEN

When the dog goes through the screen door, the simple mends of "Patching a Screen" on page 73 will not be adequate; it's time to replace the entire screen. Achieving a tight stretch with no wrinkles requires the simple tricks shown below.

1. Carefully pry up and remove all wood molding around the screen with a wood chisel. Locate the brads, and wedge the chisel as close to the brads as possible to pry up the molding. If the molding breaks, take a sample to a lumberyard to obtain a match.

2. Remove the old screening and any brads that pulled through the molding with long-nose pliers.

3. Place the door on a table or the floor with a 2 × 4 under each end. Place a third 2 × 4 across the middle of the frame, and weight it down to bow the frame (Figure A).

4. Using a utility knife, cut new screening 2 inches larger than the opening. Using a staple gun and 1/4-inch staples, staple the screening to one end of the frame, placing the staples in the sequence shown in Figure B.

5. Pull the screening tight, and staple the screening to the opposite end. Unbow the door and staple the screening to the sides, working from the center to both ends.

6. Using 1/2-inch brads and a tack hammer, fasten the screen molding. Use a hacksaw to cut new molding, if necessary.

7. Trim the excess screening by running a sharp utility knife along the outside of the molding (Figure C).

MATERIALS

- Wood molding
- Three 2 × 4s, 36" long
- Matching screening material
- 1/4" staples
- 1/2" brads

TOOLS

Wood chisel • Long-nose pliers • Heavy weights • Utility knife • Staple gun • Tack hammer • Hacksaw

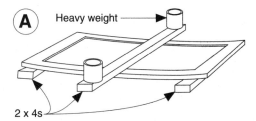

A — Heavy weight — 2 x 4s

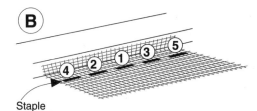

B — Staple

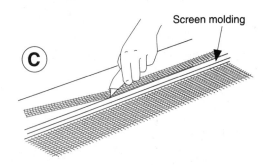

C — Screen molding

REPLACING A METAL DOOR SCREEN

Replacing the screening in a metal screen door or window is far simpler than in their wood equivalents because the screening is held in place with a spline instead of staples. Spline material is available in several diameters, so make sure you take a sample of the original when buying a replacement.

MATERIALS
- Matching screening material
- Matching tubular screen spline

TOOLS
Screwdriver • Utility knife
- Screen spline roller

1. Remove the screen panel from the aluminum door.

2. Pry up the end of the tubular screen spline with a screwdriver, and then pull it out of the channel all around the frame (Figure A). Remove the old screening.

3. Take the old screening and spline to a hardware store or home center, and purchase new materials of the same type.

4. Using a utility knife, cut the new screening at least 2 inches larger than the old piece. Then, lay it over the opening.

5. Press the screening into the channel at one end of the panel using the convex wheel of a screen spline roller (Figure B).

6. Place the spline over the screen that you just pressed into the channel, and force the spline into the channel using the concave wheel of the spline roller (Figure C). Be careful not to press too hard or the screen may break.

7. Repeat Steps 6 and 7 for the opposite end of the panel and then for the two remaining sides. Pull the screening tight, and as you insert the spline, it will automatically stretch the screening the right amount.

8. Trim the excess screening by running a sharp utility knife along the outside edge of the spline.

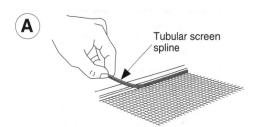

(A) Tubular screen spline

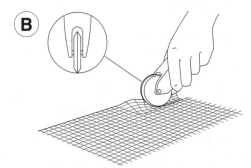

(B)

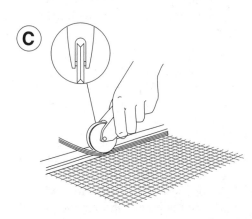

(C)

PAINTING A DOOR

Because doors take such a beating and are often handled by greasy, dirty hands, they should be painted with high-quality gloss or semigloss paint. Use exterior paint for entry doors. The top and bottom ends of nonwood doors do not need to be painted, but if the doors are wood, paint the top and bottom ends—even though not seen—to minimize shrinking and swelling.

1. Scrub the door surfaces to be painted with an abrasive scrub pad and household cleaner. Rinse the cleaner off with fresh water and let the door dry.

2. If the surfaces are glossy, apply paint deglosser with a clean rag. The deglosser provides a surface to which the paint can more readily adhere.

3. Open the door and wedge it firmly open by inserting wood shingles between the bottom edge and the floor.

4. Remove the door handle and cover all surfaces not to be painted with masking tape. Trim the tape with a utility knife. Spread a drop cloth on the floor.

5. If the door has not been painted previously, paint the entire door with a primer that is compatible with the finish coat. Let it dry.

6. If the door is flush—either solid core or hollow core—apply the finish paint with a 4 × 6-inch paint pad. Apply a second coat if the old color shows through.

7. If the door is paneled, use a high-quality, 2-inch paintbrush and follow the brushing technique shown in Figure A. Paint one section at a time, following the numbered sequence shown in Figure B.

MATERIALS
- **Household cleaner**
- **Paint deglosser**
- **Clean rag**
- **Wood shingles**
- **Masking tape**
- **Latex primer paint**
- **Gloss or semigloss, exterior or interior latex paint**

TOOLS
Abrasive scrub pad • Utility knife • Drop cloth • 4" × 6" paint pad • 2" paintbrush

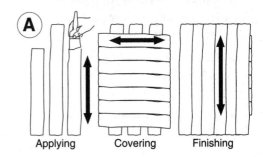

A

Applying   Covering   Finishing

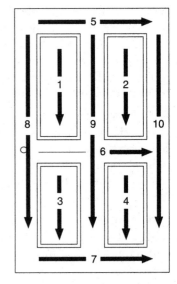

B

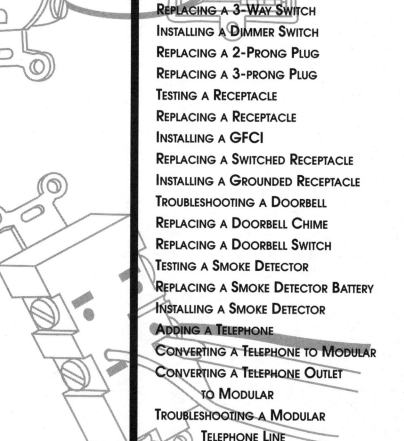

ELECTRICAL

CLEANING VCR HEADS

When a video cassette recorder (VCR) goes bad, it is invariably due to dirty video heads. Minute particles of magnetic coating from videotapes stick to the heads and interfere with the reading of the video signal. Wiping the heads with head-cleaning fluid—available at electronics stores—will restore the machine to new condition. Do not use a head-cleaning tape. It may be simple but it abrades the heads.

MATERIALS
- Masking tape
- VCR head-cleaning fluid
- Cotton swab

TOOLS
Screwdriver

1. Look at the rear panel of the VCR. If there is any question in your mind which cable plugs into which jack, use masking tape to label each cable with the name of its corresponding jack, then remove the cable. Unplug the VCR from the outlet.

2. Inspect the top cover of the VCR. It should cover both the top and the sides. Find the cover screws that secure the top and remove them. Remove the top cover.

3. Look into the interior of the VCR, and locate a silver drum about 3 inches in diameter (Figure A). That is the capstan (the actual heads are imbedded in the surface of the capstan), which you want to clean.

4. Dip a cotton swab into the head-cleaning fluid and wipe the shiny cylindrical surface of the capstan. Do not touch the shiny surface with your fingers. With your forefinger on top of the drum, rotate the drum until you have wiped the entire surface several times (Figure B).

5. When there is no longer the tiniest speck of material on the drum, replace the top cover, plug in the cables, and restore the power. You have just saved at least $15.

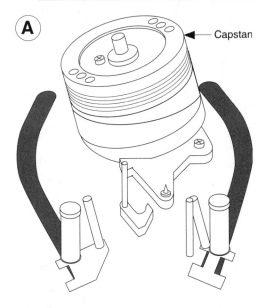

A — Capstan

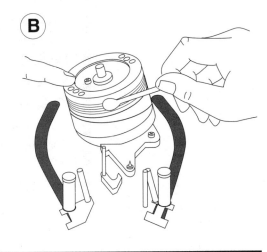

B

REPLACING A LAMP CORD

Lamp cords suffer from being walked on by adults and chewed by children and dogs. Although it is possible to splice a lamp cord, it is as simple and far safer to replace the entire cord. This technique can also be used to make your own lamp.

MATERIALS

- Lamp cord
- Electrical tape

TOOLS

Screwdriver • Diagonal-cutting pliers • Utility knife • Wire stripper

1. Unplug the lamp.

2. Remove the light bulb(s).

3. Disassemble the lamp from the top down, as shown in the illustration at right.

4. Loosen the terminal screws and remove the wire ends.

5. If threading the new cord through the lamp base appears difficult, cut the plug from the old cord with diagonal-cutting pliers, and tape the end of the new cord to the cut end of the old cord with electrical tape. Pull the old cord up through the base until the new cord appears.

6. Using a utility knife, separate the two wires of the new cord back about 2 inches.

7. Using a wire stripper, trim the insulation from each wire back 3/4 inch.

8. Tie the Underwriters' knot shown in the illustration at right.

9. Twist the end of each wire to pull the strands together. Then attach each wire by looping the end clockwise around its terminal screw and tightening the screw.

10. Reassemble the lamp.

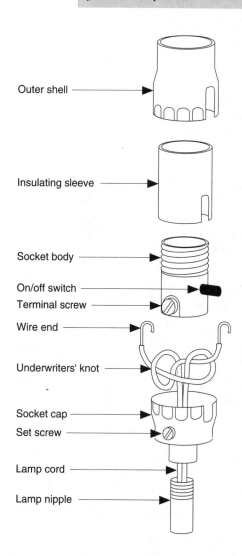

Outer shell

Insulating sleeve

Socket body

On/off switch

Terminal screw

Wire end

Underwriters' knot

Socket cap

Set screw

Lamp cord

Lamp nipple

REPAIRING A LAMP

If you have a balky lamp, don't fret. It's usually easy to fix, and the electrical components are very standardized. Hardware stores and home centers generally carry all of the common parts. If you have trouble finding a part, consult antique dealers—they may have sources.

MATERIALS
Replacement lamp socket body

TOOLS
Neon circuit tester • Screwdriver

1. First, check the lamp by switching receptacles and by replacing the bulb.

2. If the lamp still doesn't work, unplug the lamp and disassemble it from the top down (Figure A), as follows:

　1. Squeeze the socket shell at its base and work it up and off.

　2. Remove the insulating sleeve.

3. Plug the lamp in, and carefully touch the probes of a neon circuit tester to the two exposed terminal screws, making sure not to touch the tips against any metal. If the neon bulb lights, go to Step 4. If not, see "Replacing a Lamp Cord" on page 79.

4. Unplug the lamp again, and remove the two terminal screws and wires.

5. Take the old socket body to a hardware store or home center, and buy a replacement.

6. Install the socket body by looping the wire ends under the terminal screws of the new socket body and tightening the screws (Figure B).

7. Slide the insulating sleeve over the socket, and press the socket shell down until it snaps into place.

8. Screw in the bulb and plug in the lamp.

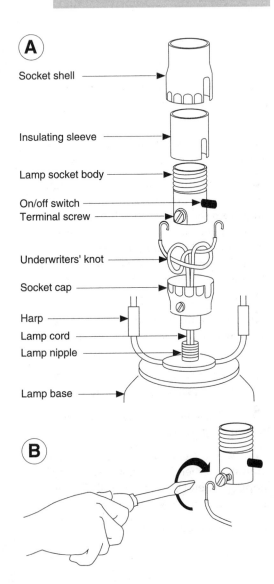

A

Socket shell

Insulating sleeve

Lamp socket body

On/off switch
Terminal screw

Underwriters' knot

Socket cap

Harp
Lamp cord
Lamp nipple

Lamp base

B

REPLACING A LIGHT FIXTURE

Except for a fresh coat of paint, nothing brightens up a room more than a new light fixture. Replacement is simple since the hard work of running the house wiring has already been done.

MATERIALS
- **Fixture mounting strap**
- **Replacement light fixture**
- **2 wire nuts**

TOOLS
Screwdriver • Wire stripper

1. Turn off the power to the fixture at the wall switch and at the main panel.

2. Remove the fixture screws and lower the fixture so it hangs by its wires.

3. The old fixture will have one white wire and one black wire—or a white wire with black tape around its end— both screwed to terminals or connected with wire nuts. Remove the old fixture from the wires.

4. If there isn't a fixture mounting strap in place, install one (Figure A). If there is a bare or green ground wire in the junction box, unscrew it from the box, and install it under the green screw of the mounting strap.

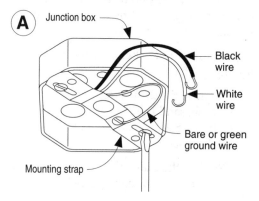

A   Junction box

Black wire

White wire

Bare or green ground wire

Mounting strap

5. Splice the new fixture wires to the house wires—black to black and white to white—using wire nuts. To splice, trim the insulation of the individual wires back 3/4 inch with a wire stripper. Place the bare tips of the two wires together, insert into the wire nut, and twist the wire nut clockwise (Figure B). Test the connections by tugging on the wires.

6. Tuck the wires into the box and fasten the new fixture with screws into the threaded holes in the mounting strap.

7. Install the light bulb, restore the power, and test the fixture.

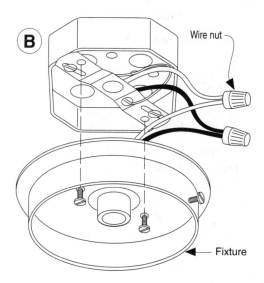

B

Wire nut

Fixture

TROUBLESHOOTING A FLUORESCENT LIGHT

A number of factors can cause a fluorescent light to act up: low room temperature, a tired bulb, a broken starter, or a bad ballast. The procedure below should find the problem before you have replaced the entire fixture—which, by the way, is sometimes the best solution.

MATERIALS
Fine sandpaper

TOOLS
None

Before concluding that anything requires replacement, check that the circuit breaker is on, that the temperature of the room is at least 50°F, and that the bulb is seated properly in the end sockets.

If the bulb only flickers, try the following options:

• Remove the diffuser panel, remove the bulb, sand the pins, and reinsert the bulb. (See "Replacing a Fluorescent Bulb" on page 84.)

• Replace the bulb. (See "Replacing a Fluorescent Bulb" on page 84.)

If the bulb doesn't even flicker, try the following options:

• If you have a starter-type light (Figure A), replace the starter. (See "Replacing a Fluorescent Starter" on page 85.)

• Replace the bulb. (See "Replacing a Fluorescent Bulb" on page 84.)

• If you have a rapid-start-type light (Figure B), replace the ballast. (See "Replacing a Fluorescent Ballast" on page 86.) Check the prices before doing this; it may be as cheap or cheaper to replace the fixture!

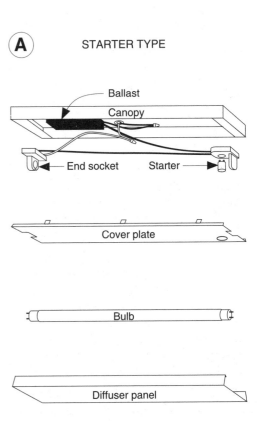

A   STARTER TYPE

Ballast
Canopy
End socket   Starter

Cover plate

Bulb

Diffuser panel

If the bulb is blackened, try the following options:

• If the bulb is blackened only at one end, remove the bulb, turn it end to end, and replace the bulb. (See "Replacing a Fluorescent Bulb" on page 84.)

• If you have a starter-type light (Figure A), replace both the bulb and the starter. (See "Replacing a Fluorescent Bulb" on page 84 and "Replacing a Fluorescent Starter" on page 85.)

If the bulb glows at the ends only, try the following options:

• If you have a starter-type light (Figure A), replace the starter. (See "Replacing a Fluorescent Starter" on page 85.)

• If you have a rapid-start-type light (Figure B), replace the ballast if you think the cost is justified. (See "Replacing a Fluorescent Ballast" on page 86.)

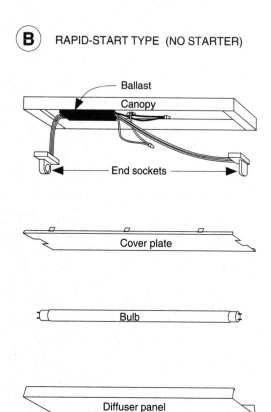

B RAPID-START TYPE (NO STARTER)

Ballast

Canopy

End sockets

Cover plate

Bulb

Diffuser panel

REPLACING A FLUORESCENT BULB

You probably already know how to change fluorescent bulbs. In case you are new to fluorescent lighting, however, here's how. Bulbs should be replaced when they burn out or begin to flicker. Spent bulbs often are black at the ends.

MATERIALS
Replacement fluorescent bulb

TOOLS
None

1. Turn off the power to the light at the main panel.

2. Remove the diffuser panel—if there is one—by pulling one edge upward and away from the fixture (Figure A).

3. Remove the bulb by rotating 90 degrees and pulling one end straight down. With one end free, the other end can be withdrawn.

4. Write down the type, wattage, and length of the old bulb, and purchase a replacement at a hardware store or home center.

5. Align the pins of the new bulb vertically with the slots in the end sockets, push the bulb straight up into the end sockets, and twist the bulb 90 degrees in either direction. You should feel the pins seat in the socket cutouts (Figure B).

6. Replace the diffuser panel. Restore the power, and switch on the light.

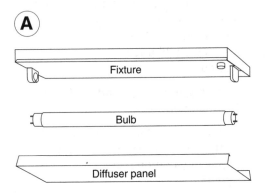

A

Fixture

Bulb

Diffuser panel

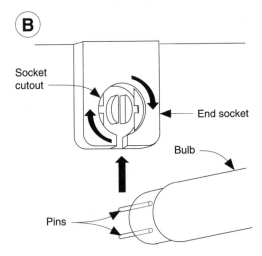

B

Socket cutout

End socket

Bulb

Pins

REPLACING A FLUORESCENT STARTER

Older fluorescent fixtures sometimes require starters—they look like little aluminum cans—that switch on the light when you turn on the power. Starters are so inexpensive that they are the first thing you should replace when your fluorescent light acts up. You can tell if you have starters by pulling down the diffuser panel and looking.

MATERIALS
Replacement fluorescent starter

TOOLS
None

1. Turn off the power to the light at the main panel.

2. Remove the diffuser panel—if there is one—by pulling one edge upward and away from the fixture (Figure A).

3. Remove the old starter by pressing it in and twisting counterclockwise.

4. Take the old starter to a hardware store or home center, and purchase a new one of the same type.

5. Install the new starter by inserting its contacts into the starter socket and twisting the starter clockwise (Figure B).

6. Replace the diffuser panel. Restore the power, and switch on the light.

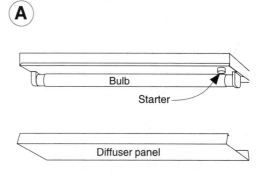

A

Bulb

Starter

Diffuser panel

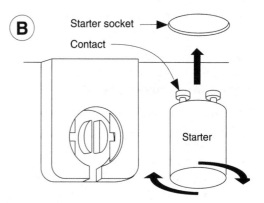

B

Starter socket

Contact

Starter

REPLACING A FLUORESCENT BALLAST

Fluorescent ballasts are simple to install. Before purchasing a replacement, however, compare the costs of a ballast and a complete fixture. The new fixture may cost even less than the ballast alone.

1. Turn off the power to the light at the main panel.

2. Remove the diffuser panel by pulling one edge upward and away from the fixture (Figure A).

3. Remove the bulb by rotating 90 degrees and pulling one end straight down.

4. Remove the cover plate. Most often this means squeezing it to release the tabs on its edges from the slots in the canopy.

5. Wrap masking tape around each of the wires to the old ballast. Mark each with pairs of numbers: 1 and 1, 2 and 2.

6. Disconnect any ballast wires held by wire nuts. Cut other wires at the center of the tape with diagonal-cutting pliers so that each wire is numbered (Figure B).

7. Remove the old ballast with a screwdriver, and take it to a hardware store or home center to buy a replacement.

8. Install the new ballast. If you cut the wires earlier, strip back the insulation from them 3/4 inch with a wire stripper, and connect them by inserting the bare ends of each pair of wires into a wire nut and twisting the nut clockwise (Figure C).

9. Tuck all the wires into the canopy, and replace the cover plate.

10. Replace the bulb and diffuser panel, and restore the power.

MATERIALS
- **Masking tape**
- **Replacement fluorescent ballast**
- **Wire nuts**

TOOLS
Diagonal-cutting pliers
- **Screwdriver • Wire stripper**

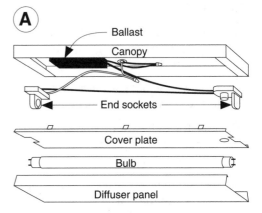

A

Ballast
Canopy
End sockets
Cover plate
Bulb
Diffuser panel

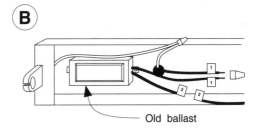

B

Old ballast

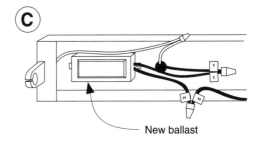

C

New ballast

REPLACING A SINGLE-POLE SWITCH

Since they contain moving parts, switches are subject to wear. Fortunately, they cost little and they are easy to replace. Note the difference between single-pole and three-way switches, however. They are not interchangeable.

MATERIALS
Replacement single-pole switch

TOOLS
Screwdriver • Neon circuit tester

1. Turn off the power to the switch circuit at the main panel.

2. Remove the switch cover plate and the two screws fastening the switch to the box.

3. Holding the switch by the fastening tabs at top and bottom, pull it straight out of the box, being careful not to touch the screw terminals to the box (Figure A).

4. Touch one probe of a neon circuit tester to each of the screw terminals on the side of the switch (Figure B). If the tester glows, you have not shut off the power; try again.

5. Inspect the switch. If there are three wires, it is a three-way switch; see "Replacing a 3-Way Switch" on page 88.

6. Remove the switch by loosening the terminals and removing the wires.

7. Purchase a replacement switch of the same type at a hardware store. If your house wiring is aluminum—silver color— make sure the switch is marked CO/ALR, indicating compatibility with both copper and aluminum wiring.

8. Fasten the wires to the terminals on the new switch. The order makes no difference, but make sure that the word *OFF* faces up on the switch.

9. Fold the wires into the box, refasten the receptacle, and restore the power.

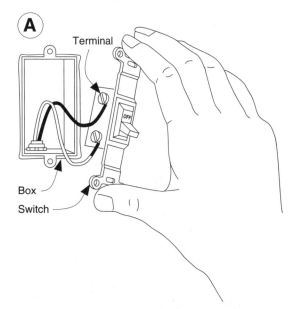

A — Terminal / Box / Switch

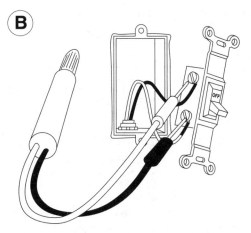

B

REPLACING A 3-WAY SWITCH

A pair of three-way switches allows you to control a light from two different locations. The three-way switch has three terminals instead of the usual two, but replacement is no more difficult. Before replacing the switch, however, try a new bulb.

MATERIALS
- Replacement 3-way switch
- Masking tape

TOOLS
Screwdriver • Neon circuit tester

1. Turn off the power to the switch circuit at the main panel.

2. Remove the cover plate and the two screws fastening the switch to the box.

3. Holding the switch by the fastening tabs at top and bottom, pull it straight out of the box, being careful not to touch the terminals to the box (Figure A).

4. Touch one probe of a neon circuit tester to each of the screw terminals on the side of the switch (Figure B). If the tester glows, you have not shut off the power; try again.

5. With masking tape, label the wire under the darkest of the three terminals *COM* (Figure C).

6. Remove the switch by loosening the terminals and removing the wires.

7. Purchase a replacement three-way switch at a hardware store. If your house wiring is aluminum—silver color—make sure the switch is marked *CO/ALR*, indicating compatibility with both copper and aluminum wiring.

8. Refasten the wires to the terminals on the new switch, making sure the wire labeled *COM* goes to the darkest screw.

9. Fold the wires into the box, fasten the switch, and restore the power. If the light doesn't go on, replace the other switch with the one you just removed.

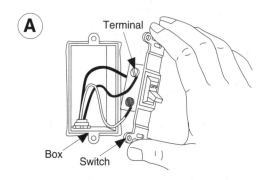

A   Terminal

Box   Switch

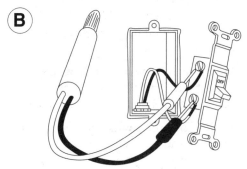

B

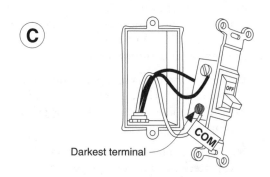

C

Darkest terminal — COM

INSTALLING A DIMMER SWITCH

Do you want to add ambience to your dining experience? Instead of burning candles, use a dimmer switch. A dimmer switch can produce nearly any degree of warmth you wish. Dimmer switches don't work with fluorescent lights.

MATERIALS

- Masking tape
- Dimmer switch
- 2 or 3 wire nuts

TOOLS

Screwdriver • Long-nose pliers

1. Turn off the power at the main panel.

2. Remove the cover plate and the two switch screws, and pull the switch straight out (Figure A).

3. Determine the type of switch you have: a single-pole—the most common—has two screws; the three-way—controlled from two locations—has three screws. If there are three screws, mark the wire under the darkest screw with masking tape. Then loosen the terminal screws and remove the wires.

4. Purchase the same type—single-pole or three-way—of dimmer switch at a hardware store or home center.

5. Straighten the ends of the feed wires with long-nose pliers.

6. Connect each of the dimmer wires to the feed wires by placing the tips of matching wires together and screwing on wire nuts (Figure B). If there are three wires, the red dimmer wire connects to the wire you marked in Step 4.

7. Test the connections by tugging on the wires to be sure they are tight, then fold the wires back into the box, allowing room for the switch.

8. Screw the new switch to the box.

9. Replace the cover plate, restore power, and test your new dimmer.

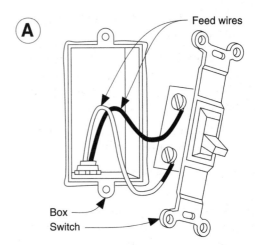

Feed wires
Box
Switch

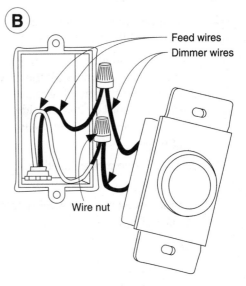

Feed wires
Dimmer wires
Wire nut

REPLACING A 2-PRONG PLUG

Replacing a two-prong plug is simple since the invention of the "quick-connect" replacement plug. The only reason you need a wire stripper is to cut the cord to the desired length, if necessary. A pair of heavy-duty scissors will serve as well. Note the difference between polarized and nonpolarized plugs. Do not substitute one for the other.

MATERIALS
"Quick-connect" replacement plug

TOOLS
Diagonal-cutting pliers

1. Cut off the old plug with diagonal-cutting pliers.

2. Take the old plug to the hardware store, and purchase a "quick-connect" replacement plug having the same prong pattern (Figure A), as follows:

 • The prongs of a nonpolarized plug are of the same width.

 • One prong of a polarized plug is wider than the other.

3. Separate the prong assembly of the new plug from its casing by squeezing the prongs together and pulling the casing off.

4. Without removing any insulation, insert the old cord through the casing.

5. Spread the prongs and push the cord into the prong assembly all the way (Figure B). *Important:* If the plug is polarized, orient the cord so that the side with the groove goes into the side with the wider prong.

6. Squeeze the two prongs together (Figure C).

7. Push the closed prong assembly into the plug casing (Figure D).

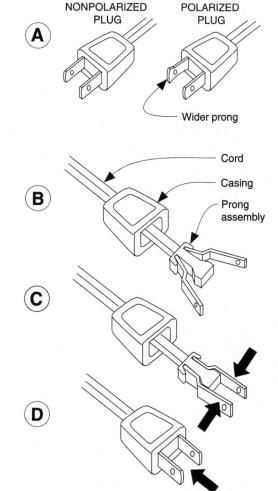

(A) NONPOLARIZED PLUG / POLARIZED PLUG — Wider prong

(B) Cord / Casing / Prong assembly

(C)

(D)

REPLACING A 3-PRONG PLUG

Three-prong plugs are not available in "quick-connect" versions, but they are still easy to replace. The most difficult part of replacing one is tying the Underwriter's knot. If that looks too difficult, purchase a three-prong plug with a screw clamp for gripping the cord.

MATERIALS
Replacement 3-prong plug

TOOLS
Diagonal-cutting pliers • Utility knife • Wire stripper • Screwdriver

1. Using diagonal-cutting pliers, cut off the old plug. Take it to the hardware store, and purchase a replacement rated at the same amps and volts (Figure A).

2. Remove the insulated disk of the new plug, exposing the inside.

3. Insert the cord through the rear of the new plug.

4. Using a utility knife, slit the cord sheathing back 2½ inches and remove it.

5. Using a wire stripper, strip ½ inch of insulation from the end of each wire.

6. If there is room inside the plug, tie the black and white wires into an Underwriter's knot to eliminate strain on the terminals (Figure B). Pull on the cord until the knot bottoms in the plug.

7. Twist the end of each wire to pull the wire strands together. Then secure each wire under its screw by looping the end clockwise around the screw and tightening the screw (Figure C). Place the white wire under the silver screw, the black wire under the brass screw, and the green wire under the green or darkest screw. Make sure no errant strands of wire are touching the adjacent screw.

8. Replace the insulated disk.

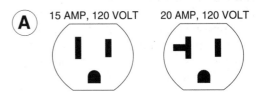

A — 15 AMP, 120 VOLT   20 AMP, 120 VOLT

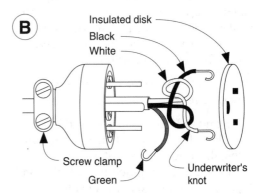

B — Insulated disk
Black
White
Screw clamp
Green
Underwriter's knot

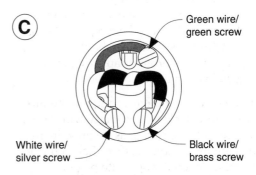

C — Green wire/ green screw
White wire/ silver screw
Black wire/ brass screw

TESTING A RECEPTACLE

Too few homeowners and apartment dwellers know about the $5 receptacle tester and the equally low-cost neon circuit tester. It's a good idea to test every receptacle in and around your home to anticipate problems before they zap you. Improperly connected receptacles can shock you, damage electronic equipment, and cause fires.

MATERIALS
None

TOOLS
Receptacle tester • Neon circuit tester

If the receptacle has three slots (see Figure A of "Replacing a Receptacle" on the opposite page), plug in a receptacle tester (Figure A). Match the pattern of lights to those shown on the tester label. Figure B shows a typical label.

If the receptacle has two slots (see Figure A of "Replacing a Receptacle" on the opposite page), use a neon circuit tester (Figure C). Holding the probes of the tester by their insulated sleeves, touch them to the long slot (L), the short slot (S), and the ground screw (G) in the following order:

• L and S: The tester should glow. If not, there is no power to the circuit.

• S and G: If the tester glows, the receptacle box is grounded, and you can install a three-slot receptacle. (See "Installing a Grounded Receptacle" on page 97.) If not, go to the next test.

• L and G: If the tester glows, the black and white wires to the receptacle may be reversed. If not, the receptacle box is not grounded, and you should not use a two-to-three prong adapter nor should you install a three-slot receptacle.

To rectify any problems, compare the miswired receptacle to a properly wired one, and reroute the wiring as if you were replacing the receptacle. (See "Replacing a Receptacle" on the opposite page.)

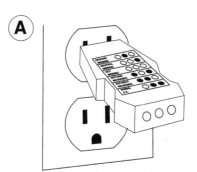

(A)

(B) **TYPICAL TROUBLESHOOTING GUIDE**
(Black is Illuminated light)

○ ● ○	GROUND MISSING	Ground (bare or green) wire missing or disconnected
○ ○ ●	NEUTRAL MISSING	Neutral (white) wire missing or disconnected
○ ○ ○	HOT MISSING	Hot (black) wire missing or disconnected
● ○ ●	HOT/GND REVERSED	Hot (black) and ground (bare or green) wires reversed
● ● ○	HOT/NEUT REVERSED	Hot (black) and neutral (white) wires reversed
○ ● ●	WIRING O.K.	All wires properly connected

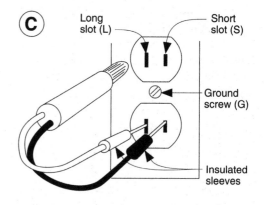

(C) Long slot (L) — Short slot (S) — Ground screw (G) — Insulated sleeves

REPLACING A RECEPTACLE

Receptacles do wear out and break. If one of yours is giving you trouble, first try bending or spreading the prongs of the plug that you're plugging into the receptacle. This will help the receptacle make a stronger contact. If the receptacle still doesn't work, replace it; new ones cost less than a fast-food quarter pounder.

1. Check your receptacle to determine if you have a grounded or polarized receptacle (Figure A).

2. Turn off power at the main panel. Test the receptacle with a neon circuit tester or receptacle tester to make sure the power is off. (See "Testing a Receptacle" on the opposite page.)

3. Remove the receptacle cover plate and the screws securing the receptacle to the box, and pull the receptacle out.

4. Before removing any wires, label each with masking tape: *S* for silver screws, *B* for brass screws, and *G* for a green screw (Figure B). Loosen the terminal screws, and remove the wires.

5. Purchase an identical receptacle at a hardware store. Do not replace a two-prong with a three-prong receptacle unless you know that the box is grounded. (See "Testing a Receptacle" on the opposite page and "Installing a Grounded Receptacle" on page 97.) If any tabs are missing on the old receptacle, remove them on the new receptacle as well to separate the two outlets electrically. Use long-nose pliers.

6. Reconnect the labeled wires. Fold the wires back into the box, refasten the receptacle, and restore power. Test the receptacle again as in Step 1 to be sure it is installed correctly.

MATERIALS
- Masking tape
- Replacement receptacle

TOOLS
Screwdriver • Neon circuit tester • Receptacle tester • Long-nose pliers

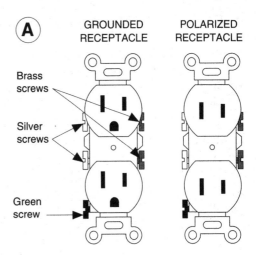

A GROUNDED RECEPTACLE POLARIZED RECEPTACLE

Brass screws

Silver screws

Green screw

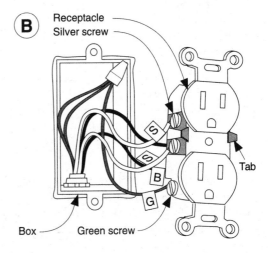

B Receptacle Silver screw

Tab

Box   Green screw

INSTALLING A GFCI

A ground fault circuit interrupter (GFCI) has a built-in circuit breaker that protects you against lethal shocks by shutting down a circuit or receptacle when it detects a problem. You should install GFCI receptacles in bathrooms, kitchens, and outdoors.

MATERIALS
- 4" of 12-2 NM cable with ground
- GFCI receptacle
- 3 wire nuts
- GFCI cover plate

TOOLS
Neon circuit tester • Screwdriver
• Diagonal-cutting pliers
• Wire stripper • Long-nose pliers

1. Turn off the power to the circuit at the main panel.

2. If there is more than one receptacle to test, test each receptacle—they may be on different circuits—by inserting the probes of a neon circuit tester into the two rectangular slots of each outlet. If the bulb glows, you haven't found both circuits; try again.

3. Remove the receptacle cover plate and the receptacle screws, and pull the receptacle straight out (Figure A).

4. Disconnect all wires from the receptacle. The black and white wires may be held by screws on the side, or they may be inserted into holes in the back of the receptacle. Inserted wires may be released by inserting the blade of a narrow screwdriver or a thin nail into the slots adjacent to the wires and pulling the wires out (Figure B).

5. Cut off a 4-inch length of 12-2 NM cable with ground with diagonal-cutting pliers. Pull the insulated wires out of the sheathing, and strip ¾ inch of insulation from both ends of each wire with a wire stripper.

6. Using long-nose pliers, make a circle of one end of the black wire, insert it under the GFCI terminal labeled *LINE-BLACK*, and tighten the screw clockwise (Figure C).

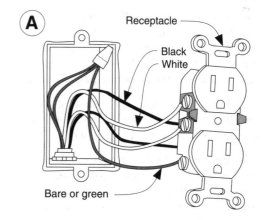

A

Receptacle

Black
White

Bare or green

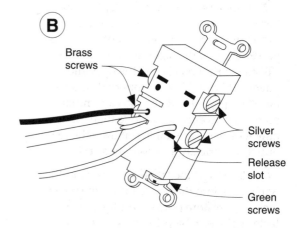

B

Brass screws

Silver screws

Release slot

Green screws

7. Fasten one end of the white wire to the GFCI terminal labeled *LINE-WHITE* in the same manner.

8. Fasten the one end of the bare wire under the GFCI green screw.

9. Connect the loose ends of all of the white wires by holding their ends together, inserting the wires into a wire nut, and twisting the wire nut clockwise until tight. Check the connection by pulling on each of the wires (Figure D).

10. Repeat Step 9 with all of the black wires and, again, with all of the bare wires.

11. Carefully fold all of the wires back into the box. Then insert and secure the GFCI, making sure none of the bare wires are contacting any of the screw terminals at the sides of the GFCI. If the box is too small to hold the wires and the receptacle, purchase a box extension at a home center.

12. Install the special GFCI cover plate.

13. Restore the power, and test the GFCI by pushing on the button labeled *TEST*. The GFCI breaker should click and turn off the power to the outlet.

14. Restore the power to the GFCI by pushing the button labeled *RESET*.

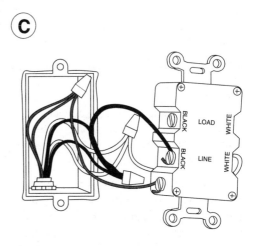

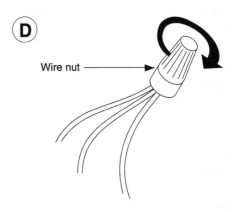

Wire nut

REPLACING A SWITCHED RECEPTACLE

A switched receptacle is used for controlling table and floor lamps from a wall switch. If you label the wires as suggested, you will have no problem replacing it.

MATERIALS

• Masking tape
• Replacement receptacle

TOOLS

Screwdriver • Neon circuit tester • Receptacle tester • Long-nose pliers

1. Turn off power at the main panel. Test both sockets in the receptacle with a neon circuit tester or receptacle tester to make sure the power is off. (See "Testing a Receptacle" on page 92.)

2. Remove the receptacle cover plate and the two screws fastening the receptacle to the box, and pull the receptacle out (Figure A).

3. Before removing any wires, label each with masking tape: *US* for the upper silver screw, *LS* for the lower silver screw, *UB* for the upper brass screw, *LB* for the lower brass screw, and *G* for the green screw (Figure B). Loosen the terminal screws and remove the wires.

4. Purchase an identical receptacle at a hardware store or home center.

5. Refasten the wires to the new receptacle, using the labels as your guide. Make sure you connect the wires that are labeled *UB* and *LB* as they were to keep the switched half of the receptacle in the same position. If any tabs are missing on the old receptacle, remove them from the new receptacle as well to separate the outlets electrically. Use long-nose pliers.

6. Fold the wires back into the box, refasten the receptacle, and restore power. Test the receptacle again as in Step 1 to be sure it is installed correctly.

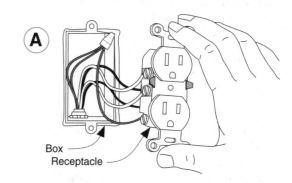

Box
Receptacle

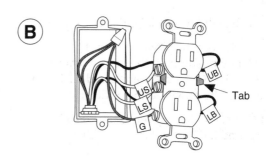

Tab

INSTALLING A GROUNDED RECEPTACLE

Many older homes have two-slot receptacles. If the metal box housing your two-slot receptacle is grounded, it can be converted to a three-slot, grounded receptacle. To determine whether yours can be converted, perform the tests in "Testing a Receptacle" on page 92.

1. Turn off power at the main panel. Test the receptacle with a neon circuit tester to make sure the power is off.

2. Remove the receptacle cover plate and the screws securing the receptacle to the box, and pull the receptacle out.

3. Before removing any wires, label each wire with masking tape: *S* for silver screws, *B* for brass screws, and *G* for the green screw, as shown in the illustration at right. Loosen the screws and remove the wires.

4. Purchase a three-slot receptacle and two grounding pigtails, one with a screw. If any tabs are missing on the original unit, remove them on the new receptacle as well to separate the two outlets electrically. Use long-nose pliers.

5. Reconnect the wires, using the labels as your guide. Fasten a grounding pigtail under a screw at the back of the box and a second pigtail under the green screw on the new receptacle. Then twist the tips of the two wires together and screw on a wire nut. Tug on the wires to make sure they're tight.

6. Fold the wires back into the box, re-fasten the receptacle to the box, and restore the power. Test the new receptacle to be sure it's installed and grounded properly. (See "Testing a Receptacle" on page 92.)

MATERIALS
- Masking tape
- 3-slot grounding receptacle
- 2 grounding pigtails, one with a screw
- Wire nut
- Grounding adapter plug

TOOLS
Neon circuit tester • Screwdriver • Receptacle tester • Long-nose pliers

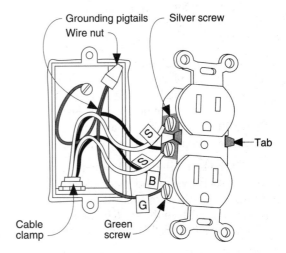

Grounding pigtails — Silver screw
Wire nut
Tab
Cable clamp
Green screw

TROUBLESHOOTING A DOORBELL

Doorbells are really quite simple. As the illustration shows, a doorbell consists of nothing more than a transformer, a bell, and one or more doorbell switches to activate the bell. Here's how to find out why your bell is no longer ringing.

MATERIALS
None

TOOLS
Neon circuit tester • Multitester • Screwdriver

1. Look for the bell transformer near the main panel. You're looking for one rated between 6 volts AC and 24 volts AC output, as marked on its case or on a label.

2. Check the transformer input—the wires from the main panel to the transformer, which are accessible from inside the mounting box. Place neon tester probes into the wire nuts or on the terminals of the black and white wires only. If the neon bulb fails to light, call an electrician to check the wiring.

3. If the neon bulb lights, check the transformer output with a multitester set to 50 volts AC. Place the probes on the transformer output terminals, trying all possible pairs. If the meter reads less than half of its labeled voltage, have an electrician replace the transformer.

4. If the bell still doesn't ring, remove the doorbell switch and place a screwdriver across the terminals. If the bell now rings, replace the switch. (See "Replacing a Doorbell Switch" on page 100.)

5. If the bell doesn't ring, remove the wires from the switch and twist them together. Then, remove the chime cover. Measure the voltage between the chime assembly terminals with the multitester. If the reading is the same as in Step 3, replace the chime. (See "Replacing a Doorbell Chime" on the opposite page.) If there is no voltage, call an electrician.

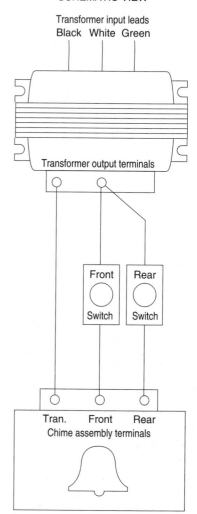

SCHEMATIC VIEW

Transformer input leads
Black   White   Green

Transformer output terminals

Front Switch   Rear Switch

Tran.   Front   Rear
Chime assembly terminals

REPLACING A DOORBELL CHIME

You probably didn't realize that you could change the personality of your doorbell. Home centers offer a wide variety of chimes, from the simplest "dong" to the most fanciful tune. Whether you need to replace a broken chime or want a chime with a new sound, make sure the new chime takes the same voltage as the old.

MATERIALS
- Masking tape
- Replacement chime assembly
- 4 drywall screws

TOOLS
Screwdriver • Multitester

1. If you are replacing the chime because it doesn't ring, first verify that it is the chime assembly that is faulty. Remove the switch at the door, and twist the wires together (Figure A). Then remove the chime cover, and touch the probes of a multitester to the chime terminals to verify that there is voltage present (Figure B). If there is no voltage, see "Troubleshooting a Doorbell" on the opposite page.

2. Turn off the power to the doorbell at the main panel.

3. Before disconnecting the chime, make a sketch showing the colors of the wires to each of the terminals: *FRONT, TRAN.* (transformer), *REAR.* If all wires are the same color, label each with masking tape.

4. Loosen the terminal screws and remove the wires, then unscrew the chime from the wall. Take the old chime to a home center, and purchase a new unit that uses the same voltage.

5. Feed the wires through the back of the new chime assembly, and screw the chime to the wall.

6. Secure each wire by looping the end clockwise around its terminal screw and tightening the screw.

7. Install the chime cover, restore the power, and test the new unit.

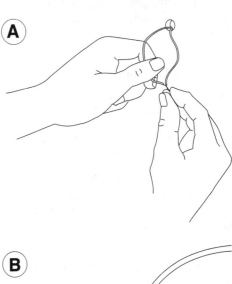

A

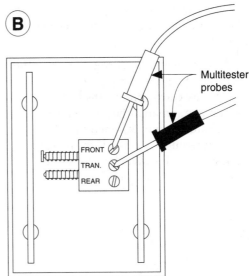

B

Multitester probes

FRONT
TRAN.
REAR

REPLACING A DOORBELL SWITCH

If a doorbell switch is exposed to weather, its contacts can corrode, rendering it inoperative. Don't try to repair the switch. Replacement switches cost just a few dollars, and replacing one takes about five minutes.

MATERIALS
Replacement doorbell switch

TOOLS
Screwdriver

1. If you are replacing the switch because the bell doesn't ring, first verify that it is the switch that is faulty. (See "Troubleshooting a Doorbell" on page 98.)

2. Turn off the power and unscrew the doorbell switch from the wall.

3. Disconnect the wires from the switch terminals.

4. Take the faulty switch to a home center, and purchase a replacement.

5. Secure each wire to the replacement switch by looping the end clockwise around its terminal screw and tightening the screw. Press the button to test.

6. If the bell now rings, push the wires back into the wall, and screw the switch to the wall.

7. If the bell doesn't ring, unscrew the wires and sand or scrape the ends to remove any corrosion. Reattach the wires and make sure that the bare ends of the wires are securely fastened under the switch terminal screws. If the bell still doesn't ring, the switch is defective; return it for a replacement.

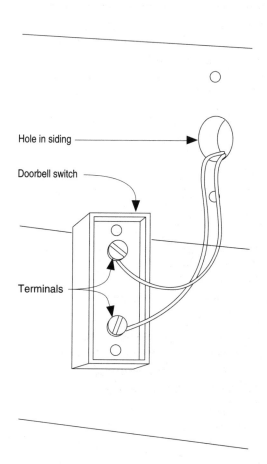

Hole in siding

Doorbell switch

Terminals

TESTING A SMOKE DETECTOR

Most people complain that their smoke detector is too sensitive. I say, better annoyed than dead! If your alarm hasn't sounded in the last month, it would be a good idea to test it. Check the battery by pressing the test button and the detector circuit by wafting smoke in its direction.

MATERIALS
• Matches
• Long candle

TOOLS
None

1. If the smoke detector has a battery and it's more than one year old, replace the battery. (See "Replacing a Smoke Detector Battery" on page 102.) Press the battery-test button to make sure the battery is properly connected (Figure A).

2. Light a long candle and hold it 6 inches below the detector so that the heated air will rise into the detector.

3. If the alarm doesn't sound within 15 seconds, blow out the flame and hold the candle so that the smoke rises into the detector (Figure B). Make sure the smoke reaches the detector. If it doesn't, light the candle again and repeat the test.

4. If the alarm still doesn't sound, replace the smoke detector. (See "Installing a Smoke Detector" on page 103.)

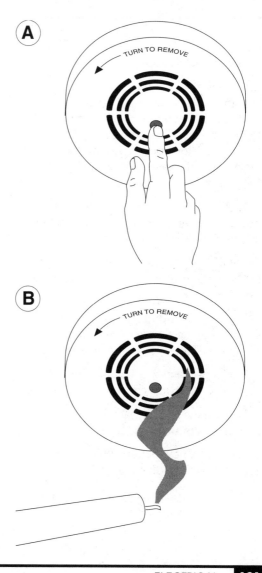

REPLACING A SMOKE DETECTOR BATTERY

A smoke detector can save you from fire only if on duty! Battery-powered smoke detectors must have their batteries replaced once a year. To avoid confusion, replace the batteries in all of your smoke detectors on New Year's Day—a new year's resolution to be more safety-minded. Battery-powered smoke detectors may look different, but they all use the same type of 9-volt battery.

MATERIALS
Replacement 9-volt alkaline battery

TOOLS
Stepladder

1. Position a stepladder or chair under the smoke detector.

2. Look for a tab on the perimeter of the smoke detector case (Figure A). If you find one, pull it down to open the case. If there is no tab, try pulling the edge down at various points. If that doesn't work, twist the case counterclockwise (Figure B).

3. After you have opened the case, note how it should be closed. It could be confusing later.

4. Grip the rectangular 9-volt battery between your thumb and forefinger and pull it out of the restraining tabs.

5. Use your thumbnail to separate the electrical connector from the battery and remove the battery from the detector.

6. Connect a new 9-volt alkaline battery to the electrical connector (Figure C).

7. Push the battery back into its restraining tabs and close the case.

8. Test the new battery. (See "Testing a Smoke Detector" on page 101.)

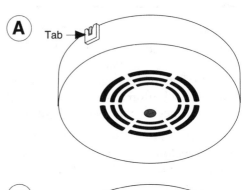

A Tab

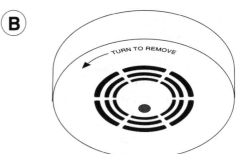

B TURN TO REMOVE

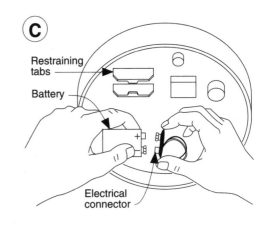

C
Restraining tabs
Battery
Electrical connector

INSTALLING A SMOKE DETECTOR

Smoke detectors are credited with saving thousands of lives every year. In fact, they are required by code in new homes. You should install at least one on each floor of your home. Since fire, heat, and smoke tend to travel upward, smoke detectors should be installed near the ceiling at the heads of stairways between floors.

MATERIALS
- Plastic screw anchors
- 9-volt alkaline battery
- Smoke detector

TOOLS
Drill and pilot bit • Hammer
• Screwdriver

1. Your fire department can offer advice on where to install smoke detectors. Or, refer to Figure A for some basic guidelines. Install smoke detectors:

- On each floor

- Close to the heads of stairways

- In the middle of a hall ceiling or on a wall about 8 inches below the ceiling

- Away from corners, ends of halls, or exterior doors, windows, or vents

2. Remove the smoke detector cover and hold the base against the wall or ceiling. Locate the mounting screw holes inside the detector and use a pencil to mark the screw locations on the wall or ceiling.

3. Drill pilot holes slightly smaller in diameter than the plastic screw anchors. Tap the screw anchors into the holes with a hammer. Insert the screws through the mounting holes in the detector and into the screw anchors, and tighten the screws (Figure B).

4. Install the battery (see "Replacing a Smoke Detector Battery" on the opposite page), and replace the cover.

5. Test the smoke detector. (See "Testing a Smoke Detector" on page 101.)

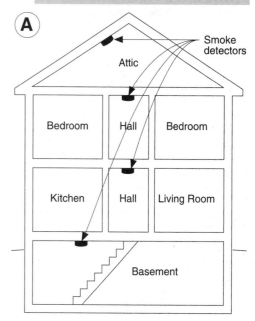

A — Smoke detectors; Attic; Bedroom; Hall; Bedroom; Kitchen; Hall; Living Room; Basement

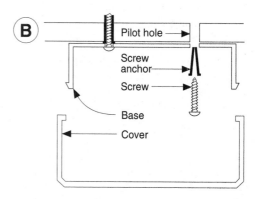

B — Pilot hole; Screw anchor; Screw; Base; Cover

ADDING A TELEPHONE

Telephone lines have enough power to operate at least five telephones at once. Considering the low price of new telephones, why not add a few and save running from room to room? You can add another telephone to an existing jack or to any telephone line running along a baseboard.

MATERIALS

- Screws
- Modular jack
- Dual-outlet adapter

TOOLS

Long-nose pliers • Wire cutters
• 6d common nail • Hammer
• Screwdriver • Wire stripper

To tap a new telephone into an existing line, follow these steps:

1. Using long-nose pliers, remove staples and pull up a 3-inch loop of telephone line near where you would like a new phone (Figure A). You may have to change the line routing to obtain 3 inches. Using wire cutters, cut the line at the top of the loop.

2. Position the base of a new modular jack where you want it on the wall, and mark the locations of the two mounting screws with a pencil (Figure B).

3. Using a 6d common nail and hammer, punch 1/8-inch-deep pilot holes for the screws, and then drive the screws into the wall.

4. Using the pliers, snap off the two knock-outs in the side of the base.

5. Using a wire stripper, strip 1 inch of insulation from the wire ends (Figure C), insert each colored pair of wires into their color-coded terminal slot, and tighten the screws. Attach the cover.

To add a second telephone to an existing modular jack, follow these steps:

1. Remove the plug of the telephone from the modular jack and plug a dual-outlet adapter into it (Figure D).

2. Plug each telephone into one of the dual-outlet adapter jacks.

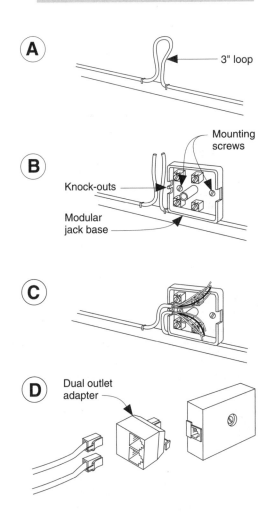

A — 3" loop

B — Mounting screws / Knock-outs / Modular jack base

C

D — Dual outlet adapter

CONVERTING A TELEPHONE TO MODULAR

Just because you have upgraded your system with modular jacks doesn't mean you should throw away your old telephones if they're still working. As they say, they don't make them like they used to. Here is how to install a modular plug on the end of an older telephone line.

MATERIALS
Line cord converter

TOOLS
Screwdriver • Wire stripper

1. Check the end of the line that leads from your old telephone. The wires should either have spade connectors or the insulation on each wire should be stripped back 1/2 inch (Figure A). If the line has been cut and the wires in it are not exposed, strip the outer sheath back 2 inches and the insulation on the individual wires back 1/2 inch, using a wire stripper.

2. Buy a line cord converter at a hardware store or home center and remove its cover plate (Figure B).

3. Note that there are four screws, color-coded to match the red, green, yellow, and black wires. Loosen the screws, then insert the bare ends of the wires from your telephone into the screw terminal slots of the matching color. If the wires have spade connectors, insert the connectors under the screws. Tighten the screws.

4. Fold the wires inside the converter body, place the telephone line in the line slot, and attach the cover plate.

5. Plug the converter into a working modular jack and test the telephone (Figure C).

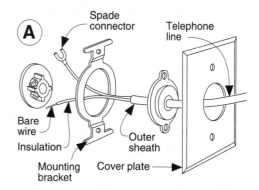

Figure A: Spade connector, Telephone line, Bare wire, Insulation, Mounting bracket, Outer sheath, Cover plate

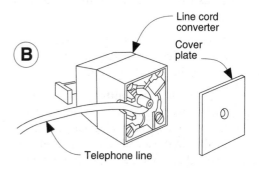

Figure B: Line cord converter, Cover plate, Telephone line

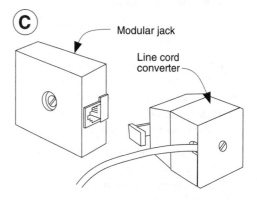

Figure C: Modular jack, Line cord converter

CONVERTING A TELEPHONE OUTLET TO MODULAR

Any new telephone, answering machine, or facsimile machine you buy will come equipped with a modular plug. Here's how to convert an older style telephone outlet to the newer modular jack you'll need to accommodate this equipment.

If the existing outlet has a four-prong receptacle (Figure A), follow these steps:

1. Disconnect the present telephone.

2. Buy a four-prong-to-modular converter at an electronics store and plug it into the four prong receptacle.

3. Plug the new modular telephone or facsimile machine into the modular converter.

If the existing telephone is hard-wired to a flush-mounted wall outlet (Figure B), follow these steps:

1. Remove the cover plate, exposing the connections inside the junction box in the wall (Figure C).

2. Using diagonal-cutting pliers, cut each of the wires leading from the terminal screws to the telephone about 1/2 inch from the terminals. Be careful not to cut the wires leading from inside the wall to the terminals.

3. Buy a flush-mounted modular jack converter like that shown in Figure C.

4. Loosen each of the terminal screws and slip the spade connectors of the modular jack converter under the screws, matching the colors of the new and old wires. Tighten the screws.

5. Fasten the converter to the mounting bracket, and replace the cover plate. Plug in your telephone.

MATERIALS

- 4-prong-to-modular converter
- Flush-mounted modular jack converter
- Modular jack converter

TOOLS

Screwdriver • Diagonal-cutting pliers

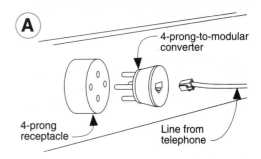

A 4-prong-to-modular converter

4-prong receptacle

Line from telephone

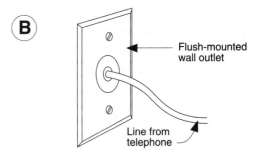

B Flush-mounted wall outlet

Line from telephone

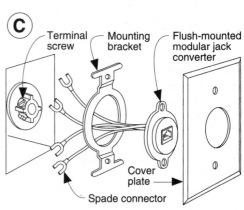

C Terminal screw — Mounting bracket — Flush-mounted modular jack converter

Cover plate

Spade connector

If the existing telephone is hard-wired to a 42A baseboard block (Figure D), follow these steps:

1. Using a screwdriver, remove the cover of the baseboard block.

2. Using diagonal-cutting pliers, cut each of the colored wires leading from the terminal screws to the existing telephone about 1/2 inch from the screws, and remove the existing cord. Be careful not to cut the wires leading from inside the wall to the terminals.

3. Buy a modular jack converter. Loosen each of the terminal screws and, matching the colors of the new and old wires, replace the old wires with the spade connectors from the new jack converter (Figure E). Tighten the screws.

4. Attach the converter cover with the cover screw, and plug in your telephone.

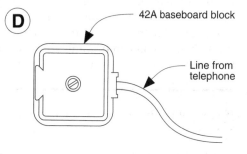

42A baseboard block

Line from telephone

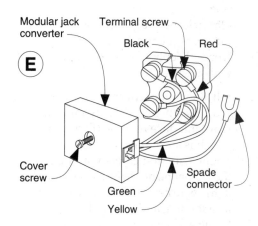

Modular jack converter

Terminal screw

Black

Red

Cover screw

Green

Yellow

Spade connector

TROUBLESHOOTING A MODULAR TELEPHONE LINE

Ever since the government split up Ma Bell, the telephone wiring and equipment inside your home has been your property and responsibility. Fortunately, with the simple troubleshooting guide below, you can become your own expert telephone system analyst.

MATERIALS
Radio interference filter

TOOLS
Screwdriver • Two telephones

If you get no dial tone, try the following options:

• Dial a number. If the number does not ring, unplug Telephone 1 from its modular jack and plug Telephone 2 into the same jack (Figure A). If Telephone 2 works, Telephone 1 is broken; replace it with a new telephone.

• If Telephone 2 doesn't work either, plug Telephone 1 directly into the network interface module (Figure B), which is located near where the telephone wire first enters your home. If the telephone now works, the trouble is in the wire between the network interface module and the modular jack. Using a screwdriver, remove the covers of both the network interface module (Figure C) and the modular jack (Figure D), and disconnect the red and green wires. Telephone lines come with an extra pair of yellow and black wires, so substitute these—yellow for red and black for green—at the network interface module and at the modular jack.

• If the telephone does not work even when plugged into the network interface module, the trouble is in the telephone company's wires. Call the phone company for assistance . . . on your neighbor's phone, of course.

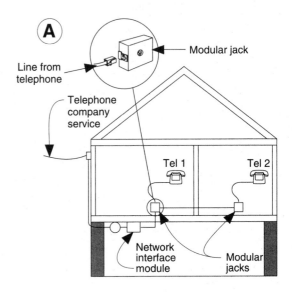

Figure A: Modular jack; Line from telephone; Telephone company service; Tel 1; Tel 2; Network interface module; Modular jacks

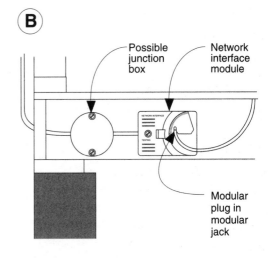

Figure B: Possible junction box; Network interface module; Modular plug in modular jack

If you get a continuous dial tone, even when dialing, the red and green wires are probably reversed. Try the following options:

• If you have the same problem on all of your telephones, use a screwdriver to remove the network interface module cover and switch the red and green wires leading to the phones (Figure C).

• If the problem affects only one telephone, use a screwdriver to remove the cover of the modular jack serving that telephone (Figure D), and reverse the red and green wires leading from the jack to the telephone.

If there is noise or unwanted interference on the line, buy a plug-in radio interference filter at an electronics store and install it between the modular jack and the telephone (Figure E). If that doesn't cure the noise, call the telephone company for assistance.

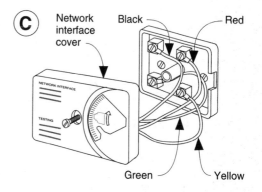

C Network interface cover — Black — Red — Green — Yellow

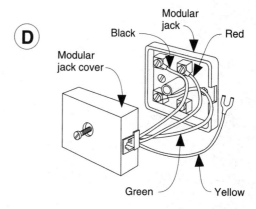

D Modular jack cover — Modular jack — Black — Red — Green — Yellow

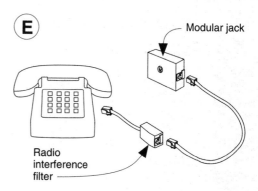

E Modular jack — Radio interference filter

FLOORS

REFASTENING LOOSE VINYL TILE

When individual vinyl tiles begin to lift, take fast action before water and loose debris collect under the tiles and damage them beyond repair. A few hours of simple preventive maintenance can avoid the need for an entire new floor.

MATERIALS

- Vinyl tile adhesive
- Plastic wrap
- Adhesive solvent

TOOLS

Cotton dish towel • Clothes iron • Putty knife or wood chisel • Vacuum cleaner • Notched adhesive spreader • Rolling pin • Bucket • Large book

1. Lay a cotton dish towel over the affected area of tile, then apply a clothes iron set on low heat over the dish towel to warm the tile.

2. Curl back the loose area of the tile and using a putty knife or wood chisel, scrape the old adhesive from the tile and floor. If the adhesive is not soft enough to scrape, try a higher temperature setting on the clothes iron.

3. Vacuum the area beneath the tile to remove debris. Spread new vinyl tile adhesive on the floor with a small notched adhesive spreader (Figure A).

4. Press the tile back into place and squeeze out the excess adhesive with a rolling pin (Figure B). If the rolling pin is wood, wrap it first in plastic wrap to protect it from the adhesive.

5. Clean up the excess adhesive with the solvent recommended on the adhesive can—usually paint thinner.

6. Weight down the repaired area for 24 hours with a bucket of water on a large book (Figure C).

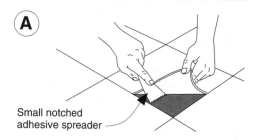

Small notched adhesive spreader

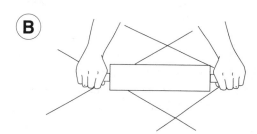

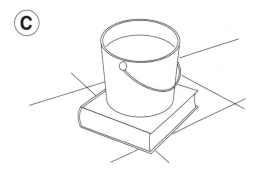

FIXING A BUBBLE IN VINYL TILE

Unless you were wiser than most and squirreled away a few leftover tiles, finding an exact match for vinyl tile is difficult. That is why you should try repairing a bubbled tile before replacing it.

MATERIALS

- Aluminum foil
- Vinyl tile adhesive
- Plastic wrap
- Adhesive solvent

TOOLS

Clothes iron • Utility knife • Putty knife • Rolling pin • Large book • Bucket

1. Cover the bubbled tile with aluminum foil, and thoroughly warm and soften it with a clothes iron set to medium heat.

2. Using a utility knife, slit the tile across the middle of the bubble (Figure A). Make sure you have cut all the way through.

3. Using a putty knife, lift one half of the bubble and force vinyl tile adhesive into the pocket (Figure B). Slide the putty knife in and out and all around the pocket to distribute the adhesive.

4. Repeat Step 3 for the other half of the bubble.

5. Squeeze out the excess adhesive by rolling from the bubble edges toward the slit, using a rolling pin. If the rolling pin is wood, wrap it first in plastic wrap to protect it from the adhesive.

6. Clean up the excess adhesive with the solvent recommended on the adhesive can—usually paint thinner.

7. Weight down the repaired area for 24 hours with a bucket of water on a large book (Figure C).

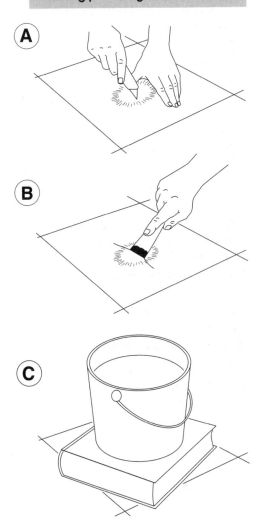

REPLACING A VINYL TILE

Use the method on this page for replacing individual vinyl tiles. The key to success is finding a tile that is an exact match to the existing floor. To patch vinyl flooring, see "Patching a Vinyl Floor" on page 114.

MATERIALS

- Replacement tile
- Adhesive solvent
- 100-grit sandpaper
- Vinyl tile adhesive
- Plastic wrap

TOOLS

Hair dryer • Wood chisel or putty knife • Vacuum cleaner • Notched adhesive spreader • Rolling pin • Bucket • Large book

1. Before attempting to remove the damaged tile, make sure you have a matching replacement tile. If you are lucky, you may find leftovers from the original installation. Otherwise, try flooring stores and flooring contractors.

2. Warm the damaged tile with a hair dryer set to high heat. Heat the tile until you can just stand keeping your hand on it.

3. While the tile is warm, chip it away with a wood chisel. Apply more heat as necessary, and be careful not to damage adjacent tiles (Figure A).

4. Remove the old adhesive down to the subfloor with the chisel or a putty knife. You may have to use adhesive solvent.

5. Orient the replacement tile to the pattern—if any—and test its fit. Sand the edges with 100-grit sandpaper to fit, if necessary. Vacuum up all debris from the floor.

6. Spread vinyl tile adhesive on the subfloor with a notched adhesive spreader. Press the tile into place and squeeze out the excess adhesive with a rolling pin (Figure B). If the rolling pin is wood, wrap it first in plastic wrap to protect it from the adhesive.

7. Clean up the excess adhesive with the solvent recommended on the adhesive can.

8. Weight down the tile for 24 hours with a bucket of water on a large book (Figure C).

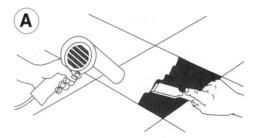

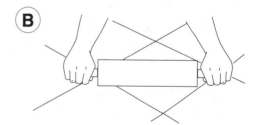

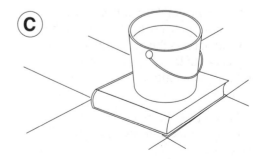

PATCHING A VINYL FLOOR

If your vinyl floor suffers a permanent stain, burn, or gouge, don't assume the floor must be replaced. First look for a piece of matching vinyl flooring. If you can find an exact match, the method below can produce a patch that only you will see.

MATERIALS
- Scrap of matching flooring
- Duct tape or masking tape
- Adhesive solvent
- Vinyl tile adhesive

TOOLS
Carpenter's square • Utility knife
- Putty knife or wood chisel
- Notched adhesive spreader

1. Locate a scrap of matching flooring. Unless you have a leftover piece of the original flooring, try flooring stores to see if the pattern is still in production. Your last resort would be to remove a piece from an inconspicuous area such as under the refrigerator.

2. Place the replacement piece over the damaged area so that the damage is covered completely and the pattern lines up (Figure A). Tape the edges of the piece in place with duct tape or masking tape.

3. Using a carpenter's square and a sharp utility knife, carefully cut through both layers of the vinyl (Figure B).

4. When you are sure you have cut through both layers, remove the tape and set the replacement patch aside.

5. Using a putty knife or wood chisel, remove the cut-out damaged vinyl flooring and scrap away the old adhesive down to the subfloor. You may have to use adhesive solvent.

6. Apply vinyl tile adhesive to the back side of the patch with a notched adhesive spreader. Press the patch into place and squeeze out the excess adhesive with a rolling pin wrapped in plastic wrap to protect it.

7. Remove the excess adhesive with the solvent recommended on the adhesive can.

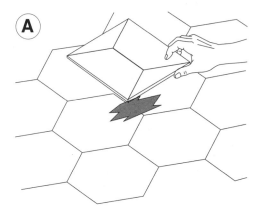

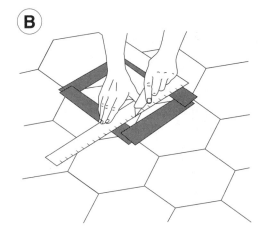

REPAIRING A SCRATCHED WOOD FLOOR

The key to this repair is caution. Just as you cannot cut a stick to make it longer, you can't stain a floor to make it lighter. If the stain turns out to be too light, you can always darken it a little by adding a second coat. Also keep in mind that the final stain plus varnish finish will be approximately the color of the wet stain when you first apply it. If the stain lightens as it dries, don't panic—the varnish will bring back the wet color.

MATERIALS

- Can of wood stain
- Paint thinner
- Cotton swabs
- Paper towels
- Varnish

TOOLS

Screwdriver • Teaspoon
• Cupcake pan • Artist's brush

1. Using a stain brochure from a paint store, select a stain that best matches the color of the floor finish.

2. Stir the stain thoroughly, then prepare mixes of paint thinner and stain in ratios of 4:1, 2:1, and 1:1. Use a teaspoon to measure and a cupcake pan to hold the mixes.

3. Using cotton swabs, apply a small bit of each mix, from lightest to darkest, to a small area of the scratch until you find the mix that best matches the color of the original finish (Figure A). Blot the excess with paper towels.

4. Apply the selected mix to all of the scratches. Be careful to apply stain only to the scratch and not to the adjacent unmarred areas. Wipe up any excess stain immediately.

5. Buy a varnish with a gloss that matches the gloss of the floor.

6. After the stain dries, use an artist's brush to apply two coats of varnish to the stained areas, following the manufacturer's directions for drying and sanding between coats (Figure B).

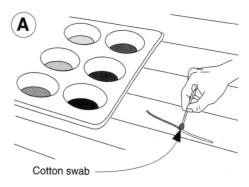

A

Cotton swab

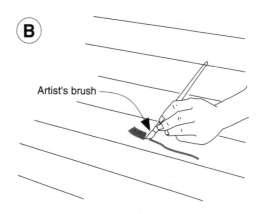

B

Artist's brush

REPAIRING WOOD FLOORING

Wood floors take a lot of abuse, but scrapes and gouges can be repaired easily. If the floor has a clear finish, the following steps will produce a patch that is barely discernable. If your wood floor is painted or covered with carpet, you need not go through the color-matching process. Just fill the gouge, sand, and paint over the patch.

1. Using a putty knife, fill the gouge with wood putty (Figure A).

2. While the putty can is open, spread five test patches on a scrap of wood.

3. After 24 hours, sand the putty even with the floor using 100-grit, then 200-grit sandpaper. Lightly sand the test patches as well. Wrap the sandpaper around a small block of wood to help achieve a level surface (Figure B).

4. Using a stain brochure from a paint store, select a stain just a little darker than the background color of your floor.

5. Stir the stain thoroughly, then prepare mixes of paint thinner and stain in ratios of 8:1, 4:1, 2:1, and 1:1. Use a teaspoon to measure and a cupcake pan to hold the stain mixtures.

6. Using a clean rag for each, apply the stain mixes, as well as the undiluted stain, to the test patches. Wipe up any excess stain.

7. Purchase a wiping varnish (a varnish thinned with paint thinner that is easier to wipe on than full-strength varnish), such as Waterlox, with a gloss that matches the the original finish of the floor. Apply it to each patch with a clean rag. You will immediately see which stain mix best matches the floor.

MATERIALS
- **Can of wood putty**
- **Scrap of wood**
- **100-, 200-, and 400-grit sandpaper**
- **Can of wood stain**
- **Clean rags**
- **Paint thinner**
- **Wiping varnish**

TOOLS
Putty knife • Block of wood
• Teaspoon • Cupcake pan
• Dark felt-tip pen

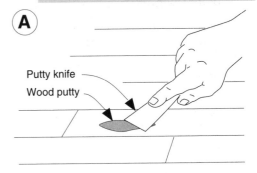

A

Putty knife
Wood putty

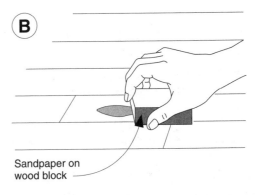

B

Sandpaper on wood block

8. Apply the matching stain to the puttied gouge area and allow it dry, according to the manufacturer's directions.

9. If the wood grain on the rest of the floor is conspicuous, use a dark felt-tip pen to simulate the grain before applying the varnish (Figure C).

10. Apply several coats of thinned varnish with a clean rag, sanding lightly between each coat with 400-grit sandpaper, until the gloss closely matches that of the original finish.

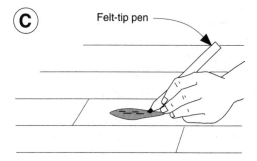

Felt-tip pen

REPLACING WOOD FLOORING

If a strip of your hardwood floor is cracked or stained, you can replace it, as described below. Then just color match the new strip and finish it.

1. Chisel out the center of the damaged flooring strip with a wood chisel and hammer until the board is split lengthwise in two (Figure A).

2. Pry out the remainder of the strip with the chisel and pull any nails out with the claw end of the hammer.

3. Take a scrap of the flooring to a flooring store and purchase a new strip that matches the wood.

4. Measure the length needed to replace the original strip and lay out the cut on the replacement strip with a try square and pencil. Using a back saw, cut the replacement strip along the mark.

5. Orient the replacement strip with its tongue ready to slip into the groove of the adjacent flooring and mark its bottom groove cheek. Then, flip the strip over to remove the marked groove cheek with the chisel and hammer (Figure B).

6. Coat the tongue and groove of the new strip with carpenter's glue. Install it by first inserting the tongue and then pressing the other edge down (Figure C).

7. Drill pilot holes at the ends and every 2 feet along the groove edge of the strip and nail with 6d small-head spiral siding nails (Figure D). Using a nail set, set the nails and cover them with a colored wax touch-up stick.

8. Color match and finish the new strip. (See "Repairing Wood Flooring" on page 116.)

MATERIALS

- Replacement wood-flooring strip
- Carpenter's glue
- 6d small-head spiral siding nails
- Colored wax touch-up stick

TOOLS

Wood chisel • Hammer • Try square
• Back saw • Drill with pilot bit
• Nail set

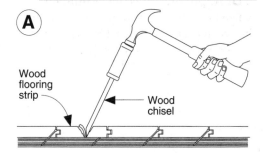

Wood flooring strip

Wood chisel

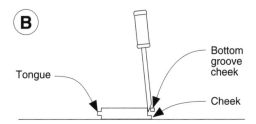

Tongue

Bottom groove cheek

Cheek

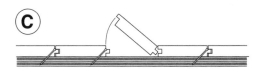

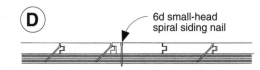

6d small-head spiral siding nail

REFASTENING BUCKLED WOOD FLOORING

If a floor is laid down when the wood is too dry, the wood strips may absorb moisture and expand. The pressure can buckle the floor and loosen the nails. If you have access to the underside of your floor, you can pull the strips into their original position with screws.

1. Using a piece of chalk, mark the area of loose flooring (Figure A). Drive a 6d finish nail through the center of the area as a reference point. (If the flooring is hardwood, first drill a pilot hole to avoid splitting the wood.)

2. Go below the floor and find the tip of the nail. Mark the extent of the loose flooring there with the chalk.

3. Look for a water pipe that penetrates the floor and measure the thickness of the floor with a tape measure (Figure B).

4. Purchase #8 roundhead wood screws of a length 1/4 inch less than the floor thickness. Allow four screws per square foot of loose flooring.

5. From below, draw lines across the damaged area a foot apart and at right angles to the finish flooring. Make a mark every 3 inches on your lines to indicate where the screws will go.

6. Mark the length of one of the wood screws on a 1/8-inch pilot bit with masking tape. Drill the pilot holes to the mark.

7. Using a 3/16-inch bit, drill clearance holes through the subfloor for the screw shanks.

8. Starting at the edges and working toward the center, place washers on the screws and drive them, drawing the finish flooring down (Figure C).

MATERIALS
- Chalk
- 6d finish nail
- #8 roundhead wood screws
- Masking tape
- #8 flat washers

TOOLS
Hammer • Drill with 1/8" and 3/16" bits • Tape measure • Screwdriver

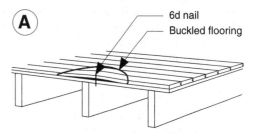

A — 6d nail / Buckled flooring

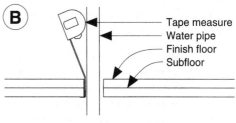

B — Tape measure / Water pipe / Finish floor / Subfloor

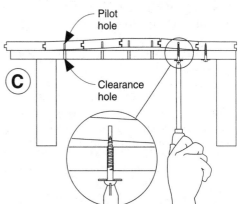

C — Pilot hole / Clearance hole

REPLACING A CERAMIC FLOOR TILE

Ceramic floor tiles can break if not fully supported underneath, but they're not hard to replace if they break. The toughest part is finding a matching replacement tile—unless, of course, you or your builder kept a few leftover tiles on hand. If you can't find one, try a professional tile installer. They often keep samples from their jobs.

MATERIALS
- Waterproof tile mastic
- Replacement ceramic tile
- Block of wood
- Box of powdered ceramic tile grout

TOOLS
- Beer-can opener • Grout saw
- Cold chisel • Hammer
- Goggles • Wood chisel • Vacuum cleaner • Sponge • Putty knife
- Bucket • Rubber-edged grout float

1. Remove the grout from around the damaged or missing tile, using a beer-can opener (Figure A). If the grout is too hard for the beer-can opener or if you are replacing a large number of tiles, you can purchase a special grout saw at a tile store.

2. Using a cold chisel and hammer, carefully chip out the damaged tile, starting near the center of the tile (Figure B). Wear goggles to protect your eyes against flying chips. Try not to damage adjacent tiles, or you will find yourself replacing these as well.

3. Using a wood chisel, remove most of the old tile mastic from the floor. You don't have to achieve a smooth surface; the new mastic will fill any irregularities.

4. Vacuum up all debris from the floor. It wouldn't hurt to wipe the area with a damp sponge to get up all the powder. The mastic sticks best to clean, solid surfaces.

5. Spread 1/8 inch of waterproof tile mastic on the back of the replacement tile with a putty knife, staying 1/4 to 1/2 inch from the edges of the tile (Figure C).

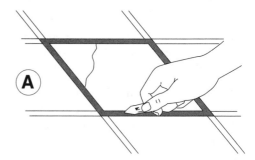

A

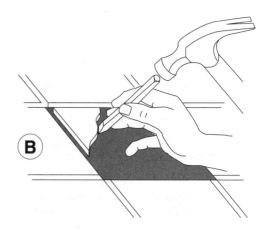

B

6. Place the tile so that its edges line up with the edges of the adjacent tiles, and tap the tile level, using a block of wood and hammer. Be gentle so you don't crack the new tile (Figure D).

7. Place a bucket of water or a few heavy books over the tile for 24 hours to hold it in place and keep people from stepping on it.

8. After 24 hours, fill the joints around the tile with ceramic tile grout. Mix the powdered grout, following the manufacturer's directions. Apply the mixed grout with your bare forefinger (Figure E). If you are replacing a large number of tiles, apply the grout by wiping diagonally across the entire surface with a rubber-edged grout float. Wipe the grout in several directions to fill the joints.

9. Wipe up the excess grout with a damp, but not saturated, sponge. Be careful not to remove too much grout from the joint.

10. After the grout dries, wipe the tiles again to remove any residue.

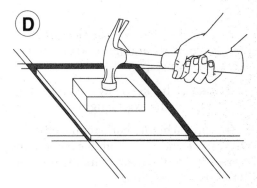

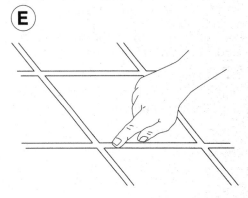

FASTENING A CARPET EDGE

The edges of carpets in doorways and other places where they abut different types of flooring should be protected by special binder bars. Otherwise, the edge of the carpet can fray and tear. It is never too late to install binder bars, and they are available in a variety of styles and lengths at carpet stores and home centers.

MATERIALS
Tackless binder bar with nails

TOOLS
Tape measure • Hacksaw • Block of wood • Hammer

1. Use a tape measure to measure the length of the carpet edge to be fastened down.

2. Purchase the necessary length of tackless binder bar (Figure A) at a home center or carpet store.

3. Using a hacksaw, lay out and cut the binder bar to the exact length.

4. Slip the binder bar over the edge of the carpet, and place both the bar and the carpet flat on the floor. Mark the position of the bar on the floor.

5. Remove the carpet from the bar, line the bar up to the positioning marks, and nail the bar to the floor (Figure B).

6. Insert the edge of the carpet again into the secured binder bar.

7. Using a block of wood and a hammer, hammer the binder bar closed over the carpet (Figure C).

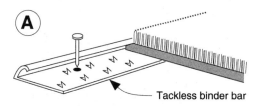

A

Tackless binder bar

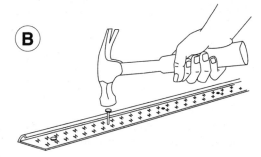

B

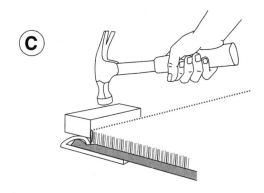

C

REPAIRING A DAMAGED CARPET

If you have a burn spot or stain in your favorite carpet, it can be patched or "plugged," just like a golf green. Use the smallest diameter plug that will cover the damaged area to minimize its visibility.

MATERIALS

- Matching carpet scrap
- Paint can lid
- Two 6d common nails
- Double-sided carpet tape

TOOLS

Hammer • Utility knife • Vacuum cleaner • Bucket • Large book

1. Before you start, make sure you have an extra scrap of carpet that matches the area to be patched. If you know you won't be moving a couch or dresser for the life of the carpet, you can cut a patch from that area. Be aware, however, that the hidden area may be less faded than the area to be patched.

2. Using a hammer and two common 6d nails, nail a clean paint can lid over the damaged area of carpet. Leave the nail heads sticking up so that you can remove them later (Figure A).

3. Using the can lid as a guide, cut all the way through the carpet with a very sharp utility knife. Keep the knife blade vertical and try to make the cut in a single pass (Figure B).

4. Remove the nails and lid with the hammer, and renail the lid over the matching carpet scrap. If the carpet has a pattern, make sure the scrap matches the circle removed. Cut the patch as in Step 3, again keeping the blade vertical.

5. Remove the nails, lid, and patch, and set them aside.

6. Vacuum the floor area where the patch will be placed, and cover the hole with double-sided carpet tape. Remove the paper backing from the tape, and press the patch into place. Weight the patch overnight with a bucket of water on a large book (Figure C).

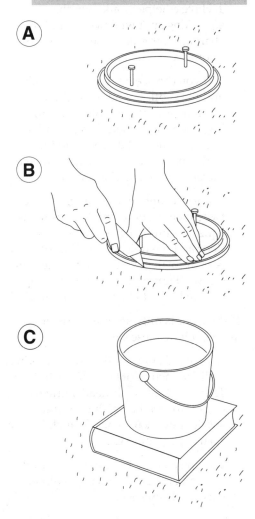

A

B

C

SILENCING A SQUEAKING FLOOR

Wood floor and stair squeaks are caused by wood rubbing against wood. To eliminate squeaks, you must prevent the movement between the wood members. Here are three ways to tighten up the floor and silence the squeaks.

MATERIALS
- Wood shingle
- Carpenter's glue
- 6d small-head spiral siding nails
- Colored wax touch-up stick

TOOLS
Hammer • Drill with $3/32$" bit • Screwdriver • Nail set

If the floor is accessible from below, follow these steps:

1. Have a helper walk over the squeaking spot while you stand on a chair and carefully observe the subfloor and joists.

2. If you can see light between a joist and the subfloor and the gap changes with the squeak, the solution is to coat both sides of a wood shingle with carpenter's glue and drive it into the gap with a hammer until just snug to avoid increasing the gap (Figure A).

3. If you cannot detect any motion between the subfloor and the joists, the squeak is probably between the subfloor and the finish floor. The solution is to draw the two floors together with screws (Figure B). (See "Refastening Buckled Wood Flooring" on page 119.)

If the floor is only accessible from above, follow these steps:

1. To avoid splitting the finish flooring, drill $3/32$-inch pilot holes $3/4$ inch deep. Then drive 6d small-head spiral siding nails through the finish floor into the subfloor every 6 inches, $3/4$ inch in from each edge (Figure C).

2. Using a nail set, set the heads of the nails and cover them with a colored wax touch-up stick.

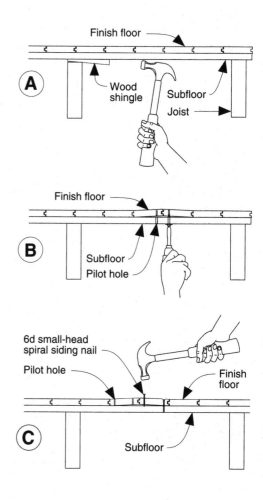

SILENCING A SQUEAKING STAIR

As with wood floors, squeaking stairs are caused by wood rubbing on wood. The only way to eliminate stair squeaks is to tighten the offending adjacent wood members with nails or wedges. Both methods are described here.

1. Locate and mark the offending stair.

2. Measure the distance *(X)* by which the tread extends beyond the riser and add ³/₈ inch. Mark this dimension on the top of the stair tread, and using a try square, draw a line at this mark across the width of the stair (Figure A).

3. Using a ³/₈-inch bit, hold the tips of the bit and one 6d small-head spiral siding nail together, and mark the length of the nail on the bit with masking tape.

4. Drill pairs of angled pilot holes along the marked line, through the tread and into the riser to the depth of the mark on the bit.

5. Using a hammer, drive the nails into the pilot holes (Figure B) and set them with a nail set. Cover the nail heads with a colored wax touch-up stick, if they are exposed.

6. If the squeak persists, apply carpenter's glue to wood stair wedges and drive them between the rear of the tread and the riser above. Use the hammer and a scrap of wood to avoid marring the stair (Figure C).

7. Trim the wedges flush with the riser using a sharp wood chisel.

8. If you find the wedges unsightly, cover the tread/riser joint with a strip of ½-inch quarter-round molding and fasten the molding with brads.

MATERIALS

- 6d small-head spiral siding nails
- Masking tape
- Colored wax touch-up stick
- Carpenter's glue
- Wood stair wedges
- ¹/₂" quarter-round molding
- Brads

TOOLS

Tape measure • Try square • Drill and ³/₃₂" bit • Hammer • Scrap of wood • Nail set • Wood chisel

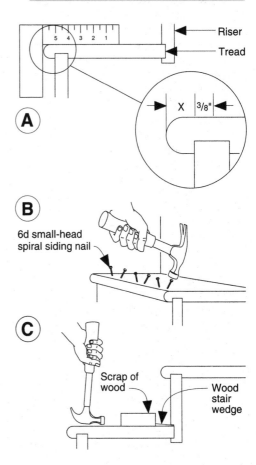

A — Riser / Tread / X ³/₈"

B — 6d small-head spiral siding nail

C — Scrap of wood / Wood stair wedge

TIGHTENING A NEWEL POST

If the handrail on your banister seems loose, first check to see whether just the balusters are loose or if the newel posts are loose as well. Tighten balusters, as shown in "Tightening a Loose Baluster" on the opposite page. Tighten newel posts with wood screws, as shown below.

MATERIALS
- #10 × 3½" flathead wood screws
- Can of wood putty
- Matching paint or stain and varnish

TOOLS
Drill and combination countersink and pilot bit for #10 wood screws (or ⅛", ³⁄₁₆", and ⅜" bits) • Screwdriver

1. Lay out the screw locations about 1 inch above the bottom of the newel post (Figure A).

2. Using a combination countersink and pilot bit, drill pilot, clearance, and countersink holes for #10 × 3½-inch flathead wood screws at each location. Angle the holes down at 45 degrees so that the screws will enter the floor beneath the newel post.

3. If you don't have a combination countersink and pilot bit, drill the hole in three steps starting with a ⅛-inch bit for the pilot hole, followed by a ³⁄₁₆-inch bit for the shank clearance hole, and finishing up with a ⅜-inch bit for the countersink, as shown in Figure B.

4. Drive the screws firmly into the newel post until the heads are just below the surface.

5. Cover the screw heads with wood putty, and paint or stain and varnish to match the surrounding finish. (See "Repairing Wood Flooring" on page 116.)

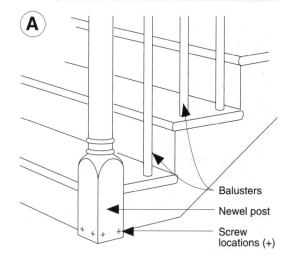

Balusters
Newel post
Screw locations (+)

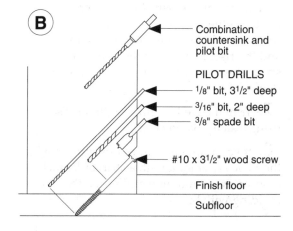

Combination countersink and pilot bit

PILOT DRILLS
⅛" bit, 3½" deep
³⁄₁₆" bit, 2" deep
⅜" spade bit

#10 x 3½" wood screw

Finish floor
Subfloor

TIGHTENING A LOOSE BALUSTER

A baluster is one of numerous vertical posts supporting a handrail. A loose baluster is more of an annoyance than a danger, but securing it is a simple, 20-minute project.

1. Determine whether the top of the baluster is flush against the bottom of the handrail or set into the handrail (Figure A). If it is set into the handrail, go to Step 3.

2. Squirt carpenter's glue straight from the nozzle into the gap between the top of the baluster and the bottom of the handrail until it comes out of all sides (Figure B). If the glue container doesn't have a suitable nozzle, use a small plastic gluing syringe, which can be purchased at a hardware store.

3. Using a 1/16-inch drill bit, drill two pilot holes at 45-degree angles through the top of the baluster and slightly into the handrail.

4. Hammer 6d—2 inch long—finish nails into each pilot hole. Countersink the nails with a nail set (Figure C).

5. Wipe away excess glue with a sponge dampened with hot water.

6. Cover the nail heads with a colored wax touch-up stick.

MATERIALS

- Carpenter's glue
- Plastic gluing syringe
- 6d finish nails
- Colored wax touch-up stick

TOOLS

Drill and 1/16" bit • Hammer • Nail set • Sponge

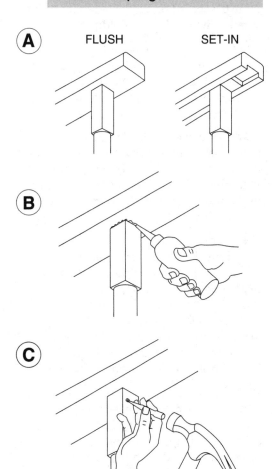

(A) FLUSH   SET-IN

(B)

(C)

REPLACING A BASEBOARD

Baseboards most often require replacement because the wall abutting and behind them is damaged. If you are very careful, you can remove a baseboard intact. Don't be hard on yourself if you fail, however—it happens to the best of carpenters.

1. Compare your baseboard to Figure A to determine if it consists of a single large baseboard or a large baseboard plus smaller shoe and edge moldings.

2. Cut through any paint film by running a sharp utility knife along the wood joints and the wall. If you don't do this, you'll either split the wood or damage the wall as you remove the baseboard.

3. To remove the small moldings, use a nail set and hammer to drive the nails all the way through the moldings (Figure B). After the moldings have been removed, pull out the nails with locking pliers, such as Vise-Grips.

4. To remove the large molding, drive wide putty knives between the molding and the wall, then drive the flat end of a pry bar between the two putty knives (Figure C). As soon as the gap between the molding and the wall grows to 1/8 inch, drive a wooden shingle or other wedge into the gap to hold it. Move the putty knives to another location and repeat the process.

5. After the molding has been wedged out along its entire length, remove the shingles, and tap the molding back into place. This should slightly pop the nails out of the molding so that you can remove them with the hooked end of the pry bar.

MATERIALS

- Scrap wood shingles
- Replacement moldings
- 8d and 4d finish nails
- Colored wax touch-up stick
- Drywall joint compound
- Matching paint or stain and varnish

TOOLS

Utility knife • Nail set • Hammer • Locking pliers • 2 wide putty knives • Pry bar • Paintbrush

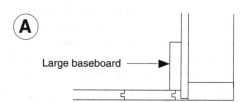

(A)

Large baseboard

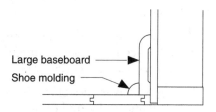

Large baseboard

Shoe molding

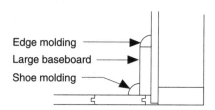

Edge molding

Large baseboard

Shoe molding

6. If you've damaged any of the molding while removing it, take a sample to a lumberyard, and ask for a replacement of the same design. Before purchasing it, ask if they will cut the new molding to match the old, including any mitered—angled—cuts. If they won't, find another lumberyard, or ask a friend with a miter box to cut them for you.

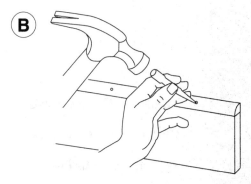

7. Lay the old and new baseboards together, and transfer the location of the nailholes from the old to the new. Marking the old hole positions should assure that you will be nailing into the 2 × 4 studs in the wall instead of just the thin drywall or plaster.

8. Nail the new baseboard into place using 8d finish nails. Set the nails with a nail set.

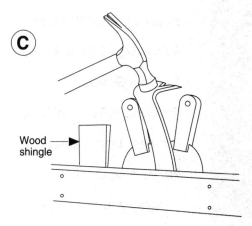

Wood shingle

9. Renail the small moldings, if any, with 4d finish nails, and set the nails with a nail set. If the nail holes are now too large for the 4d nails to hold, nail them in different locations since you'll be nailing into the large baseboard not the wall studs.

10. If the baseboard is stained, fill the nail holes, using a colored wax touch-up stick before finishing. If the baseboard is painted, fill the nail holes with drywall joint compound, and then paint to match.

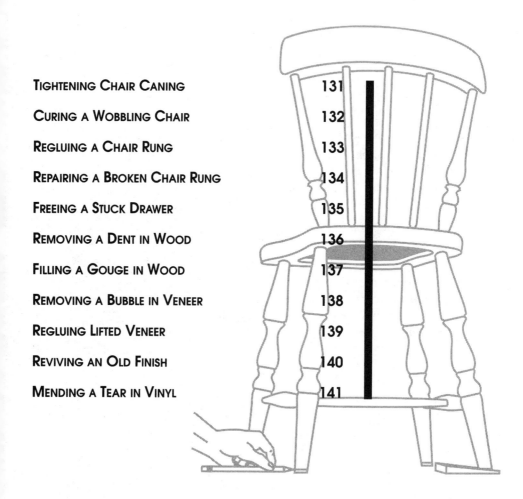

TIGHTENING CHAIR CANING

When a cane seat sags, most people start looking in the Yellow Pages for recaning services. But there may be a simpler solution. Natural fibers often shrink when wet thoroughly and then dried. Before spending money on recaning, try shrinking the caning, as shown below.

MATERIALS
None

TOOLS
Rectangular cake pan • Tea kettle • Hand towels

1. Find a rectangular cake pan large enough to cover the entire area of caning.

2. Set the cake pan on a countertop and the chair upside down over the cake pan so that the caning is within the edges of the pan, as shown in the illustration at right.

3. Heat water in a tea kettle to boiling.

4. Slowly pour the hot water over the caning until the cake pan is full. If the caning does not protrude enough above the chair seat frame to remain immersed, spread a hand towel over it, and pour the hot water over the towel.

5. Let the caning stand in the water for five minutes.

6. Remove the chair from the pan and set it upright. Dry the wooden parts with a dry towel, and let the caning dry for at least 24 hours before putting any weight on it.

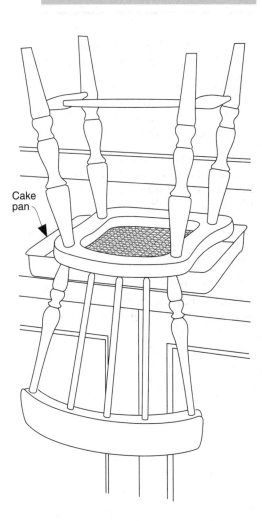

Cake pan

CURING A WOBBLING CHAIR

There is nothing worse than watching your dinner guests wobble back and forth on your dining chairs. Curing the problem requires cutting a small amount from each leg, and this method is fool-proof. Any other method, if applied without pre-cise measurement, will usually result in more and more cutting and shorter legs!

MATERIALS
- **Wood shingle**
- **100-grit sandpaper**

TOOLS
Utility knife • Pencil • Hacksaw
• Block of wood

1. Using a utility knife, split off 1/2-inch-wide strips from a wood shingle.

2. Place the wobbly chair on a level surface—such as the kitchen floor—and gently wedge a shingle strip under the shortest leg until the chair stops wobbling.

3. Lay a cylindrical or hexagonal pencil flat on the floor, and draw layout lines around all four legs, as shown in the illustration at right.

4. Lay the chair on its side and, using a hacksaw, carefully cut each leg along the layout lines.

5. If the chair still wobbles slightly, use 100-grit sandpaper wrapped around a block of wood to sand the longest leg.

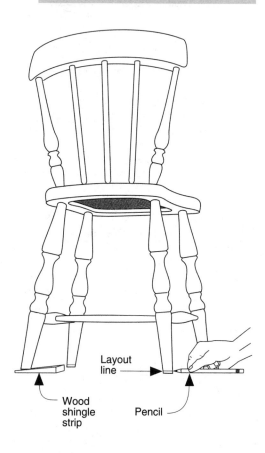

Layout line

Wood shingle strip

Pencil

REGLUING A CHAIR RUNG

Most chair rungs eventually loosen up, and many homeowners try unsuccessfully to reglue them. The most common mistakes are leaving the old glue in place and not applying enough pressure to the joints while the glue is drying. Here is a simple way to remove the old glue and an ingenious method of applying pressure without resorting to large, expensive clamps. If you can't find wood stair wedges at a lumberyard or home center, ask a friend with a table saw to make some for you.

MATERIALS
- 100-grit sandpaper
- Wood stair wedges
- Carpenter's glue

TOOLS
Utility knife • Wooden spoon • Backsaw • Rubber mallet or hammer • Block of wood

1. Gently pry apart the chair legs to remove the loose rung.

2. Remove all traces of the old glue from the joints by scraping the rung ends with a utility knife (Figure A) and reaming out the leg sockets with 100-grit sandpaper wrapped around the end of a wooden spoon handle (Figure B).

3. Using a backsaw, cut slots into both ends of the rung (Figure C).

4. Using the utility knife, trim wood stair wedges to the exact length and width of the slots you have just cut in the rungs.

5. Apply carpenter's glue to the rung ends and leg sockets, insert the wedges halfway into the rung slots (Figure C), and replace the rung in the leg sockets.

6. With a rubber mallet or hammer and block of wood, gently tap on the chair legs until the rungs are fully seated. When the wedge hits the bottom of a socket, tapping the rung further drives the wedge into the rung slot, expanding the rung for a tight fit. Since the rung is tightly wedged, there is no need to clamp the chair—just don't use it for 24 hours.

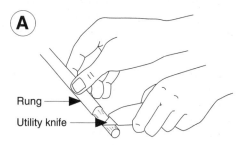

A

Rung

Utility knife

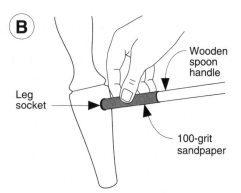

B

Wooden spoon handle

Leg socket

100-grit sandpaper

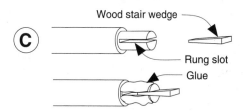

Wood stair wedge

C

Rung slot

Glue

REPAIRING A BROKEN CHAIR RUNG

If a chair rung is broken within 1 or 2 inches of a chair leg, it can be reinforced with a dowel that extends through the leg and down the axis of the rung. If you regularly use a power drill, you should have no trouble drilling the precise dowel hole required. A rung with a break near its center should be replaced with a new rung, using the technique described in "Regluing a Chair Rung" on page 133.

MATERIALS

- Carpenter's glue
- Masking tape
- 3/16" wood dowel

TOOLS

Bungee cord • Tape measure
- Drill and 3/16" bit • Utility knife
- Hammer

1. Using carpenter's glue, glue both surfaces of the break in the rung, and quickly wrap a bungee cord around the legs (Figure A).

2. Measure the distance from the outside of the leg to 1/2 inch beyond the break in the rung.

3. Using masking tape, mark a 3/16-inch drill bit with the measured distance. Purchase a longer bit, if necessary.

4. Without removing the bungee cord, drill a 3/16-inch hole straight through the chair leg and down the center of the rung as far as the mark on the bit (Figure B).

5. Using a utility knife, cut a 3/16-inch dowel about 1/4 inch longer than the depth of the hole.

6. Squirt carpenter's glue into the hole and coat the dowel with glue.

7. Hammer the dowel into the hole until it hits the bottom of the hole (Figure C). It should project about 1/4 inch.

8. Using the utility knife, cut the dowel flush and wipe up the excess glue. Let the glue dry for 24 hours before removing the bungee cord.

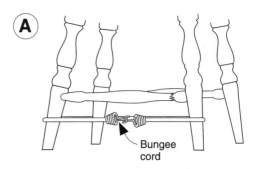

A

Bungee cord

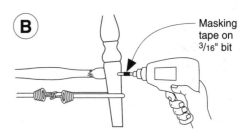

B

Masking tape on 3/16" bit

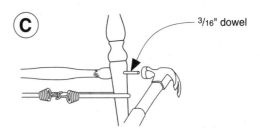

C

3/16" dowel

FREEING A STUCK DRAWER

Who doesn't have a drawer that sticks? The usual cause is a drawer front that is simply too large for its opening. But sometimes the drawer sides are the culprits. The obvious cure is to make the drawer a bit smaller with the judicious use of a hand plane. Before making a lot of wood shavings, however, try the simple task of rubbing the drawer edges with canning wax.

MATERIALS
Block of canning wax

TOOLS
Block plane

If only the drawer front sticks, it is too large and requires hand planing. Follow these steps:

1. Carefully observe the drawer front while opening and closing the drawer to determine whether it is the top or bottom edge that sticks.

2. Remove the drawer and hand plane the offending edge several strokes (Figure A).

3. Replace the drawer and check the fit.

4. If the drawer still sticks, continue hand planing and checking the fit until the drawer closes easily.

If the drawer sticks while you are opening or closing it, the sides are binding. Follow these steps:

1. Remove the drawer and rub both top and bottom edges with a block of canning wax (Figure B).

2. If the wax doesn't cure the binding, remove the drawer and hand plane the top edges of its sides (Figure C).

3. Continue hand planing and checking the fit until the drawer closes easily. Then, apply more wax to the planed edges.

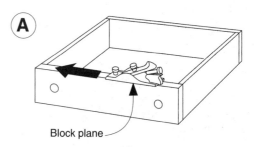

Block plane

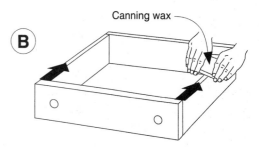

Canning wax

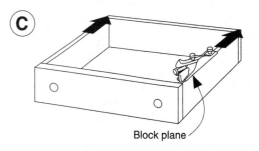

Block plane

REMOVING A DENT IN WOOD

Dented wood is a little like freeze-dried food: Adding water to its cells will—to some extent—re-inflate the cells to their original shape. This method involves forcing moisture into the cells through tiny holes in the wood finish. It will never remove the dent entirely but may make it acceptable.

MATERIALS
Gauze pad

TOOLS
Flashlight • Chalk or water-soluble marker • Push pin or common pin • Clothes iron

1. Identify the full extent of the dent by feel and by shining a flashlight at a low, grazing angle to the wood surface. Mark the dented area with a piece of chalk or a water-soluble marker.

2. Using a push pin or a common pin, prick the entire surface of the dent every 1/4 inch to just break through the finish (Figure A). The holes should be small so that they won't be obvious, but they need to penetrate the surface finish in order to pass moisture into the wood.

3. Cut a gauze pad just large enough to cover the dent.

4. Wet the gauze pad, place it on the dent, and press it with the tip of a hot clothes iron for a few seconds (Figure B). The object is to drive steam through the pin pricks into the wood.

5. Check the dent. Repeat applications of the hot iron until the dent disappears, or until the gauze pad is dry.

6. The hot steam may discolor the finish. If the finish is still discolored after a week, repair the damage. (See "Reviving an Old Finish" on page 140.)

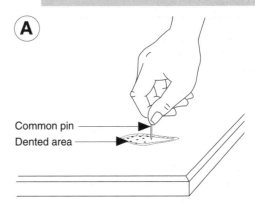

(A) Common pin — Dented area

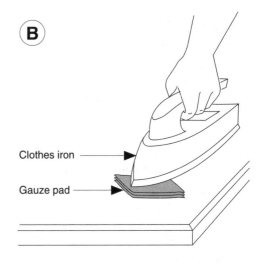

(B) Clothes iron — Gauze pad

FILLING A GOUGE IN WOOD

Over years of daily use, furniture is bound to receive bumps and bruises. If your furniture has a clear finish, these steps will produce a repair that is barely discernable. If your furniture is painted, you need not go through the color-matching process. Just fill the gouge, sand, and paint over the patch.

MATERIALS
- Can of wood putty
- Scrap of wood
- 200-grit sandpaper
- Matching stain
- Clean rags
- Wiping varnish

TOOLS
Utility knife • Putty knife
- Block of wood • Teaspoon
- Cupcake pan • Paintbrush
- Felt-tip pen

1. Using a utility knife, cut away any loose splinters. Using a putty knife, fill the gouge with wood putty and overfill slightly (Figure A). While the can is open, spread five small test patches of wood putty on a scrap of wood.

2. After 24 hours, sand the putty level, using 200-grit sandpaper wrapped around a block of wood (Figure B).

3. Using a stain brochure from a paint store, select a stain that is slightly darker than the finish. Stir the stain thoroughly, then prepare four mixes of paint thinner and stain in ratios of 8:1, 4:1, 2:1, and 1:1. Use a teaspoon to measure and a cupcake pan to hold the stain mixtures. Using a clean rag for each, apply the straight stain and each stain mix to the five putty patches.

4. Purchase a wiping varnish (a varnish thinned with paint thinner), such as Waterlox, with a gloss that matches the original finish of the furniture. Apply it to each patch with a clean rag. You will immediately see which mix matches best.

5. Using a dark felt-tip pen, simulate wood grain by continuing the grain lines across the repair, if desired (Figure C).

6. Apply the selected mix plus two coats of wiping varnish to the puttied gouge. For even better results, sand and refinish the entire surface.

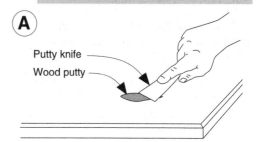

A Putty knife
Wood putty

B Sandpaper on block of wood

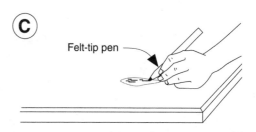

C Felt-tip pen

REMOVING A BUBBLE IN VENEER

Replacing the veneer on a piece of furniture is an expensive process best left to professional furniture restorers. But, if moisture has raised a bubble in the veneer of a prized piece of furniture, don't call the professional until you have tried this simple cure.

MATERIALS
- **Clean rags**
- **Carpenter's glue**
- **Wax paper or plastic wrap**

TOOLS
Clothes iron • Utility knife • Plastic gluing syringe • Bucket • Large book

1. Wood veneer is very fragile, so work carefully. First, soften the bubbled veneer by placing a clean damp rag over the bubble and pressing it with a clothes iron on low heat for ten seconds. Repeat until the veneer becomes pliable.

2. Using a sharp utility knife, slit the bubble in the direction of the wood grain (Figure A).

3. Using a small plastic gluing syringe (available at a hardware store), inject carpenter's glue under both sides of the bubble (Figure B).

4. Press down on the bubble to squeeze out excess glue. Wipe up the excess glue with a damp rag.

5. Place wax paper or plastic wrap over the bubble, then weight the bubble down for 24 hours with a bucket of water on a large book (Figure C).

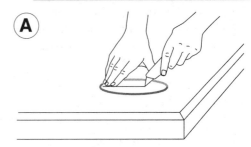

(A)

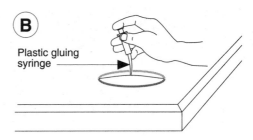

(B)

Plastic gluing syringe

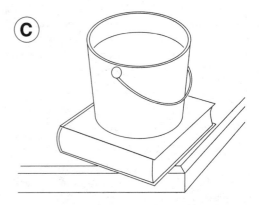

(C)

REGLUING LIFTED VENEER

This repair is similar to "Removing a Bubble in Veneer" on the opposite page, except that the edge of the veneer has come unglued instead of the center. Be careful when scraping off the old glue not to leave any glue particles in the crevice between the veneer and the base. Even tiny particles will show through the veneer as bumps, just as the pea did under the princess's mattresses.

MATERIALS
- Clean rag
- Carpenter's glue
- Wax paper or plastic wrap

TOOLS
Clothes iron • Putty knife or utility knife blade • Stiff paintbrush • Rolling pin • Bucket • Large book

1. Wood veneer is very fragile, so work carefully. First, soften the bubbled veneer by placing a clean damp rag over the bubble and pressing it with a clothes iron on low heat for ten seconds. Repeat until the veneer becomes pliable (Figure A).

2. Using a putty knife or the blade from a utility knife, scrape away as much of the old glue as possible. Make sure that the surfaces are smooth.

3. Using a stiff paintbrush, spread a thin layer of carpenter's glue over the substrate (Figure B).

4. Press the veneer down, working from the sound area toward the loose edge. If the reglued area is large, use a rolling pin to squeeze out the excess glue, rolling toward the edges of the veneer.

5. Wipe up the excess glue with a damp rag.

6. Place wax paper or plastic wrap over the glued area, then weight the veneer down for 24 hours with a bucket of water on a large book (Figure C).

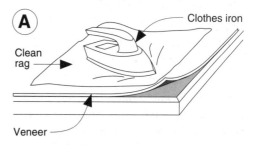

A — Clothes iron — Clean rag — Veneer

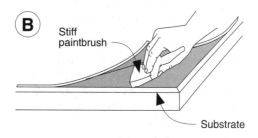

B — Stiff paintbrush — Substrate

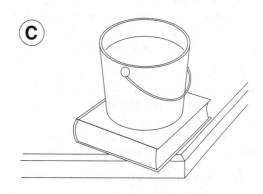

C

REVIVING AN OLD FINISH

Stripping the entire finish from an old piece of furniture is expensive, messy, and often unnecessary. Moreover, an entirely new finish may not have the charming patina that only age can produce. A cleaning and touch-up, followed by a new coat of finish, may produce a better result.

1. Inspect the surface carefully to make sure the finish isn't cracked. Note any scratches, gouges, and water rings.

2. Clean the entire surface with mineral spirits and clean rags. Wipe the surface at least three times, using a clean rag each time. Let the piece dry thoroughly.

3. Remove any white water rings in the finish by rubbing just the ring area with extra-fine steel wool and auto-body rubbing compound (this functions as liquid sandpaper but is finer in grit). Be careful not to penetrate the finish all the way to bare wood.

4. Fill deep scratches and gouges with colored wax touch-up sticks (Figure A). Match the finish color by alternating different colors of sticks until the blend is right. Remove any excess wax by scraping with the blade of a utility knife.

5. Apply three coats of spray urethane varnish to the entire surface (Figure B). Spray in long strokes parallel to the wood grain, and wait 15 minutes between coats.

6. After 24 hours, rub the entire piece with extra-fine steel wool and auto-body rubbing compound. Make sure you compound every area, including recesses, or the finish will not look uniform. Remove the compound with clean, damp rags.

7. Apply furniture paste wax and buff.

MATERIALS

- Mineral spirits
- Clean rags
- Extra-fine steel wool
- Auto-body rubbing compound
- Colored wax touch-up sticks
- Spray urethane varnish
- Furniture paste wax

TOOLS

Utility knife blade

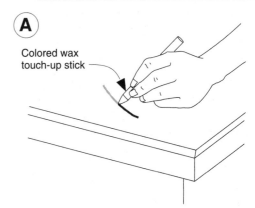

A

Colored wax touch-up stick

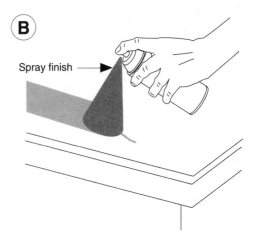

B

Spray finish

MENDING A TEAR IN VINYL

Automobile seats are the most common candidates for this repair. Though vinyl can be made to look like leather, beneath the surface it is just plastic, subject—like all plastics—to hardening and cracking. If your car seats crack, get a few more years out of them by cementing the cracks back together. The cardboard will quickly break down and not be uncomfortable to sit on.

MATERIALS

- Thin cardboard
- Common pins
- Tube of vinyl cement
- Cotton swabs

TOOLS

Scissors • Plastic gluing syringe

1. Using scissors, cut a piece of thin cardboard—an old cardboard notebook cover is perfect—2 inches by the length of the tear.

2. Slide the cardboard piece through the tear, using common pins to maneuver it until it is centered underneath the tear.

3. Pin one edge of the tear to the cardboard with common pins (Figure A).

4. Remove the plunger from a plastic gluing syringe (available at a hardware store), squeeze about 1 tablespoon of vinyl cement into the barrel, and replace the plunger.

5. Using the syringe, apply a thin bead of cement to each edge of the tear in the vinyl (Figure B).

6. Quickly draw the edges of the tear together and push common pins through both the vinyl and cardboard to hold the edges together.

7. Remove any excess cement, using as many cotton swabs as necessary to do a neat job (Figure C).

8. Leave the pins in place for the curing time, as specified on the tube of cement.

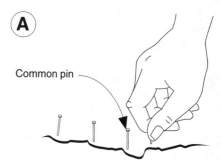

(A) Common pin

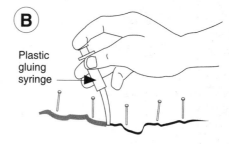

(B) Plastic gluing syringe

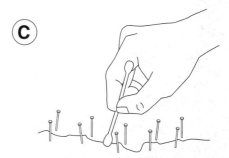

(C)

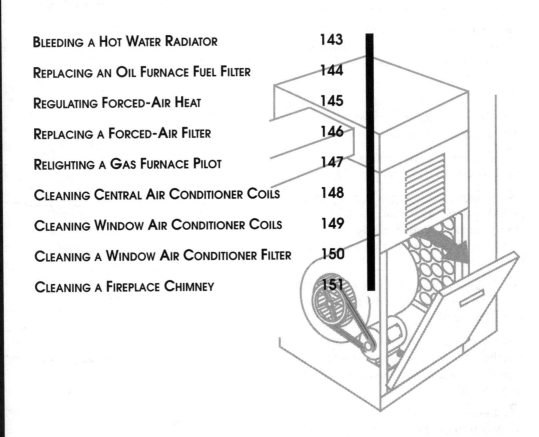

H
E
A
T
I
N
G
&
C
O
O
L
I
N
G

BLEEDING A HOT WATER RADIATOR

If you are getting heat from some but not all of your baseboard convectors or radiators, the cool ones may have air locks. This air has built up in the pipes and is preventing heated water from flowing up into the unit. The cure is to remove the air through the bleeder valve.

MATERIALS
None

TOOLS
Screwdriver • Cup • Square socket valve key

1. Trace the supply lines for each heating zone in the house back to the furnace, making sure any manual valves in the loop are open.

2. Turn up the thermostats in your house until the heating system comes on. Wait until at least one baseboard convector (Figure A) or radiator (Figure B) gets warm.

3. Check each radiator or baseboard convector in the house. Note any units that remain cold. Also note any units that make loud gurgling or banging sounds. It is normal for them to creak and ping as they warm, however.

4. On each of the problem units, turn the inlet valve—with a handle, knob, or screw—fully counterclockwise to make sure the unit is open to flow.

5. Hold a cup next to the bleeder valve (there may be just one bleeder valve for all the baseboard convectors in a room). Using a screwdriver, turn the screw counterclockwise just until a steady stream of water flows out. (Many older radiators require a square socket valve key—available at a hardware store—to open the bleeder valve.) Quickly close the screw by turning it fully clockwise.

6. If the unit is still cold after ten minutes, call your heating contractor.

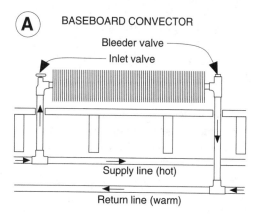

A BASEBOARD CONVECTOR
Bleeder valve
Inlet valve
Supply line (hot)
Return line (warm)

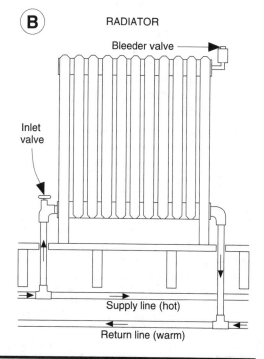

B RADIATOR
Bleeder valve
Inlet valve
Supply line (hot)
Return line (warm)

REPLACING AN OIL FURNACE FUEL FILTER

An oil heat system usually has a fuel filter between the fuel storage tank and the oil burner to trap impurities before they clog the tiny opening in the oil burner nozzle. The filter should be replaced every heating season before it becomes completely clogged and cuts off the fuel supply.

MATERIALS
- **Paper towels**
- **Replacement fuel filter cartridge**

TOOLS
Cake pan • Adjustable wrench

1. Turn off the house thermostats and the red emergency furnace switch that controls power to the furnace. It is usually located at the entrance to the basement or furnace room.

2. Locate the fuel filter between the fuel tank and the oil burner (Figure A). Close the fuel shutoff valve (Figure B) by turning it clockwise. If the handle is a lever, turn it perpendicular to the fuel line.

3. Place a large cake pan under the filter and, holding the filter body with one hand, turn the top bolt counterclockwise with an adjustable wrench.

4. When the body drops, remove the filter cartridge and the rubber gasket and place both in the pan (Figure C). Empty the body and wipe the inside clean with paper towels.

5. Empty the cartridge and take it to an auto-parts store to buy a replacement.

6. To improve the new filter's seal, smear its gasket with fuel oil from the cake pan and insert the gasket into the groove in the body.

7. Place the new filter cartridge in the body, seat the body under the cap, and tighten the bolt securely.

8. Turn on the fuel shutoff valve and then, after five minutes, turn on the emergency switch and thermostats.

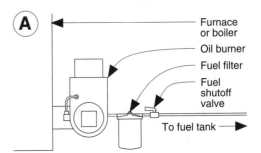

Furnace or boiler
Oil burner
Fuel filter
Fuel shutoff valve
To fuel tank →

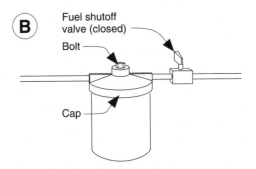

Fuel shutoff valve (closed)
Bolt
Cap

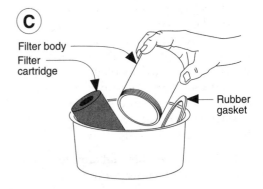

Filter body
Filter cartridge
Rubber gasket

REGULATING FORCED-AIR HEAT

Some rooms in a house with forced-air heat have higher heat loss than others because of differences in insulation and the number of doors and windows. By opening or closing dampers in the air ducts or registers, you can regulate the rate of heat flow into the rooms. Try this on a cold night when the rooms won't be affected by heat from the sun.

MATERIALS
None

TOOLS
None

1. To maximize the efficiency of the heating system, you want as much free air flow as possible, so begin by opening all floor and wall registers fully in each room. Also, make sure that none of the registers are covered by rugs or other furnishings.

2. In the basement, trace all of the ducts leading from the supply plenum (the common air chamber from which all the supply [warm] ducts leave), looking for damper handles (Figure A). Turn all damper handles parallel to the direction of the ducts (Figure B).

3. Adjust the thermostat until the coldest room is at the desired temperature. (Some of the rooms will be too warm.)

4. Partially close the supply registers, if adjustable, or partially close the dampers in the supply ducts leading to the rooms that are too warm.

5. Wait an hour for the room temperatures to stabilize. If the too-warm rooms are still too warm, close the registers or dampers further. If too cool, partially open the registers or dampers. Continue waiting and adjusting until all rooms are at the desired temperatures.

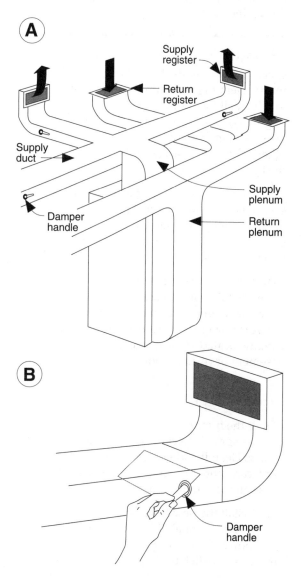

A

Supply register

Return register

Supply duct

Supply plenum

Return plenum

Damper handle

B

Damper handle

REPLACING A FORCED-AIR FILTER

Heating and cooling systems often share the same forced-air duct system, which contains a large fibrous air filter. The filter removes airborne dust returning from the living space and generally keeps the house and the system cleaner. A dirty filter makes the furnace or central air conditioner work harder, so replace the inexpensive filter several times during the year.

1. Use the furnace manual or visual inspection to locate the filter that covers the return plenum (the common air chamber to which all the return [cool] ducts go) (Figure A). Some filters fit into an exposed slot in front of the blower, but others can only be accessed by removing the blower access panel.

2. If necessary, remove the blower access panel (Figure A). Most panels simply pull up and out. Others may require first turning a handle or removing several screws.

3. Turn the furnace or air conditioner off and let it cool, if necessary. Make sure the red emergency furnace switch (which controls power to the furnace) is off. It's usually located at the entrance to the basement or furnace room.

4. Remove the furnace filter by sliding it out (Figure B).

5. If the filter is washable—not cardboard—spray it forcefully with a garden hose to clean it. Otherwise, take it to a hardware store or home center and purchase an exact replacement.

6. Install the new filter, replace the blower access panel, if necessary, and restore power to the system. Turn the red emergency switch back on.

MATERIALS
Replacement furnace filter

TOOLS
Screwdriver • Garden hose

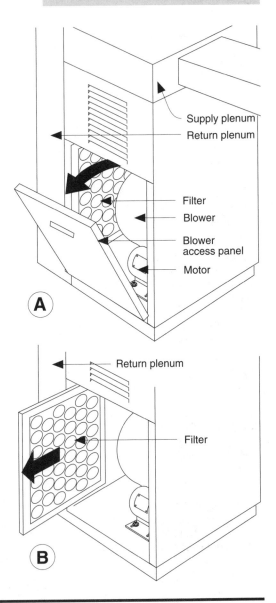

Supply plenum
Return plenum
Filter
Blower
Blower access panel
Motor

A

Return plenum
Filter

B

RELIGHTING A GAS FURNACE PILOT

A gas furnace pilot may go out because of a sudden gust of wind or because the gas was temporarily cut off. A thermocouple near the pilot flame senses when the pilot is off and shuts off the gas supply before an explosive situation develops. The pilot is easily relit following these steps, but first read your furnace manual or check the outside of your furnace for the manufacturer's specific directions.

MATERIALS
Gas grill lighter or long wood match

TOOLS
None

1. Find the instructions on your furnace and read the directions for lighting the pilot. Locate each of the elements—inlet valve, etc.—named in the directions before proceeding.

2. Turn off the gas inlet valve (*OFF* is perpendicular to the gas line) and the manual control knob (Figure A). Allow 30 minutes for any accumulated gas to dissipate. If you still smell gas after 30 minutes, call the gas company.

3. Turn the house thermostats off.

4. Turn the manual control knob to the *PILOT* position and hold it in place as you light the pilot. Use a gas grill lighter (Figure B) or a long wood match. Keep the manual control knob in the *PILOT* position for a full minute before releasing it.

5. Turn the manual control knob to *ON*.

6. If the pilot now goes out, the thermocouple may be defective. Turn the manual control knob to *OFF* and call the gas company.

7. If the pilot stays on, turn the house thermostats to a high setting to verify that the main burner comes on. If not, call the gas company.

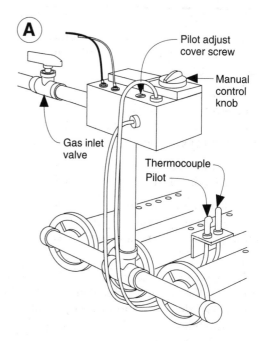

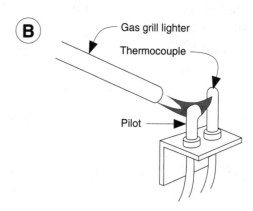

CLEANING CENTRAL AIR CONDITIONER COILS

The coil that dissipates the heat from your house air conditioner resembles a car radiator. To remove the heat, air is drawn through the honeycomb-like fins of the coil. The smallest deposit of dirt on the fins reduces the efficiency of the air conditioner and increases your cooling bill. Clean the coils annually.

MATERIALS

- Drop cloth or large plastic bag
- 3-in-1 or general purpose oil

TOOLS

Toothbrush • Vacuum cleaner
• Garden hose

1. Turn off the power to the outdoor air conditioning unit and remove the cover (Figure A).

2. Loosen the dirt on the outside face of the condenser coil using a toothbrush or other stiff, nonmetallic brush. Take care not to bend the fins.

3. Either vacuum up or blow away the loosened dirt from the coil (Figure B).

4. Cover all of the air conditioner, except the condenser coil, with a drop cloth or large plastic bag to protect the electrical components.

5. Spray the condenser coil from the inside of the unit toward the outside, using a garden hose and maximum water pressure (Figure C).

6. Remove the drop cloth or plastic bag and replace the cover.

7. Restore the power.

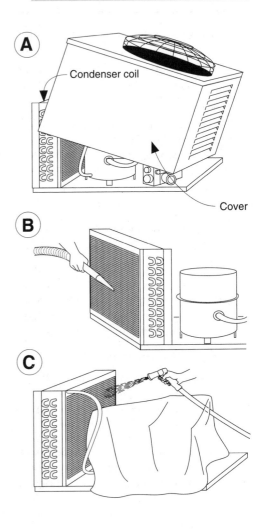

A Condenser coil

Cover

B

C

CLEANING WINDOW AIR CONDITIONER COILS

The coil that dissipates the heat from a window air conditioner resembles a car radiator. To remove the heat, air is drawn through the honeycomb-like fins of the coil. A small deposit of dirt on the fins reduces the efficiency of the air conditioner and increases your cooling bill. Clean the coils annually.

MATERIALS
None

TOOLS
Screwdriver • Toothbrush • Vacuum cleaner

1. Unplug the air conditioner and remove the snap-on front panel (Figure A).

2. Before removing the air conditioner unit from its exterior metal housing, have a table or other horizontal surface ready on which to place the unit. *Warning:* The unit will weigh at least 50 pounds.

3. Remove the screws or other fasteners that secure the unit inside its exterior metal housing.

4. Slide the unit forward into the room from the housing. If the unit suddenly resists, look for a green grounding wire attached to the housing. If there is one, unscrew it. Replace the screw so that it will not be misplaced.

5. Place the unit on the table or other horizontal surface (Figure B).

6. Use a toothbrush to loosen the dirt from the outdoor side of the coil. Vacuum to remove the dirt (Figure C).

7. Slide the unit back into its exterior metal housing, reattach the green grounding wire if there is one, and replace the front panel and the power plug.

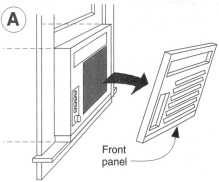

Front panel

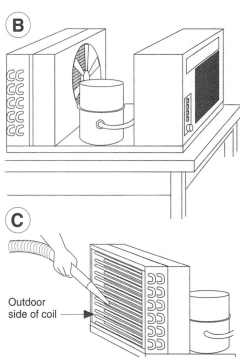

Outdoor side of coil

CLEANING A WINDOW AIR CONDITIONER FILTER

Behind the front panel of a window air conditioner is a fibrous filter intended to prevent dust from entering your home. The more efficient the filter, the more often it needs cleaning. If your air conditioner is not working as well as it used to, it may be because the filter needs cleaning.

MATERIALS
None

TOOLS
Garden hose

1. Remove the snap-on front panel (Figure A).

2. Pull out the flexible filter (Figure B). If it is torn, buy a replacement at the hardware store. If it is still intact, you can wash it.

3. Take the filter outdoors, and place it face down on a deck, driveway, or other clean surface.

4. Spray the filter with maximum water pressure from a garden hose until no more dirt comes out (Figure C).

5. Slap the filter on the deck or driveway repeatedly to shake out the moisture, and let the filter dry in the sun.

6. Replace the filter and front panel on the air conditioner.

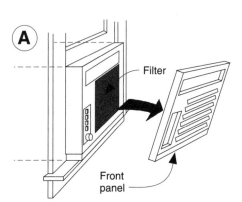

Filter

Front panel

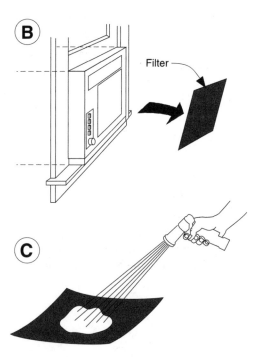

Filter

CLEANING A FIREPLACE CHIMNEY

Burning wood causes creosote to build up in the chimney, which may result in a dangerous, runaway chimney fire. Clean your chimney as soon as the deposits reach ¼ inch thickness. The cleaning process is simple, but don't attempt it unless you are comfortable on the roof. Also, be sure to wear a paper breathing mask, old clothes, and gloves.

MATERIALS
- Plastic sheeting
- Duct tape

TOOLS
Paper breathing mask • Tape measure • Chimney-cleaning brush • Extension handles • Stiff brush and dust pan

1. If your chimney has a metal cap, remove it. Measure the inside dimensions of the flue. Lined chimney flues come in standard sizes and shapes for which special cleaning brushes are available (Figure A).

2. Purchase the brush that best matches your flue dimensions from a home center or woodstove dealer. You'll also need enough extension handles to reach the full height of the chimney (Figure A).

3. Move or cover all fabric-covered furnishings and carpet within 10 feet of the fireplace. Seal the fireplace opening with plastic sheeting and duct tape.

4. From the roof, lower the brush into the chimney flue and work it up and down to loosen the soot (Figure B). Work from the top down, adding extensions after each section is clean.

5. If the wind is blowing, seal the top of the chimney with plastic sheeting to prevent downdrafts.

6. Remove the sheeting over the fireplace opening. Reach up inside the flue and clean off any dislodged soot from the smoke shelf.

7. Brush up the soot. Do not use your best vacuum cleaner because it will never be clean again! Remove the sheeting from the top of the chimney.

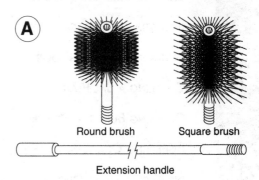

(A)

Round brush   Square brush

Extension handle

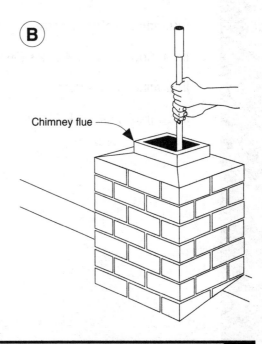

(B)

Chimney flue

INSTALLING A DOOR SWEEP

Wood doors shrink in winter, opening a drafty crack between the door and the threshold. You can bridge that gap with an aluminum and vinyl door sweep that can be adjusted seasonally if necessary. Door sweeps are available in 3-foot lengths and most include fastening screws.

MATERIALS

- Aluminum and vinyl door sweep
- Panhead self-tapping screws

TOOLS

Tape measure • Hacksaw
- Fine-point felt-tip pen
- 8d finishing nail • Hammer
- Drill and pilot bit • Screwdriver

1. Measure the width of the door at the bottom. Purchase an aluminum and vinyl door sweep at a hardware store or home center.

2. Mark the door width on the door sweep, and check the measurement by holding the door sweep against the bottom of the door.

3. Using a hacksaw, cut the door sweep to the exact length (Figure A).

4. Hold the cut door sweep firmly in position against the bottom of the door, with the flexible sweep against the threshold, and trace the screw slots with a fine-point felt-tip pen (Figure B).

5. With an 8d finishing nail and hammer, punch starter holes in the door at the center of each screw slot tracing so that up and down adjustments will be possible later.

6. At the punched holes, drill pilot holes of a diameter about two-thirds that of the supplied screws.

7. Install the sweep with the supplied screws. If the door is metal, substitute panhead self-tapping screws.

8. Close the door, back the screws out slightly, adjust the door sweep so it closes tightly against the threshold, and tighten the screws securely (Figure C).

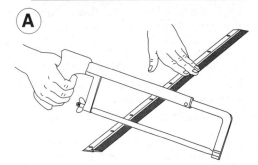

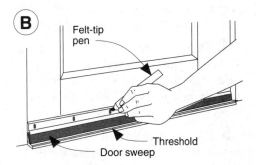

Felt-tip pen

Threshold
Door sweep

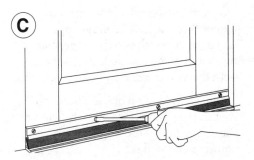

WEATHER-STRIPPING A WINDOW

If candles flicker in your house on windy nights, your windows are probably leaking air. Air leaks contribute to about one quarter of the heating bill in the average home. Once you have learned to apply V-strip to one window, you'll be able to weather-strip each additional window in about 15 minutes.

MATERIALS
- Clean rag
- Self-adhesive, vinyl V-strip weather strip
- Staples

TOOLS
Wire brush • Scissors • Stapling gun • Hammer • Nail set

1. Using a wire brush, brush all surfaces to which the weather strip will be applied and wipe with a clean, damp rag. Raise the lower sash as far as possible.

2. Cut a length of V-strip (Figure A) equal to the width of the window sash. Remove the backing and apply the V-strip to the bottom of the lower sash with the V-opening facing out (Figure B).

3. Cut two lengths of V-strip 1 inch longer than the height of the lower sash. Apply the strips to the lower half of the interior side channels in the window frame with the V-opening facing out (Figure B).

4. Drop the upper sash halfway so that its bottom rail is exposed. With the V-opening down, apply V-strip to the inside edge of its bottom rail (where the rails meet when the window is closed).

5. Drop both sashes all the way. Apply V-strip to the top of the upper sash with the V-opening facing out (Figure B).

6. Cut two lengths of V-strip 1 inch longer than the height of the upper sash, and apply the strips to the upper half of the exterior side channels in the frame with the V-opening facing out (Figure B).

7. If the adhesion of the V-strip seems weak, staple both ends of each strip with a stapling gun. Set the staples flush with a hammer and nail set.

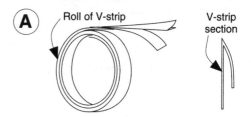

Roll of V-strip

V-strip section

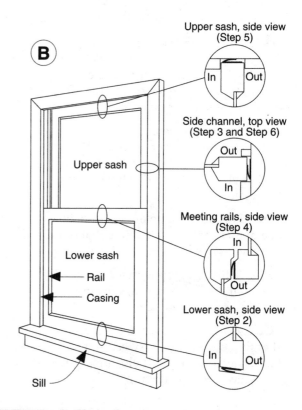

Upper sash, side view (Step 5)

In   Out

Side channel, top view (Step 3 and Step 6)

Out

In

Meeting rails, side view (Step 4)

In

Out

Lower sash, side view (Step 2)

In   Out

Upper sash

Lower sash

Rail

Casing

Sill

WEATHER-STRIPPING A DOOR

Weather stripping will prevent your heating dollars from floating out the door. New prehung doors are already weather-stripped, but you will have to weather-strip old wood doors yourself. Of the dozens on the market, the one with the best combination of tightness, longevity, and ease of installation is the V-strip, available in plastic, aluminum, and bronze. Metal outlasts plastic four to one.

MATERIALS

Bronze, V-strip door weather-strip kit

TOOLS

Tape measure • Utility knife • Hammer• Long-nose pliers • Nail set • Wide putty knife

1. Purchase a bronze V-strip door weather-strip kit at a hardware store or home center with enough weather strip to cover the top and both vertical door edges.

2. Measure the width of the door frame and cut a strip to that length from the roll or from the shortest length of V-strip, using a sharp utility knife.

3. Hold the top strip in place on the top of the door frame, butted against the door stop with the V-opening facing the outside (Figure A). Drive one of the nails into the center of the strip.

4. Working from the center toward the ends, drive nails every 2 inches. Hold the tiny nails with long-nose pliers to get them started. Use a nail set or a common nail held backwards against the supplied nails for the final blows to avoid denting the soft V-strip.

5. Cut the hinge-side strip to length. Angle the top end to avoid interfering with the top strip. Again, nail from the center toward the ends.

6. Cut two latch-side pieces to skip over the strike plate (Figure B). Nail as with the other pieces.

7. If the seal isn't tight enough, bend the V-strip outward, using a wide putty knife.

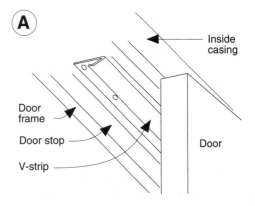

A — Inside casing / Door frame / Door stop / V-strip / Door

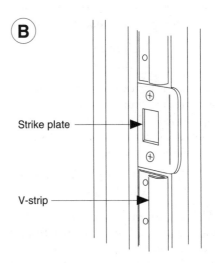

B — Strike plate / V-strip

INSULATING A GARAGE DOOR

You probably don't heat your garage, but if the garage is under or next to the house, a small amount of heat escapes from the heated living space into the garage. If you insulate the inside of your garage door, the garage will remain a few degrees warmer and the car will be easier to start on frigid mornings.

If your door has recessed panels (Figures A and B), follow these steps:

1. With a carpenter's square and utility knife, cut foil-faced, structural cardboard sheathing, such as Simplex's Thermoply, to match the door or door segments.

2. Load and prepare a cartridge of construction adhesive in a caulking gun. (See "Caulking Building Cracks" on page 159.)

3. Lay a continuous bead of construction adhesive around the outside of each recessed panel.

4. Staple the sheathing over the adhesive, forming air pockets at each recess.

If your door is flush and one piece (Figure C), follow these steps:

1. Frame the inside perimeter of the door with 1 × 2 furring strips. Cut the strips to size with a crosscut saw and fasten them by driving drywall screws through them into the door.

2. Install vertical strips every 16 inches across the back of the door.

3. Using a carpenter's square and utility knife, cut foil-faced structural cardboard sheathing to cover the door. Staple the panels to the furring strips.

MATERIALS
- **Foil-faced, structural cardboard sheathing**
- **Cartridge of construction adhesive**
- **Staples**
- **1 × 2 furring strips**
- **Drywall screws**

TOOLS
Carpenter's square • Utility knife
• Screwdriver • Caulking gun
• Stapling gun • Crosscut saw

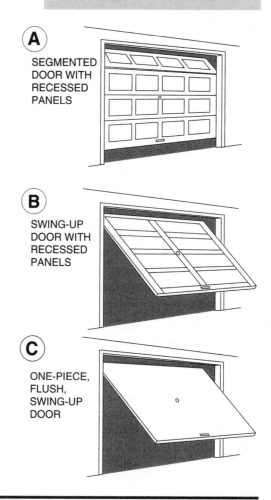

A SEGMENTED DOOR WITH RECESSED PANELS

B SWING-UP DOOR WITH RECESSED PANELS

C ONE-PIECE, FLUSH, SWING-UP DOOR

INSULATING UNDER A FLOOR

Crawl spaces or basements can get pretty cold in the winter, making your floors feel frosty. But, if you insulate the floor, you'll be able to go barefoot in the kitchen and also save as much as 10 percent on your heating bill. However, under-floor water pipes in very cold climates may freeze unless also protected. (See "Insulating Water Pipes" on page 161.)

1. Measure the on-center spacing (*OC*) of the floor joists (Figure A). If the spacing equals 16 or 24 inches, this is the nominal width of insulation to purchase.

2. Measure the depth (*D*) required to bring the insulation level to the bottom edges of the joists (Figure A).

3. At a home center, select unfaced fiberglass batts of the width closest to the joist spacing (*OC*) and of the determined depth (*D*). Purchase enough fiberglass insulation to cover the underside of the floor. (If your joist spacings does not match the standard widths of either 16 or 24 inches, purchase wider batts and cut the batts lengthwise. An easy way to cut the batts is to compress them with a long board and cut along it with a utility knife.)

4. Wearing goggles, long sleeves, a paper breathing mask, and gloves, press the batts into place, fitting them around pipes and ducts. Hammer roofing nails into the bottom edges of the joists and string nylon fishing line in a zigzag pattern to hold the batts up (Figure B).

5. For added insulation and holding power, nail up 1-inch-thick, 2 × 8 molded polystyrene sheets at right angles to the joists, using 1¼-inch roofing nails (Figure C). Check with your building inspector, however, to see if local code allows this.

MATERIALS

- **Unfaced fiberglass batts**
- **1¼" roofing nails**
- **Nylon fishing line**
- **1" × 2' × 8' molded polystyrene sheets**

TOOLS

Tape measure • Goggles• Paper breathing mask • Gloves • Long board • Utility knife • Hammer

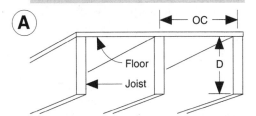

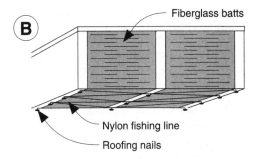

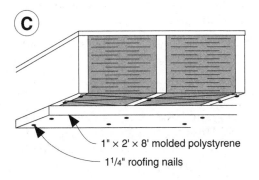

CAULKING A SILL PLATE

The largest air leak in the average home is the crack between the foundation and the wood sill plate in the crawl space or basement. A $1/16$-inch crack around the perimeter equals a 1-square-foot opening to the outdoors. You wouldn't leave a window open 6 inches all winter, which loses the same amount of heat, so caulk the sill plate.

MATERIALS
- Incense stick
- Closed-cell-foam weather strip
- Cartridge of silicone sealant
- Spray urethane foam

TOOLS
Wire brush • Toothbrush • Putty knife • Utility knife • Caulking gun

1. Determine if your sill plate/foundation joint (Figure A) is leaking air by holding a smoking incense stick on the inside of the joint on a windy day (Figure B). Try a dozen different spots along different walls. If the smoke doesn't rise straight up, you've found a leak.

2. You can caulk the crack from the inside or the outside of the building, depending on accessibility.

3. Clean dust and debris from the crack, first with a wire brush, then with a toothbrush.

4. If the crack is greater than $1/4$ inch wide, first stuff closed-cell-foam weather strip into the crack with a putty knife.

5. Load a cartridge of silicone sealant into a caulking gun. (See "Caulking Building Cracks" on the opposite page.) Seal the crack by laying a bead of silicone sealant that bulges over both sides of the crack (Figure C).

6. Spread and smooth the silicone with a moistened forefinger.

7. If the foundation is of stone and the crack is not uniform, fill the joint with spray urethane foam from an aerosol can. This type of foam can be squirted into tiny cracks where it expands to fill irregular voids.

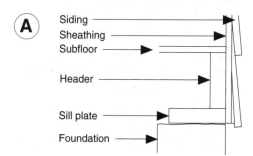

(A) Siding — Sheathing — Subfloor — Header — Sill plate — Foundation

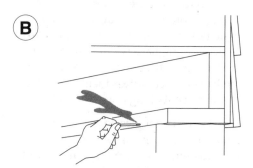

(B)

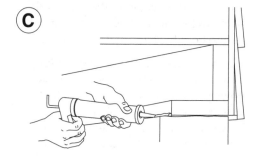

(C)

CAULKING BUILDING CRACKS

All of the tiny cracks in the average house add up to a 2-square-foot hole to the outside. You wouldn't leave a window open in the winter, which would lose the same amount of heat, so seal those cracks with caulk. Areas to be caulked include holes for electrical wires and plumbing pipes, joints between dissimilar materials such as masonry and wood, and cracks around doors and windows.

MATERIALS
- **Household cleaner**
- **Cartridge of caulk**

TOOLS
Wire brush • Scrub pad • Utility knife • Screwdriver • Caulking gun

1. Before caulking, thoroughly clean the cracks of old caulk, peeling paint, and dirt with a wire brush. If a painted surface is chalky, scrub it with household cleaner and a scrub pad, and rinse with clear water.

2. Using a utility knife, cut the nozzle of a cartridge of caulk back at an angle of 45 degrees and to an inside diameter of ³/₈ inch (Figure A).

3. Insert a screwdriver through the tip of the cartidge, puncturing the inner seal.

4. Load the cartridge into a caulking gun in the numbered order shown in Figure B. Note that to start caulk flowing, you must turn the L-shaped handle up to engage the ratchet inside the gun and then squeeze the trigger. To stop the flow, turn the L-shaped handle down to disengage the ratchet and release the pressure.

5. Squeeze a continuous bead of caulk along the joint so that it bridges but doesn't reach the bottom of the gap (Figure C).

6. Before the caulk sets, smooth the bead with a moistened forefinger.

7. If you plan to paint the area, allow several days for the caulk to cure. Note: Some caulks can not be painted.

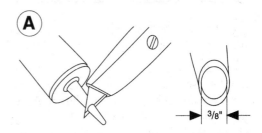

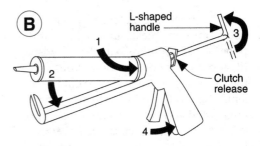

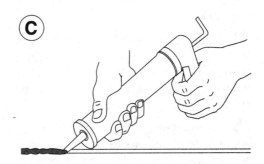

INSULATING CRAWL-SPACE WALLS

Heat flows from warmer to cooler areas—regardless of direction. You can stop the heat flow from your floor either at the floor itself (see "Insulating under a Floor" on page 157) or at the foundation walls. Insulating the walls offers the advantage of a warm crawl space where pipes will not freeze. Don't forget to remove the insulation from the foundation vents in the summer, however, or you will risk dry rot in the floor framing and sills.

1. Prepare the crawl space by emptying it out and raking the floor smooth.

2. Lay a continuous sheet of 6-mil polyethylene sheeting over the entire floor and up the walls about 6 inches (Figure A). If you plan to use the space for storage, lay sheets of plywood over the sheeting to protect it from damage.

3. Wearing goggles, long sleeves, a paper breathing mask, and gloves, cut R-19 paper-faced fiberglass batts lengthwise to fit, and press them into the cavities above the sill plates. An easy way to cut the batts lengthwise is to compress them with a long board and cut along it with a utility knife. Cut smaller sections to fit over vents. Using a stapling gun, staple the paper edges to the subfloor and sill plate (Figure B).

4. Hang fiberglass batts vertically from the sill plate, down the wall, and 2 feet onto the floor. Fasten the tops with 1 × 2 furring strips nailed to the sill plate with 6d common nails (Figure B).

5. Using an office stapler, staple the edges of adjacent batts together to form a continuous barrier and lay 2 × 4s around the perimeter to hold the batts down and against the wall (Figure B).

MATERIALS
- 6-mil polyethylene sheeting
- Plywood
- R-19, paper-faced fiberglass batts
- Staples
- 1 × 2 furring strips
- 6d common nails
- 2 × 4s

TOOLS
Rake • Goggles • Paper breathing mask • Gloves • Long board • Utility knife • Stapling gun • Hammer • Office stapler

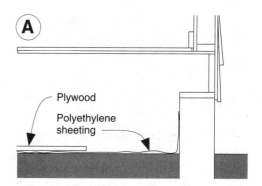

A
Plywood
Polyethylene sheeting

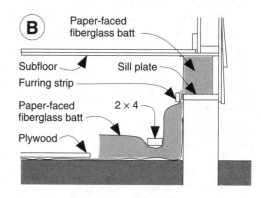

B
Paper-faced fiberglass batt
Subfloor
Sill plate
Furring strip
Paper-faced fiberglass batt
2 × 4
Plywood

INSULATING WATER PIPES

There are two reasons to insulate water pipes. The first reason is heat loss—every time you draw hot water, the heat of the water left in the supply pipe is lost to the atmosphere. The second reason is water damage. Cold-water pipes sweat in the warmer months just like cool drinks. Water from sweating pipes inside walls and ceilings can result in obvious water staining and not-so-obvious but more dangerous dry rot.

MATERIALS
- Foam pipe insulation
- Duct tape

TOOLS
Tape measure • Serrated kitchen knife

1. Measure the outside diameter and total length of pipe to be insulated. Areas of pipe to consider insulating include:

- The first 10 feet of hot-water pipe leading from the top of the water heater

- Hot-water pipes in unheated spaces such as the basement, crawl space, and garage

- Cold-water pipes that produce damaging condensation during the humid summer months

2. Purchase foam pipe insulation at a home center.

3. Using a serrated kitchen knife, cut the pipe insulation to length for each section of pipe to be insulated (Figure A).

4. Spread the insulation apart at one end and force the insulation over the water pipes.

5. At the elbows, cut the insulation at 45-degree angles to completely cover the pipes (Figure B).

6. Tape all joints with duct tape (Figure C). To prevent condensation from cold-water pipes, tape the lengthwise slit in the insulation as well.

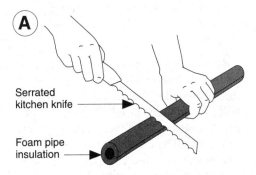

Serrated kitchen knife

Foam pipe insulation

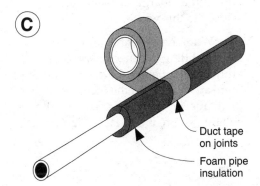

Duct tape on joints

Foam pipe insulation

INSULATING A WATER HEATER

Call your electric utility and inquire about water heater insulation. Chances are excellent that they provide free kits, if not free installation! If they don't offer insulation kits, make your own from a roll of paper-faced fiberglass insulation. Older water heaters with minimal insulation have been shown to leak an average of 29 percent of their heat through their exteriors.

1. Measure the height (*H*) and the circumference (*C*) of your water heater (Figure A).

2. Wearing goggles, long sleeves, a paper breathing mask, and gloves, cut three equal pieces from a roll of 23-inch-wide, R-11, paper-faced fiberglass insulation to match the height *H*. Fiberglass can be easily cut by compressing with a carpenter's square and cutting along the straightedge with a utility knife.

3. Lay the pieces side by side on the floor with the edges butting. Pull the adjacent paper edges up, fold them over each other, and staple every 3 inches along the fold with an office stapler (Figure B).

4. Add 12 inches to circumference *C*, and cut the fiberglass insulation assembly to this width.

5. Wrap the assembly around the heater, slitting it as necessary to fit around the pipes, and draw it snug until there are no gaps in the insulation. Using duct tape, tape the paper edge to the insulation where it overlaps (Figure C).

MATERIALS

- Roll of 23"-wide, R-11, paper-faced, fiberglass insulation
- Staples
- Duct tape

TOOLS

Tape measure • Goggles • Paper breathing mask • Gloves
• Carpenter's square • Utility knife
• Office stapler • Old scissors

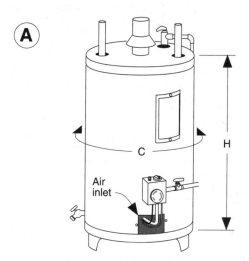

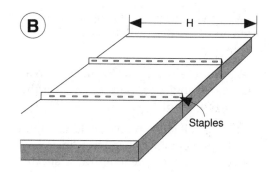

6. If the water heater is gas-fired, make sure the insulation does not block the air inlet at the bottom (Figure A).

7. If the water heater is electric—not gas—cut a cap of insulation that overhangs the insulation on the side of the water heater by 3 inches. Using a pair of old scissors, trim the fiberglass back from the heater's edge but leave the 3-inch paper overhang. Slit the cap as necessary to fit around pipes (Figure D).

8. Using duct tape, tape the overhang of the cap to the side blanket.

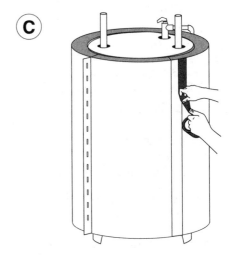

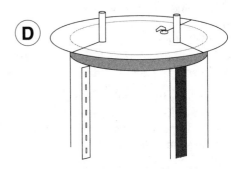

INSULATING AN ATTIC ACCESS PANEL

Everyone knows that doors lose a lot of heat in winter, but did you ever think of your attic access panel as a door leading to the outside? Attics can be nearly as cold as the outdoors, and considering how simple it is to insulate and weather-strip the access panel, it should be your first priority this winter.

MATERIALS
- Clean rag
- Sheet of rigid foam insulation
- Tube of construction adhesive
- Adhesive-backed foam weather strip

TOOLS
Felt-tip pen • Ripsaw

1. Before removing the attic access panel, trace around the edges where it meets the ceiling trim (Figure A).

2. Remove the panel and remove any old insulation from its top side. Using a clean, damp rag, clean the top side to remove dust and dirt.

3. Buy a sheet of rigid foam insulation at a home center. Since availabilty of thicknesses varies, buy what is available. Determine how many layers you'll need to use to get an R-value of 20. The R-value of a single thickness of the foam will be printed on its surface. If the R-value is 5, for example, you should use four layers.

4. Place the panel over the insulation and trace its outline with a felt-tip pen. Using a ripsaw, cut as many pieces of foam as are needed.

5. Apply construction adhesive to the attic side of the access panel and press a piece of foam onto it (Figure B). Apply adhesive and succeeding layers of foam until complete.

6. Apply adhesive-backed foam weather strip to the living-space side of the access panel between the edges and the line traced in Step 1 (Figure C).

7. Replace the panel in the ceiling.

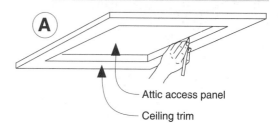

A
Attic access panel
Ceiling trim

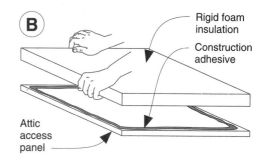

B
Rigid foam insulation
Construction adhesive
Attic access panel

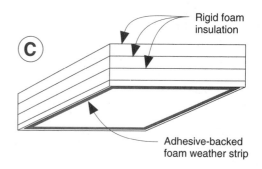

C
Rigid foam insulation
Adhesive-backed foam weather strip

INSULATING ATTIC DUCTS

It is easier to insulate an unheated crawl space or basement (see "Insulating Crawl-Space Walls" on page 160) than to insulate the heating and cooling ducts located there. Heating and cooling ducts in the attic are easily accessible, however, and should be insulated.

1. Wipe all ductwork joints with a clean, damp rag to remove dust.

2. Tape all of the joints in the ductwork with duct tape (Figure A). Tape along the seams and at the joints between sections.

3. Wearing goggles, long sleeves, a paper breathing mask, and gloves, insulate between the joists with R-19 or R-30, unfaced fiberglass batts thick enough to push up against the bottoms of the ducts (Figure B). (See "Insulating an Attic Floor" on page 166.)

4. Measure the ductwork in your attic, and buy enough rolls of 23-inch-wide, R-11, foil-faced fiberglass insulation at a home center to wrap over the tops and down the sides of the ducts. Fiberglass is easily cut by compressing with a carpenter's square and cutting along it with a utility knife. Using an office stapler, staple the edges of adjacent batts together to form a continuous barrier.

5. Butt additional unfaced, R-19 or R-30 fiberglass batts against the sides of the insulated ducts, holding the fiberglass installed in Step 4 snug against the ducts.

MATERIALS

- Clean rag
- Duct tape
- R-19 or R-30, unfaced fiberglass batts
- Rolls of 23"-wide, R-11, foil-faced fiberglass insulation
- Staples

TOOLS

Goggles • Paper breathing mask • Gloves • Carpenter's square • Utility knife • Office stapler

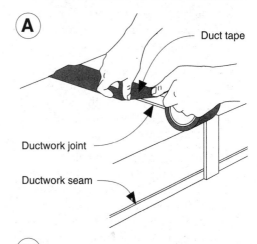

A

Duct tape

Ductwork joint

Ductwork seam

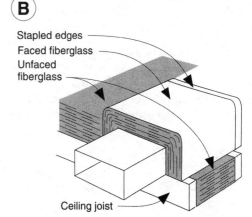

B

Stapled edges
Faced fiberglass
Unfaced fiberglass

Ceiling joist

INSULATING AN ATTIC FLOOR

Your attic floor is probably already insulated, but is it insulated well enough? Every additional inch of insulation will reduce heat loss during winter and help keep out attic heat during summer.

1. In your attic, measure the on-center spacing (*OC*) between the joists (Figure A). If the spacing equals 16 or 24 inches, this is the nominal width of insulation to purchase. (If your joist spacing does not match one of these standard widths, you can use loose-fill insulation to fill the space between the joists.)

2. Measure the thickness (*T*) required to bring the insulation level to the top of the joists (Figure A).

3. At a home center, select unfaced fiberglass batts of the width closest to the joist spacing (*OC*) and of the determined thickness (*T*). Purchase enough fiberglass batts to cover the attic floor.

4. Wearing goggles, long sleeves, a paper breathing mask, and gloves, place fiberglass batts between the joists over any existing insulation, making sure there are no gaps except 3 inches around recessed light fixtures. To cut the fiberglass, compress it with a carpenter's square and cut it with a utility knife.

5. If your attic has soffit vents, staple stiff cardboard or Styrofoam between the joists to create baffles that maintain a free path for air flow between the insulation and the roof (Figure B). You can also use premade ventilation baffles.

6. Once the joists are filled in, you can place additional batts at right angles to the joists (Figure C) for an even greater R-value.

MATERIALS
- **Unfaced fiberglass batts**
- **Cardboard, Styrofoam, or pre-made ventilation baffles**
- **Staples**

TOOLS
Tape measure • Goggles
- **Paper breathing mask • Gloves**
- **Carpenter's square • Utility knife**
- **Stapling gun**

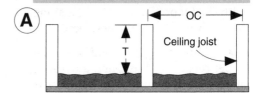

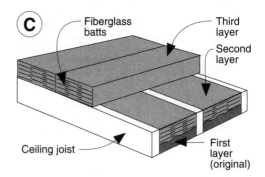

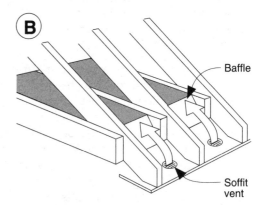

TROUBLESHOOTING A LEAKY HOSE

A lot of nearly perfect garden hoses end up in the dump prematurely. No matter where a hose is leaking, the bad section can be removed and made like new with replacement plastic couplings. You can find replacement couplings, as well as a number of other convenient hose fittings, at any hardware store or home center.

MATERIALS

• **Replacement hose washer**
• **Replacement plastic hose coupling**
• **Plastic hose clamps**
• **Double-ended plastic hose coupling**

TOOLS

Slip-joint pliers • Utility knife • Screwdriver

Inspect the hose with the water on to find the location of the leak.

If it is leaking between the coupling and nozzle or spigot, try the following options:

• The coupling may simply require tightening. Use slip-joint pliers to tighten the coupling a quarter turn.

• If tightening the coupling didn't stop the leak, unscrew the coupling with the slip-joint pliers and inspect the flat washer inside the coupling or nozzle (Figure A). If it is worn—or missing—install a new hose washer.

If the hose leaks where it joins the coupling, follow these steps:

1. Turn off the water. Using a utility knife, cut the hose about 2 inches from the leaking coupling (Figure B).

2. Take the old coupling and piece of hose to a hardware store or home center and purchase a replacement plastic coupling and clamp of the proper size for the hose.

3. Insert the plastic coupling into the hose end. Place the two halves of the clamp over the end of the hose containing the coupling and tighten the screws firmly (Figure C).

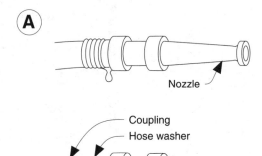

Nozzle

Coupling
Hose washer

If the hose leaks along its length, follow these steps:

1. Turn off the water. Using the utility knife, cut out the leaking section of the hose.

2. Take the piece of hose to a hardware store or home center and buy a plastic double-ended coupling and two clamps of the proper size for the hose.

3. Insert the plastic coupling into one of the cut hose ends. Push the other cut end of the hose over the other end of the coupling. Place two halves of a clamp over each end of the coupling and tighten the screws firmly (Figure D).

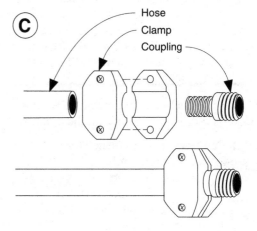

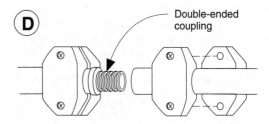

STIFFENING UP A DECK

A properly designed deck conforms to the same structural standards as a floor inside the house. The deck should not bounce up and down, nor should it sway from side to side. If your deck does move, you can add structural stiffness very simply.

If the deck is too springy, double up the joists (Figure A) by following these steps:

1. Purchase pressure-treated lumber of the same thickness and width as the existing joists at a lumberyard. If you don't want to cut the new joists to length, purchase the longest ones that will fit without cutting.

2. Hold the sister joist up against the old joist and nail the ends in place with 10d galvanized common nails (Figure A). Drive additional pairs of nails every 2 feet along the new joist.

If the deck sways, add diagonal bracing (Figure B) by following these steps:

1. Measure the lengths (*L*) of the diagonal braces required (Figure B). If the lengths are less than 6 feet, purchase pressure-treated 5/4 (five quarter) × 6 lumber. If greater than 6 feet, purchase 2 × 6 lumber for extra strength.

2. Using a combination square and a crosscut saw, cut one end of each brace at 45 degrees.

3. While a helper holds the bottom of each brace in place, nail the angled top of each brace to the post with two 10d galvanized common nails (Figure B).

4. Nail the bottom ends. Then, using a crosscut saw, trim the excess flush with the post to which it is nailed.

MATERIALS
- **Pressure-treated lumber**
- **10d galvanized common nails**

TOOLS
**Tape measure • Hammer
• Combination square • Crosscut saw**

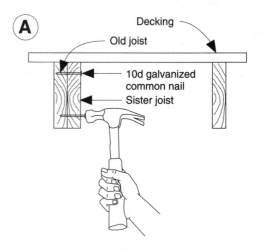

A Decking
Old joist
10d galvanized common nail
Sister joist

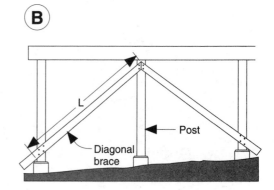

B
L
Post
Diagonal brace

REPLACING A DECK BOARD

By replacing a few bad deck boards, you might be able to put off replacing an entire deck for a few years. Here's a trick for cutting out and replacing a bad spot in about 15 minutes. And, if you use an electric saber saw in place of the keyhole saw, you can cut *that* time in half.

MATERIALS
- **Replacement pressure-treated deck board**
- **Pressure-treated 2 × 4**
- **10d galvanized common nails**

TOOLS
Carpenter's square • Keyhole saw • Crosscut saw • Drill and ⅛" bit • Hammer

1. Stick the tongue of carpenter's square between two deck boards to locate the joist nearest the damaged area. Mark the edge of the joist closest to the damaged area on the top of the damaged board. Next, find the joist nearest the opposite end of the damaged area and mark its position (Figure A).

2. Using a keyhole saw, cut the damaged board along the two lines (Figure B).

3. After sawing through both ends, take the damaged section to a lumberyard to buy a matching deck board for replacement. If the new deck board is wider than the old, ask the lumberyard attendant to rip it to the needed width.

4. While you are at the lumberyard, buy a pressure-treated 2 × 4 to make cleats to support the new deck board. From the 2 × 4, cut two cleats 6 inches longer than the width of the deck board, using a crosscut saw.

5. Drill six, evenly spaced ⅛-inch pilot holes through each 2 × 4 cleat.

6. Hold the cleats against the joists and the bottom of the decking and nail them to each joist with 10d galvanized common nails (Figure C).

7. Using the crosscut saw, cut the new deck board to length and nail it to the cleats at both ends with 10d nails.

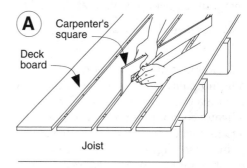

A — Carpenter's square
Deck board
Joist

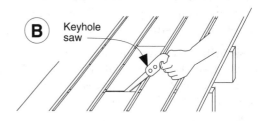

B — Keyhole saw

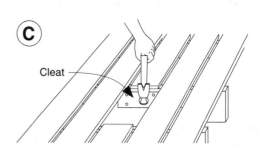

C — Cleat

REFINISHING A DECK

Any hard finish—such as paint or varnish—applied to an exposed exterior deck is bound to fail within a few years. You are better off using stain, which does not form a hard skin that can crack and peel. Here is how to switch from a hard finish to stain and a water repellent.

MATERIALS
- Tarp or polyethylene sheeting
- Liquid paint remover
- Exterior stain
- Water repellent

TOOLS
Paint scraper • Rubber gloves
• Wide paintbrushes • Putty knife
• Stiff brush

1. If there is a deck or other floor beneath the deck, cover it with a tarp or polyethylene sheeting to prevent staining by paint remover or stain that may drip.

2. Remove all loose and peeling paint with a paint scraper.

3. Remove all paint that remains with a liquid paint remover. On a cloudy day, put on a pair of rubber gloves and apply a heavy coat of paint remover to about 4 square feet of deck at a time with a wide paintbrush (Figure A). Wait—don't rebrush—until the paint blisters. Scrape up the blistered paint with a putty knife or paint scraper (Figure B). Repeat the application to stubborn areas.

4. After all of the paint has been removed, scrub the deck with a stiff brush and water to remove all traces of paint remover. Let the deck dry.

5. Apply a heavy coat of exterior stain with another wide paintbrush (Figure C).

6. After the stain dries, apply a liberal coat of water repellent.

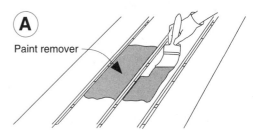

A Paint remover

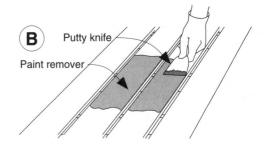

B Putty knife
Paint remover

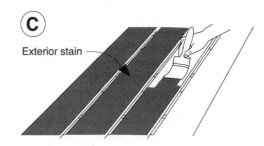

C Exterior stain

REPAIRING A ROTTED PORCH POST

If you have a broken foot or ankle, the doctor places a cast over it to take the weight while it mends. If the bottom of a porch post has rotted, you can avoid having to replace it by creating a cast of baseboards. Placing a similar cast around each of the porch posts will make the casts appear to be part of the original design. If, however, the posts are so badly rotted that the roof has sagged, the roof must be jacked level—a job for a professional carpenter.

1. Measure the thickness (*T*) of the porch post (Figure A).

2. For each rotted porch post, you will need 2 feet of pressure-treated lumber, ³/₄ inch thick × *T*-inches wide and ³/₄ inch thick × (*T*+1¹/₂) inches wide (Figure B). Have the lumberyard—or a friend with a table saw—rip the boards to the exact widths.

3. Use a tape measure and combination square to mark the boards for cutting every 12 inches. Make the cuts with a miter box and backsaw.

4. Assuming the roof is level, nail two cut pieces of each width to the base of each post with galvanized 8d finishing nails. Use 6 nails per piece—24 nails per post.

5. Cut ³/₄-inch quarter-round molding into lengths equal to the widths of the widest base pieces. Using the miter box and backsaw, make the cuts at 45-degree angles.

6. Nail the quarter-round molding to the posts with galvanized 4d finishing nails (Figure C). Fill the nail holes with wood putty and paint the casts to match the posts.

MATERIALS

- ³/₄" pressure-treated lumber
- ³/₄" quarter-round molding
- Galvanized 8d finishing nails
- Galvanized 4d finishing nails
- Wood putty
- Exterior paint

TOOLS

Tape measure • Combination square • Miter box • Backsaw • Hammer • Paintbrush

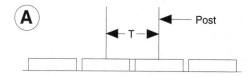

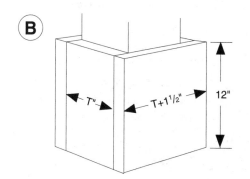

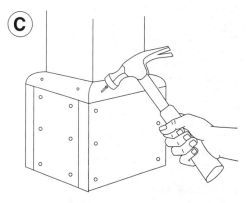

REPLACING A PORCH POST

Replacing a porch post is simple work but, if only the base is rotted, consider reinforcing it. (See "Repairing a Rotted Porch Post" on page 173.) The replacement post shown here has a simple square cross section. If your posts are fancier, look in the Yellow Pages under "Millwork" for a shop to fabricate a replacement post.

MATERIALS

- **Replacement post**
- **2' piece of 2 × 8**
- **1' piece of 2 × 8**
- **16 galvanized 12d finishing nails**

TOOLS

Tape measure • Jack post
• Crosscut saw • Pry bar
• Combination square • Drill
and ³/₃₂" bit • Hammer

1. Measure the height (*H*), width, and thickness of the post (Figure A) and buy a replacement post at a lumberyard.

2. Rent or purchase a jack post at least 3 inches shorter than *H* when collapsed.

3. Place a 2-foot piece of 2 × 8 next to the post and over the beam beneath. Put the base of the jack on the 2 × 8 and the jack pin in the highest position possible.

4. Place a 1-foot piece of 2 × 8 on top of the jack and turn the jack screw until the jack is snug. Turn one more full turn.

5. If the base of the damaged post is loose, knock it out with the new post, then pry the top down with a pry bar. *Be careful not to disturb the jack.* If the base is firm, saw through the post and remove the top and bottom with the pry bar.

6. Put the new post in position and mark its height. Transfer the mark to the post's sides with a combination square.

7. Cut the post with a crosscut saw and position it in the location of the old post.

8. Drill four ³/₃₂-inch pilot holes, angled at 45 degrees and 1 inch from the ends, at the top and bottom of the post (Figure B).

9. Fasten the post at top and bottom with galvanized 12d finishing nails and remove the jack post.

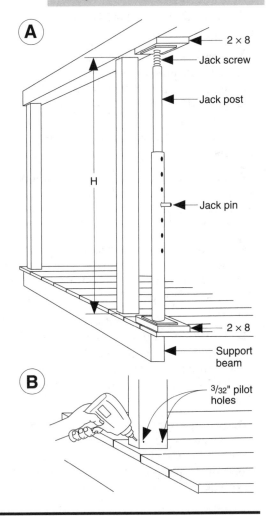

A 2 × 8 — Jack screw — Jack post — Jack pin — *H* — 2 × 8 — Support beam

B ³/₃₂" pilot holes

REPAIRING A ROTTED FENCE POST

Replacing an entire post in a wood fence is a major job. If just the base of the post has rotted, here is a quick splice that should last the remaining lifetime of the fence. Don't try to save money by using anything for the splice but a pressure-treated 2 × 4. If you use an ordinary framing stud, you will be repeating the job within five years.

1. Using blocks of wood and wood shingles, shim the fence up to the desired height.

2. Using a crosscut saw, cut through the rotted post 2 inches above ground.

3. Using a garden spade or post-hole digger, dig the rotted section out of the ground, placing the excavated soil on a large plastic trash bag. Enlarge the hole to 1 foot in diameter and 3 feet deep (Figure A).

4. Cut a 4-foot length of pressure-treated 2 × 4. Bevel the cut so that the exposed top will shed water.

5. Tamp the bottom of the hole with the square end of the new post, then set it into the hole with the beveled end next to the old post (Figure B).

6. Drill ¼-inch holes through the top end of the new post, then ⅛-inch holes about 1 inch deep into the original post (Figure C).

7. Insert galvanized ¼ × 3½-inch lag screws with ¼-inch washers into the holes, tap with a hammer to start, and tighten with an adjustable wrench (Figure C).

8. Remove any grass or roots from the excavated soil and refill the hole around the post. Tamp the soil with the remaining piece of the 2 × 4.

MATERIALS

- Large plastic trash bag
- Pressure-treated 2 × 4
- 2 galvanized ¼ × 3½" lag screws and washers

TOOLS

Blocks of wood • Wood shingles • Crosscut saw • Garden spade or post-hole digger • Drill with ¼" and ⅛" bits • Hammer • Adjustable wrench

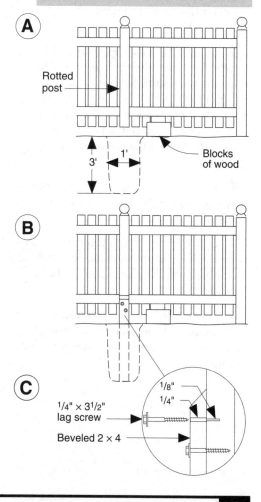

BRACING A SAGGING FENCE

If the horizontal stringers are not stiff enough, a fence similar to the one shown in Figure A will sag under the constant force of gravity. A quick fix is to cut the span of the stringers in half by supporting them at their midpoints.

MATERIALS
- 8 × 12 or 12 × 12 concrete paver
- Pressure-treated 2 × 4
- 2 galvanized 10d common nails

TOOLS
- Block of wood or concrete block
- Tape measure • Crosscut saw
- Hammer

1. Clean any debris or vegetation from under the sagging portion of fence.

2. Purchase an 8 × 12 or 12 × 12 concrete paver at a home center. Center it under the area of maximum sag (Figure A).

3. Using a 2 × 4 as a lever and a block of wood or concrete block as a fulcrum, raise the fence until the horizontal stringers are level. While in this position, have a helper measure the height of the support block required between the paver and the bottom of the bottom stringer (Figure B).

4. With a crosscut saw, cut a support block of this length from the end of a pressure-treated 2 × 4.

5. Using the lever and fulcrum again, raise the fence and insert the support block between the paver and the bottom stringer.

6. Secure the block by driving two galvanized 10d common nails through the bottom stringer into the support block (Figure C).

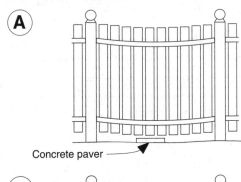

(A) Concrete paver

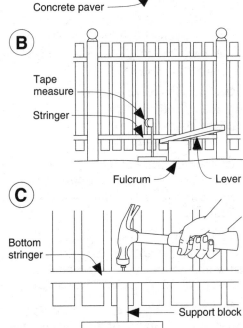

(B) Tape measure
Stringer
Fulcrum — Lever

(C) Bottom stringer
Support block
Concrete paver

BRACING A SAGGING GATE

Any gate made with solid wood parts will eventually sag, as shown in Figure A, if it does not incorporate diagonal bracing. Here is how to retrofit a sagging gate with a diagonal brace to make it as straight and strong as new.

1. Wedge blocks of wood and wood shingles under the sagging end of the gate to raise it 1/4 inch higher than level.

2. While the gate is propped up, hold a strip of lumber of the same thickness and width as the horizontal gate stringers diagonally (Figure B). Lay out cut lines across the diagonal brace with a combination square so the brace will fit snugly between the stringers. Using a crosscut saw, cut the diagonal brace along the cut lines.

3. Holding the brace in place, mark the screw locations—one at each end of the brace and two where it intersects each vertical member (Figure C).

4. Drill 3/16-inch holes through the brace (but not into the vertical members) at each marked screw location.

5. Holding the brace in place, drill 1/8-inch pilot holes through the 3/16-inch holes 1/2 inch deep into the vertical members at each end of the brace.

6. Fasten the brace by driving #10 galvanized wood screws through the two end holes. The screw lengths should be the sum of the thicknesses of the brace and the vertical member, less 1/4 inch.

7. Drill 1/8-inch pilot holes through the remainder of the 3/16-inch holes and fasten wood screws in each (Figure C).

8. Remove the temporary blocking.

MATERIALS
- Matching gate-frame lumber
- #10 galvanized wood screws

TOOLS
Blocks of wood • Wood shingles • Combination square • Crosscut saw • Drill with 1/8" and 3/16" bits • Screwdriver

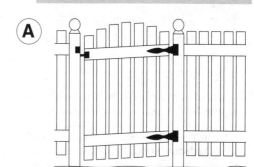

A

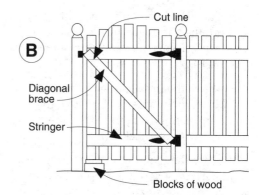

B

Cut line

Diagonal brace

Stringer

Blocks of wood

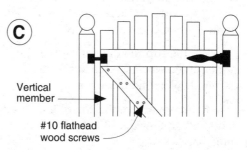

C

Vertical member

#10 flathead wood screws

REPLACING A HAMMER HANDLE

One of the good qualities of a wood hammer handle is that it can be easily replaced. Hardware stores and lumberyards carry replacement handles and the wedges required to install them. Though it sounds easier than drilling, don't put the old hammer in a charcoal fire to burn the wood handle out, as some old-timers suggest. The extreme heat will ruin the temper of the hammer head.

MATERIALS

- Replacement hammer handle with wood and metal wedges
- Paint or varnish

TOOLS

Vise • Hacksaw • Drill and ¹/₄" bit
• Large nail • Hammer • Paintbrush

1. Place the head of the hammer in a vise and saw off the old handle with a hacksaw.

2. Drill overlapping ¼-inch holes through the wood remaining in the head (Figure A).

3. Place the head of a large nail against the remaining wood, and hammer the nail point to remove all of the wood.

4. Place the head on the new handle, and rap the handle vertically against a solid surface such as a concrete floor (Figure B).

5. When the handle is snug, place the head back in the vise, and remove the wood projecting from the top of the hammer with the hacksaw.

6. Place the hammer vertically on the solid surface, insert the supplied wood wedge into the slot in the handle, and— with a second hammer—drive the wedge home (Figure C).

7. Put the supplied metal wedge at the center of the wood wedge but turned perpendicular, and drive it in.

8. Paint or varnish the end of the wood containing the wedges to seal it against moisture.

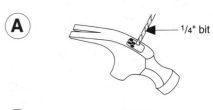

A   ¹/₄" bit

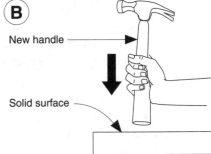

B
New handle
Solid surface

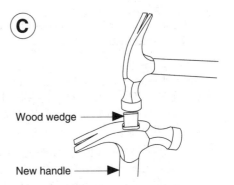

C
Wood wedge
New handle

REPLACING A SPADE OR RAKE HANDLE

Garden tools will last a lifetime if you take care to clean them after each use and oil the handles. If you have neglected yours and a handle has broken, replace the handle. The most difficult part of the process is finding the right kind of handle. If you have tried a hardware store or home center and you still cannot find one, call a local landscaping company and ask for the name of their source.

MATERIALS

- Replacement spade or rake handle
- 1/2" wood dowel
- #8 × 3/8" stainless, self-tapping screw

TOOLS

Hacksaw • Large nail • Hammer • Drill and 1/8" bit • Screwdriver

1. Using a hacksaw, cut through the head of the old rivet securing the handle to the spade or rake (Figure A).

2. Drive out the remainder of the rivet with a large common nail and hammer.

3. Hook the edge of the blade over a step, porch railing, or deck, and drive the handle from the socket with a 1/2-inch wood dowel and hammer (Figure B).

4. Insert the tapered end of the new handle into the tool socket and bang the handle vertically (rake or shove end up) against a solid surface—such as a concrete floor— to snug the handle in the socket.

5. Drill a 1/8-inch pilot hole through the rivet hole and 1/4 inch into the handle.

6. Screw a #8 × 3/8-inch, stainless, self-tapping screw through the rivet hole and into the pilot hole.

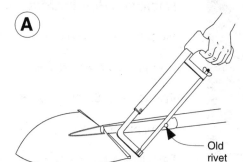

A

Old rivet

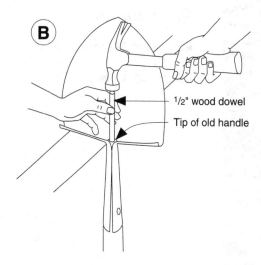

B

1/2" wood dowel

Tip of old handle

PATCHING A CRACK IN CONCRETE

There is little or nothing you can do to prevent concrete from cracking once the concrete has been poured. The best you can do is to install a patch that will fill the gap and stay in place.

MATERIALS
- Cartridge of polyurethane caulk
- Ready-mix mortar

TOOLS
Garden hose • Caulking gun
• Utility knife • Screwdriver • Hammer
• Cold chisel • Goggles • Cake pan
• Tablespoon • Small knife
• Triangular trowel • Stiff-bristled brush
• Towel

If the crack is less than ⅛ inch wide, follow these steps:

1. Clean out any debris from the crack with a high-pressure stream of water from a garden hose.

2. Let the crack dry and fill it with polyurethane caulk. (See "Caulking Building Cracks" on page 159.)

If the crack is more than ⅛ inch wide, follow these steps:

1. Wearing goggles, use a hammer and cold chisel to deepen the crack to at least 1 inch, and then undercut the sides (Figure A).

2. Clean out any debris from the crack with a high-pressure stream of water from a garden hose. Remove any remaining water with a sponge.

3. Using a cake pan and tablespoon, mix enough ready-mix mortar to fill the crack. Using a triangular trowel, fill the crack with mortar and jab the tip of the trowel repeatedly into the mix to release air pockets.

4. Smooth the surface of the mortar with the trowel (Figure B).

5. After the mortar stiffens slightly, use a stiff-bristled brush to match the texture of the surrounding concrete (Figure C). Place a wet towel over the crack and keep it damp for 24 hours.

6. Clean the tools in water.

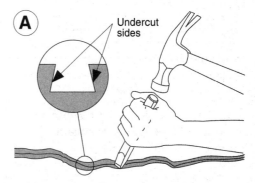

A Undercut sides

B

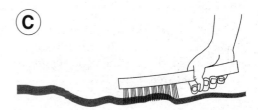

C

PATCHING A HOLE IN CONCRETE

Patching a hole in concrete is remarkably similar to filling a cavity in a tooth. Mortar simply poured into a hole in fractured concrete will not last long. If you meticulously perform each of the steps below, however, you will produce a patch that should last as long as the concrete floor.

MATERIALS

- Chalk
- Ready-mix sand mix
- Liquid bonding agent
- 1 × 4 board

TOOLS

Goggles • Hammer • Cold chisel
- Wire brush • Garden hose • Hoe
- Wheelbarrow or large plastic tub
- Old paintbrush • Scissors
- Triangular trowel • Stiff-bristled brush
- Towel

1. Wearing goggles, lightly tap around the hole with a hammer to determine the extent of the damaged area. The damaged area will sound dull whereas solid concrete will ring. Outline the damaged area with chalk (Figure A).

2. With the hammer and a cold chisel, chip away all of the damaged concrete inside the chalk line. Chisel the perimeter so that the edge is vertical and the hole is at least 1 inch deep (Figure B).

3. Clean away loose debris with a wire brush and a high-pressure stream of water from a garden hose.

4. Pour enough ready-mix sand mix into a wheelbarrow or large plastic tub to fill the hole. Add water and combine with a hoe. The mix is right when you can form a ball that neither drips water nor crumbles.

5. Scoop up about a quart of the sand mix and mix it with a liquid bonding agent, according to the directions. The mix should have the consistency of thick gravy. This mix acts like glue to bond the old and new concrete.

6. Cut the bristles of an old paintbrush to half their normal length with scissors. Use the brush to apply the bonding mix to the damaged area (Figure C).

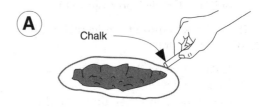

A Chalk

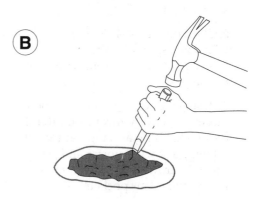

B

C Bonding mix

7. Using a triangular trowel, immediately fill the entire hole with the wet sand mix. Jab the trowel repeatedly into the mix to release air pockets.

8. Cut a 1 × 4 board about 1 foot longer than the width of the hole.

9. Use the board on edge as a leveling tool, sliding it side to side as you pull it toward you. The combined action will force out the excess mix and level the hole (Figure D).

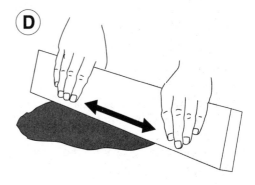

10. After 30 minutes, slide the trowel back and forth in a sweeping motion to smooth the surface further (Figure E).

11. If the surrounding concrete has a textured surface, use a stiff-bristled brush to create a matching finish (Figure F). Place a wet towel over the repaired hole and keep it damp for 24 hours.

12. Clean the tools in water.

PATCHING A CHIPPED CONCRETE STEP

This repair is often attempted but rarely succeeds. Two elements are essential for success: undercutting or dovetailing the chipped-out area and using epoxy concrete patching compound. Do not cheat!

1. Wearing goggles, use a hammer and cold chisel to remove any loose concrete around the chipped-out area. Chip away the concrete, as necessary, to undercut the sides (Figure A).

2. With a rip saw, cut a scrap of wood to the same height as the step and about a foot longer than the chipped-out area.

3. Apply clean motor oil to one side of the wood scrap with a rag to keep the wood from sticking to the concrete.

4. Wedge the oil-coated scrap against the damaged step, using a concrete block to hold it in place (Figure B).

5. Using a cake pan and tablespoon, mix epoxy concrete patching compound, according to the manufacturer's directions.

6. Using a triangular trowel, fill the chipped-out area with the compound. Jab the tip of the trowel repeatedly into the compound to release air pockets.

7. Smooth the exposed top surface of the compound with the trowel (Figure B).

8. After the compound has become stiff enough to not sag, remove the board and form the step edge with the trowel. Place a wet towel over the edge and keep it damp for 24 hours.

9. Clean the tools with water.

MATERIALS

- Scrap of wood
- Clean motor oil
- Rag
- Concrete block
- Epoxy concrete patching compound

TOOLS

Goggles • Hammer • Cold chisel
• Rip saw • Cake pan
• Tablespoon • Triangular trowel
• Towel

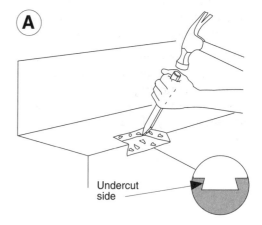

A

Undercut side

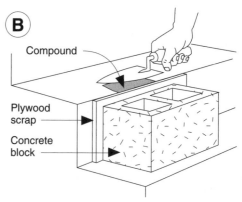

B

Compound

Plywood scrap

Concrete block

REFASTENING A RAILING IN CONCRETE

When the bolts fastening the base of a railing to concrete break out of the concrete, repair may seem impossible. But it's usually successful if you follow these steps carefully.

1. Using locking pliers and an adjustable wrench, remove the nuts and bolts from the base of the railing post. If the bolts are broken off in the holes, move the base slightly and drill new holes.

2. Place a piece of cardboard under the base and trace the outlines of the base and its holes with a fine-point felt-tip pen (Figure A). Remove the cardboard and trace the base onto the concrete as well. Cut around the outline on the cardboard and drill through the holes with a bit of the same diameter as the old bolts.

3. Wearing goggles, use a drill and 3/4-inch masonry bit to drill out the old bolt holes until you hit solid concrete (Figure B). Buy nuts and bolts long enough to fit the new holes.

4. Clean out any debris from the hole. Using an artist's paintbrush, paint the holes with a liquid bonding agent.

5. Using a cup and teaspoon, mix anchoring cement, according to the manufacturer's directions. Fill the holes with the cement and insert the new bolts, head down, to the bottom of the hole.

6. Place the cardboard template over the bolts, line the cardboard up with its outline, and adjust the bolts vertically.

7. After several hours, remove the cardboard and seal the cemented area with plastic roof cement. Refasten the railing with the nuts.

MATERIALS
- Thin cardboard
- Replacement nuts and bolts
- Liquid bonding agent
- Anchoring cement
- Plastic roof cement

TOOLS
Locking pliers • Adjustable wrench • Fine-point felt-tip pen • Scissors • Drill and 3/4" masonry bit • Goggles • Garden hose • Sponge • Artist's paintbrush • Cup • Teaspoon

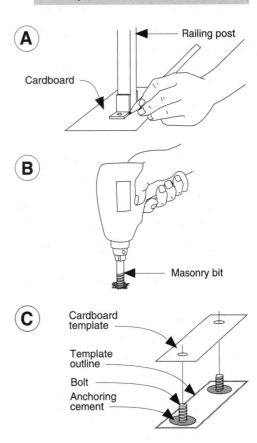

A — Railing post, Cardboard

B — Masonry bit

C — Cardboard template, Template outline, Bolt, Anchoring cement

REPLACING A SIDEWALK SLAB

Yearly freezing and thawing can eventually break up a section of sidewalk, and the steps below will help you replace it. Any obstructions like tree roots should be removed before pouring the new concrete or you'll be replacing the slab again in just a few years.

1. Wearing goggles, use a sledge hammer to break up the damaged slab (Figure A).

2. Remove all concrete chunks larger than 2 inches in diameter. Spread the rest of them uniformly across the bottom.

3. Using a garden spade, dig the grass and dirt away from the edges of the adjacent slabs for a distance of several feet (Figure B).

4. Using a crosscut saw, cut lengths of a 2 × 4 to span the gap between the slabs, plus one foot on each end.

5. Place the 2 × 4s on edge, with their top edges flush with the adjacent slabs. Backfill with dirt against the 2 × 4s and nail 1 × 3 furring strips across the ends of the 2 × 4s to hold them in place (Figure C).

6. Line the faces of the 2 × 4s and the adjacent concrete with strips of tar paper to keep the concrete from adhering to the 2 × 4s.

7. Dampen the soil and broken edges of concrete with a garden hose.

8. Using a hoe, mix a 80-pound bag of ready-mix concrete with water in a wheelbarrow or large tub. The mix is ready when you can form a ball that neither drips water nor crumbles.

MATERIALS

- 2 × 4s
- Tar paper
- 1 × 3 furring strips
- Nails
- 80-lb bag of ready-mix concrete
- 1 × 4 board
- Plastic sheeting

TOOLS

Goggles • Sledge hammer
- Garden spade • Crosscut saw
- Hammer • Garden hose • Hoe
- Wheelbarrow or large tub
- Triangular trowel • Stiff-bristled brush

A

B

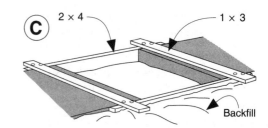

C   2 × 4   1 × 3

Backfill

9. Place the concrete in the form and keep adding it until the form is filled. Jab the tip of a triangular trowel into the concrete repeatedly to release air pockets.

10. Cut a length of 1 × 4 about 1 foot longer than the width of the slab.

11. Resting the 1 × 4 on the edges of the 2 × 4 forms, slide the 1 × 4 side to side while you pull it toward you (Figure D). The combined action will level the concrete and remove the excess. If any low spots remain, add concrete to them and repeat the leveling action.

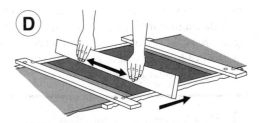

12. After 30 minutes, turn the 1 × 4 on its face and work it back and forth to create a smooth surface.

13. If the adjacent slabs have textured surfaces, use a stiff-bristled brush to create a matching texture (Figure E).

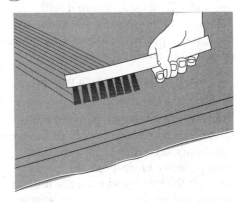

14. Clean the tools in water.

15. After an hour, remove the furring strips and 2 × 4 forms. Use a triangular trowel to smooth the concrete edges (Figure F). Wash the trowel in water when finished.

16. Place plastic sheeting over the new slab to retard evaporation. Lift the sheeting and spray the concrete with a garden hose twice a day for a week.

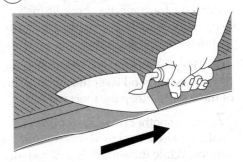

REPAIRING STUCCO

Depending on its location, cracked stucco may be merely an eyesore, or it may be an entryway for wall-damaging moisture. Repairing a small damaged area is best done while you have an extended amount of time available since it involves short steps spread over a week.

1. Wearing goggles, remove all loose stucco with a hammer and cold chisel (Figure A).

2. If the underlying mesh is loose but not badly damaged, secure it with galvanized roofing nails. If it is too far gone, nail a patch of expanded metal lath over the old mesh.

3. Mist the damaged area with a garden hose to dampen it.

4. Using a large cake pan and tablespoon, mix half a bag of ready-mix mortar with water, according to the directions. Using a putty knife, push the mortar through the mesh and level the mortar 1/2 inch below the surrounding stucco (Figure B).

5. After 30 minutes, thoroughly scratch the fresh mortar about 1/8 inch deep with a nail. Keep the mortar damp by misting every few hours.

6. The next day moisten the first layer, then apply a second layer to within 1/8 inch of the surface. Keep the mortar damp.

7. After another two days, apply the final coat. Use a steel trowel to smooth the surface. While the surface is still wet, use a stiff-bristled brush to create a texture to match the original stucco.

8. After four more days, paint the wall with exterior latex stucco paint.

MATERIALS
- Galvanized roofing nails
- Expanded metal lath
- Ready-mix mortar mix
- Exterior latex stucco paint

TOOLS
Goggles • Hammer • Cold chisel
- Garden hose • Cake pan
- Tablespoon • Putty knife
- Large nail • Steel trowel
- Stiff-bristled brush • Paintbrush

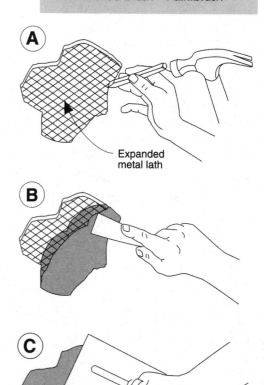

Expanded metal lath

Patching a Crack in Blacktop

Cracks in the surface of a blacktop driveway should be repaired as soon as they're noticed. Open cracks admit water, which can freeze and further damage the surface. Sealing the surface every year (see "Sealing Blacktop" on page 191) automatically seals small cracks before they require patching. Always work on blacktop when the temperature is over 60°F because the asphalt flows and adheres better when it's warm.

MATERIALS
- **Clean sand**
- **Cartridge of asphalt crack filler**
- **Paint thinner or mayonnaise**
- **Rag**

TOOLS
Wire brush • Utility knife • Screwdriver • Caulking gun • Putty knife

1. Clean loose debris from the crack with a wire brush.

2. If the crack is more than 1/2 inch deep, fill it to within 1/4 inch of the top with sand.

3. Using a utility knife, cut the nozzle of a cartridge of asphalt crack filler at an angle of 45 degrees, leaving an inside diameter of 3/8 inch. Insert a screwdriver through the tip of the cartridge and puncture the inner seal. Load the cartridge into a caulking gun in the order shown in Figure A. To start the asphalt crack filler flowing, turn the L-shaped handle up to engage the ratchet and then squeeze the trigger.

4. Apply the crack filler to the crack with the caulking gun (Figure B). Apply only enough to fill the crack.

5. Smooth and level the filler with a putty knife (Figure C).

6. Spread sand over the filled crack to prevent wet asphalt from sticking to paws and shoes.

7. Clean the tools with paint thinner or mayonnaise and a rag.

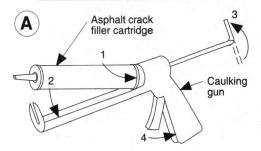

Ⓐ Asphalt crack filler cartridge / Caulking gun

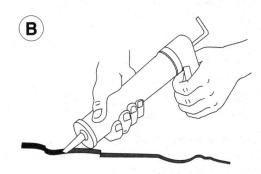

Ⓑ

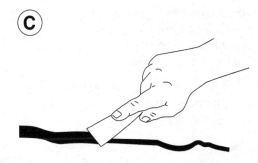

Ⓒ

PATCHING A HOLE IN BLACKTOP

Patching a hole in a blacktop driveway is best done just before sealing the surface. (See "Sealing Blacktop" on the opposite page.) Always wait for dry, warm weather—over 60°F—to work on blacktop because asphalt flows and adheres better when it's warm.

MATERIALS

- Sand
- Cold-mix asphalt
- Liquid asphalt sealer
- Paint thinner or mayonnaise
- Rag

TOOLS

Triangular trowel • 2 × 4
- Stiff-bristled push broom

1. Using a triangular trowel, remove loose, crumbly material and other debris from the edge of the hole (Figure A).

2. If the hole is deeper than 4 inches, fill it to 4 inches below the surface with sand, and tamp the sand with the end of a 2 × 4 until it is hard-packed.

3. Add 2 inches of cold-mix asphalt and spread the mix with the trowel. Jab the tip of the trowel repeatedly into the mix to release air pockets (Figure B).

4. Tamp the leveled mix with the end of the 2 × 4.

5. Add and spread a finish layer of the mix to ½ inch above the level of the driveway.

6. Using the 2 × 4, tamp the finish layer level with the driveway (Figure C).

7. Spread a thin layer of sand over the patch and drive over the patch a dozen times to further compress the mix.

8. After 24 hours, brush off the loose sand with a stiff-bristled push broom and apply liquid asphalt sealer. (See "Sealing Blacktop" on the opposite page.)

9. Clean the tools with paint thinner or mayonnaise and a rag.

(A)

(B)

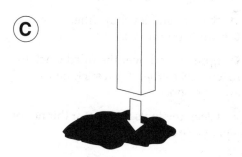

(C)

SEALING BLACKTOP

The worst enemy of a blacktop driveway is frost heave—the result of water beneath the driveway freezing and expanding. Sealing the blacktop prevents most of the water from seeping through the surface to cause trouble.

1. Brush all loose dirt and debris from the driveway with a driveway sealer brush.

2. Wet the driveway thoroughly with a garden hose, dribble household cleaner over the wet surface—1 quart of cleaner per 1,000 square feet of driveway—and brush again to loosen deposits of motor oil. Clean one section at a time if the driveway dries too quickly.

3. Hose the driveway thoroughly to rinse away all of the cleaner (Figure A).

4. When the driveway is dry, start at one end and apply coal tar sealer liberally, brushing it smooth with the driveway sealer brush (Figure B). Apply the sealer to 10 square feet or so at a time.

5. Put up a barrier at the end of the driveway to prevent traffic for 48 hours.

6. If, after 48 hours, the surface doesn't appear to be completely sealed, apply a second coat of asphalt sealer and wait another 48 hours before driving on it.

7. If you wish to save the brush, clean it with kerosene.

MATERIALS

- **Household cleaner (1 quart per 1,000 square feet of driveway)**
- **Coal tar sealer (5 gallons per 300 square feet)**
- **Kerosene**

TOOLS

Driveway sealer brush
- **Garden hose**

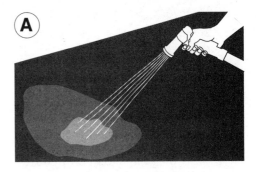

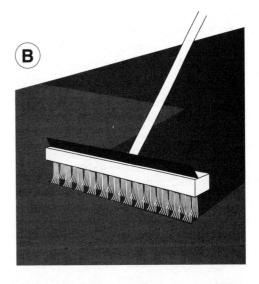

REPOINTING MORTAR JOINTS

Well-formed mortar joints prevent rain water from seeping between the bricks where it might freeze and crack the wall. Often, mortar that appears to be deteriorating is sound ½ inch below the surface. Repointing will give the wall a new appearance and an increased life span.

MATERIALS
- Ready-mix mortar
- Short, flat board

TOOLS
Goggles • Hammer • Cold chisel
• Wire brush • Garden hose
• Cake pan • Tablespoon
• Triangular trowel • Pointing tool

1. Wearing goggles, remove the crumbling mortar to a depth of ½ inch with a hammer and narrow cold chisel (Figure A).

2. Remove all loose debris with a wire brush and a high-pressure stream of water from a garden hose.

3. Using a cake pan and a tablespoon, mix ready-mix mortar with water. The mix is right when it has the consistency of peanut butter.

4. Spray the mortar joints with mist from the garden hose.

5. Using a triangular trowel, create a ³/₈-inch-thick layer of mortar on a short, flat board.

6. Holding the edge of the board against a joint, press a ½-inch-wide slice of mortar into the joint with the trowel (Figure B).

7. Use the trowel to fill gaps around the brick with mortar. Using a pointing tool, smooth the joints to match the surrounding joints. Cut off excess mortar with the trowel and brush the wall with a wire brush to remove any loose mortar (Figure C).

8. Clean the tools with water.

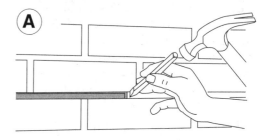

A

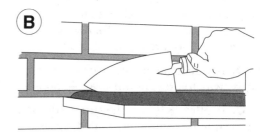

B

C

REPLACING A BRICK

Replacing a cracked or unsightly brick is not as impossible as it might seem. Patience and a lot of gentle-to-moderate tapping with a cold chisel will break up a damaged brick without cracking the surrounding masonry.

MATERIALS
- **Ready-mix mortar**
- **Replacement brick**

TOOLS
Goggles • Hammer • Cold chisels
• Garden hose • Cake pan
• Tablespoon • Triangular trowel
• Pointing tool

1. Wearing goggles, use a hammer and a narrow cold chisel to chip out the mortar surrounding the damaged brick to a depth of about 1 inch (Figure A).

2. Using the hammer and a larger cold chisel, chip away the brick (Figure B). Continue until the brick and mortar are completely removed.

3. Clean out debris and dampen the bricks with a high-pressure stream of water from a garden hose.

4. Using a cake pan and tablespoon, mix a small amount of ready-mix mortar with water. The mix is right when it has the consistency of mashed potatoes.

5. Using a triangular trowel, apply a ³/₈-inch layer of mortar to the bottom of the cavity and a similar thickness to the sides and top of the replacement brick.

6. Place the brick on the trowel next to the cavity and slide the brick into the cavity (Figure C).

7. Use the trowel to fill gaps around the brick with mortar. Using a pointing tool, smooth the joints to match the surrounding ones. Cut off excess mortar with the trowel and brush the wall with a wire brush to remove any loose mortar.

8. Clean the tools with water.

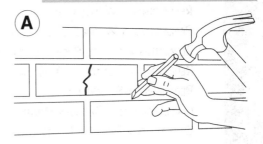

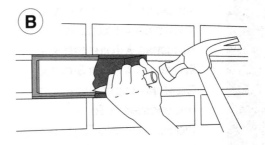

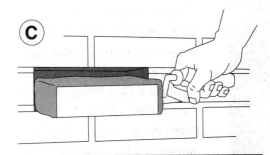

ADJUSTING A SINK POP-UP DRAIN

Most of the bathroom sink pop-up stoppers in the world have stopped working. Either they won't stay open or closed or they leak. That is because their owners have never looked under the sink. Amaze your friends and family by fixing yours.

If the stopper doesn't pop up when the lift rod is depressed, try these options:

- Pinch the spring clip and move the pivot rod down one hole in the clevis.

- Loosen the clevis screw with slip-joint pliers, pull the clevis down until the stopper pops up, and tighten the clevis screw again.

If the stopper won't hold water even when closed, follow these steps:

1. Remove the stopper by lifting it straight up or by turning and lifting it.

2. If it won't release, remove the retaining nut with groove-joint pliers, pull the pivot rod out, and pull the stopper up.

3. Clean the stopper seal or, if worn, buy and install a replacement.

If the stopper won't remain either closed or open, use the groove-joint pliers to tighten the retaining nut until the stopper stays open or closed.

If water leaks from the pivot ball, follow these steps:

1. Remove the retaining nut with groove-joint pliers. Pull out the pivot rod, gasket, and washer—if there is one.

2. Buy a replacement gasket and washer at a hardware store. Reassemble the pivot assembly.

MATERIALS
- **Replacement stopper seal**
- **Replacement pivot-ball gasket**
- **Replacement pivot-ball washer**

TOOLS
Slip-joint pliers • Groove-joint pliers

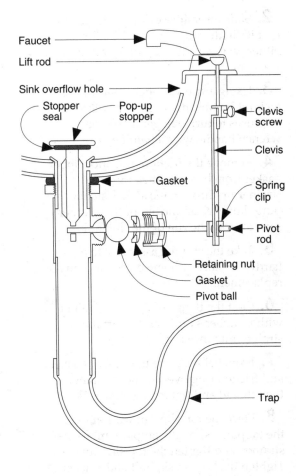

Faucet
Lift rod
Sink overflow hole
Stopper seal
Pop-up stopper
Clevis screw
Clevis
Gasket
Spring clip
Pivot rod
Retaining nut
Gasket
Pivot ball
Trap

REPLACING A KITCHEN SINK STRAINER

If your sink strainer will not hold water, try replacing the strainer basket first. Take the old one to a hardware store or home center to find a similar replacement for less than $5. If the new strainer leaks, replace the entire assembly, as described below.

MATERIALS
- **Replacement sink strainer assembly**
- **Plumber's putty**

TOOLS
Groove-joint pliers • Spud wrench • Hammer • Putty knife

1. Using groove-joint pliers, loosen the two slip nuts from the tailpiece by turning them counterclockwise.

2. Slide the tailpiece down into the trap, or if it's in the way, remove the tailpiece. In either case, save the slip nuts and their washers.

3. Using a spud wrench, remove the locknut by turning it counterclockwise. If it refuses to turn, tap gently on the wrench handle with a hammer.

4. Remove the friction ring and rubber gasket from beneath, then push the strainer up through the sink. Using a putty knife, clean the old putty or other sealant from the rim of the sink hole.

5. Take the strainer assembly to a hardware store or home center and buy a replacement.

6. Coat the flange of the new strainer with plumber's putty and insert the strainer into the sink.

7. From below, place the rubber gasket and friction ring over the new strainer, then thread and tighten the new locknut.

8. Place the top slip-nut washer over the tailpiece, slide the tailpiece up to the strainer, and tighten the top slip nut. Tighten the bottom slip nut and washer onto the trap.

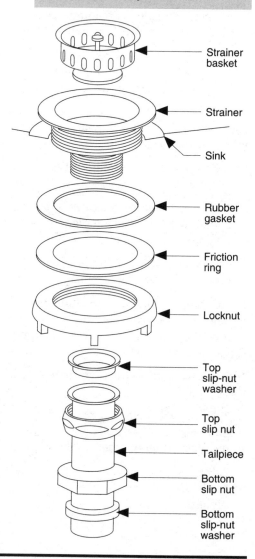

Strainer basket

Strainer

Sink

Rubber gasket

Friction ring

Locknut

Top slip-nut washer

Top slip nut

Tailpiece

Bottom slip nut

Bottom slip-nut washer

UNCLOGGING A SINK DRAIN

The best time to unclog a sink drain is before the drain becomes completely blocked. Commercial drain cleaners will usually remove accumulated grease and hair. But if the blockage becomes complete, the steps below will cure it.

1. Remove the pop-up stopper if there is one. Most stoppers lift out or will after they are turned.

2. If the stopper will not lift out, place a bucket under the trap and, using groove-joint pliers, remove the retaining nut. Pull the pivot rod straight back and lift out the stopper. Then replace the pivot rod and retighten the retaining nut (Figure A).

3. Fill the sink with water to a depth of 4 inches.

4. Stuff the sink overflow with a small towel (Figure B).

5. While a helper holds the towel in place, place a plunger over the drain and plunge up and down forcefully.

6. If that doesn't succeed in clearing the blockage, loosen the two slip nuts on the trap with the groove-joint pliers and remove the trap (Figure C).

7. Using diagonal-cutting pliers, cut a wire coat hanger and bend a hook in one end. Use the hook to fish the blockage out of the tailpiece, the trap, or the drainpipe.

8. If that doesn't succeed in clearing the blockage, call a plumber.

MATERIALS
Wire coat hanger

TOOLS
Bucket • Groove-joint pliers • Plunger • Diagonal-cutting pliers • Small towel

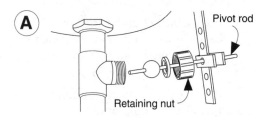

A Pivot rod / Retaining nut

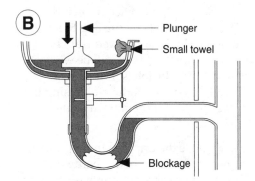

B Plunger / Small towel / Blockage

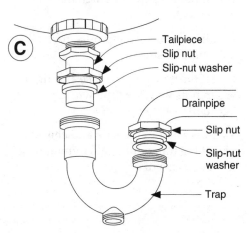

C Tailpiece / Slip nut / Slip-nut washer / Drainpipe / Slip nut / Slip-nut washer / Trap

REPLACING A SINK TRAP

Because the trap under a sink retains water and is often treated with caustic chemicals to remove blockages, it is usually the first plumbing part to fail. Exact replacements are easy to find in a hardware store or home center. Take the old trap with you, and make sure to buy new slip-nut washers at the same time.

MATERIALS
- **Replacement slip-nut washers**
- **Replacement trap**

TOOLS
Bucket • Adjustable wrench • Pipe wrench • Washcloth

1. Place a bucket under the trap. Using an adjustable wrench, remove the clean-out plug—if there is one—by turning it counterclockwise (Figure A).

2. Remove the bucket and empty it into the toilet—not the sink!

3. Using a pipe wrench, loosen the trap's two slip nuts by turning them counterclockwise as viewed from beneath (Figure B). If they will be exposed to view when the job is done, wrap the slip nuts in a washcloth before using the wrench to protect them from being scratched.

4. Remove the trap and the slip-nut washers and take them to a hardware store or home center to purchase replacements.

5. Slide on the old slip nuts, then slide on the new washers.

6. Fit the new trap in place and tighten the slip nuts with the pipe wrench (Figure B).

7. Run water in the sink and check for leaks. If the trap joints leak, tighten the slip nuts, as needed.

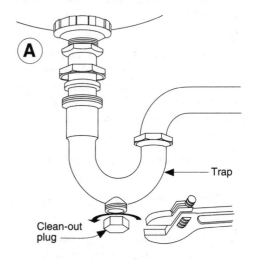

A

Trap

Clean-out plug

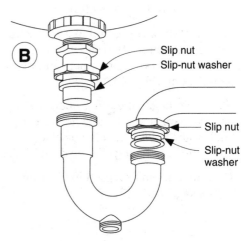

B

Slip nut
Slip-nut washer

Slip nut

Slip-nut washer

Unclogging a Sink Spray

If your sink spray is losing its oomph or is leaking, the perforated disk is probably clogged with debris or mineral deposits. Clearing the holes is a five-minute job. If the sink spray still doesn't work properly, consider replacing it since the whole assembly is not expensive.

MATERIALS
- **Plastic resealable bag**
- **Paper clip**
- **Vinegar**

TOOLS
Screwdriver or nail file

1. Using a small screwdriver, pry off the cover over the spray-head screw (Figure A).

2. Remove the screw. Place the spray-head screw cover and screw in a plastic resealable bag so you won't lose them.

3. Remove the perforated disk.

4. Clear the holes in the perforated disk with a straightened paper clip (Figure B).

5. If there are mineral deposits on the disk, soak the disk overnight in vinegar, and then clean it again with the straightened paper clip.

6. Reassemble the spray head.

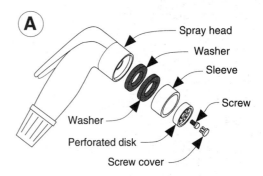

A — Spray head, Washer, Sleeve, Screw, Washer, Perforated disk, Screw cover

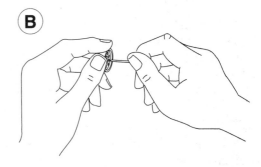

B

REPLACING A BATHROOM SINK

An inexpensive way to spruce up your bathroom is to replace the sink and toilet. Unlike toilets, bathroom sinks come in a wide variety of shapes and sizes. To avoid having to replace the vanity top as well, make sure the new sink is the same size as the old cutout. Also, make sure the new sink has the same faucet hole spacing as the old sink.

1. Look under the sink for any sink clips (Figure A). If there are any, loosen the screws. It is not necessary to completely remove the screws from the clips. Remove the sink clips.

2. Turn off the water supply valves under the sink.

3. Using an adjustable wrench, loosen both supply slip nuts at the bottom of the water supply lines (Figure B).

4. Using a pipe wrench, loosen the drain slip nuts (Figure B).

5. Lift the sink straight up and place it upside down on the counter.

6. Loosen the drain locknut with the pipe wrench and remove the sink strainer and tailpiece. To keep the strainer from twisting when you're loosening the drain locknut, insert slip-joint-plier handles into it from the other side.

7. Remove the top supply slip nuts and faucet mounting nuts with the adjustable wrench. Then loosen the clevis screw with slip-joint pliers, pull up the lift rod, and remove the faucet set. (See "Adjusting a Sink Pop-Up Drain" on page 195.)

8. Purchase a new sink and matching drain assembly that requires the same counter cutout and the same spacing between the faucet supply holes.

MATERIALS

- Replacement sink
- Drain assembly
- Plumber's putty
- Tube of clear silicone sealant

TOOLS

Screwdriver • Adjustable wrench • Pipe wrench • Slip-joint pliers

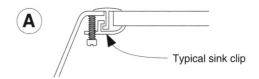

A — Typical sink clip

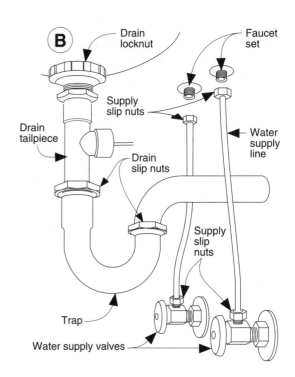

B
Drain locknut
Faucet set
Supply slip nuts
Drain tailpiece
Water supply line
Drain slip nuts
Supply slip nuts
Trap
Water supply valves

9. Apply plumber's putty to the base of the faucet set (Figure C), insert the faucet set into the supply holes in the new sink, and fasten it with the mounting nuts, using the adjustable wrench.

10. Using your fingers, apply plumber's putty to the flange of the new drain assembly (Figure D), insert the assembly into the new sink drain hole, and fasten it with the drain locknut, using the pipe wrench.

11. Apply clear silicone sealant under the sink rim, lower the sink into the countertop cutout, and reattach the sink clips, if any.

12. Slide the lift rod down through the hole in the faucet set and into the top of the clevis. Tighten the clevis screw.

13. Squeezing the spring clip with your fingers, slide the pivot rod through the spring clip and one of the clevis holes (Figure E). See "Adjusting a Sink Pop-Up Drain" on page 195 if you need help determining into which clevis hole the pivot rod should go.

14. Attach the supply lines with the bottom supply slip nuts.

15. Slide the trap up over the bottom of the drain tailpiece and tighten the drain slip nut.

16. Turn on the water supply valves and check both the drain and the supply lines for leaks. Tighten the slip nuts and locknut, if necessary.

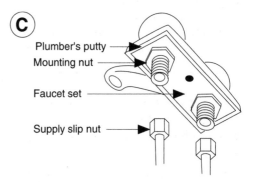

C

Plumber's putty
Mounting nut
Faucet set
Supply slip nut

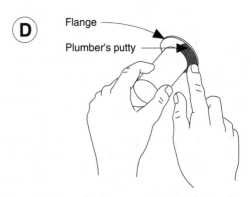

D

Flange
Plumber's putty

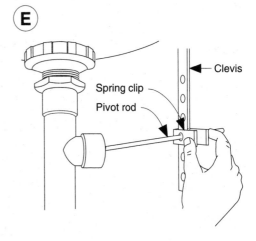

E

Clevis
Spring clip
Pivot rod

CLEANING A FAUCET AERATOR

If you have your own water supply or if your main water supply valve has been worked on recently, your faucet aerator screen may have collected some debris. Cleaning the screen is a simple task.

MATERIALS
- **Masking tape or rubber jar opener**
- **Vinegar**
- **Paper clip**

TOOLS
Groove-joint pliers

1. Wrap several turns of masking tape around the aerator body. You could also hold a rubber jar opener around the aerator body.

2. Using groove-joint pliers, grip the protected aerator body and unscrew it counterclockwise.

3. Disassemble the aerator and lay the parts out in order. Rinse out any debris from the perforated disk and screen.

4. If there are mineral deposits on the perforated disk and screen, soak both in vinegar overnight.

5. Remove any material clogging the disk or screen with a straightened paper clip. Rinse.

6. Reassemble the aerator and screw it back on, protecting its surface as you did in Step 1.

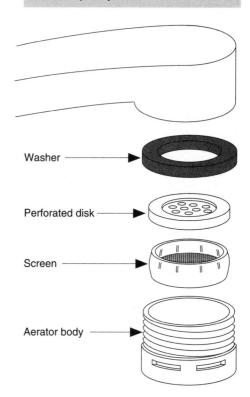

Washer

Perforated disk

Screen

Aerator body

REPAIRING A ROTATING BALL FAUCET

If your single-lever faucet has a round cap just under the handle, it is probably a rotating ball faucet. If the faucet is dripping, it may be fixed as simply as tightening the cap clockwise with groove-joint pliers. But if it still leaks, your best bet is to buy a repair kit.

MATERIALS
- Plastic resealable bag
- Faucet repair kit
- Waterproof grease

TOOLS
Allen wrench • Groove-joint pliers
• Screwdriver

1. Turn off the water supply valves under the sink.

2. Find an Allen wrench that fits snugly into the setscrew in the faucet handle and turn the setscrew counterclockwise until the handle lifts off.

3. Using groove-joint pliers, grip the knurled ring around the cap and turn it counterclockwise to remove it.

4. Remove the cam, rubber cam seal, and ball. Using a small screwdriver, lift out the rubber inlet seals and springs.

5. Remove the spout by twisting and lifting at the same time.

6. Remove the O-rings.

7. Place the cam, cam seal, ball, inlet seals, springs, and O-rings in a plastic resealable bag, and take them to a hardware store to purchase a kit with matching parts.

8. Coat the new O-rings with waterproof grease and seat them in their grooves.

9. Install the remaining replacement parts. If the ball contains a slot, align the slot with the alignment pin in the body. Fit the tab on the cam into the notch in the body before screwing down the cap.

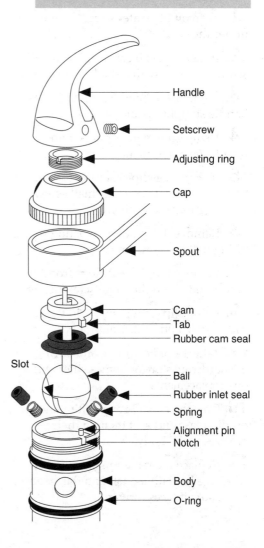

Handle
Setscrew
Adjusting ring
Cap
Spout
Cam
Tab
Rubber cam seal
Slot
Ball
Rubber inlet seal
Spring
Alignment pin
Notch
Body
O-ring

REPAIRING A CARTRIDGE FAUCET

The majority of single-lever—and some double-lever—faucets are of the cartridge type. There are literally dozens of cartridge styles, so be sure to take the old cartridge with you to the hardware store or home center to buy a replacement. The color of the replacement cartridge doesn't matter—just the geometry.

MATERIALS
- **Replacement cartridge**
- **Large O-rings**
- **Waterproof grease**

TOOLS
Screwdriver • Groove-joint pliers • Long-nose pliers • Slip-joint pliers

1. Turn off the water supply valves under the sink.

2. If there is a cap covering the handle screw, pry it off with a small screwdriver.

3. Remove the handle screw. Lift the handle straight up and off.

4. Using groove-joint pliers, remove the plastic retaining nut.

5. If there is a clip retaining the cartridge, remove it with the small screwdriver or long-nose pliers.

6. Remove the spout by twisting it and lifting it at the same time.

7. Remove the large O-rings from the faucet body with the small screwdriver.

8. Using slip-joint pliers, grip the cartridge stem and pull straight up.

9. Take the old cartridge and O-rings to the hardware store or home center and buy replacements.

10. Coat the new O-rings with waterproof grease and seat them in their grooves in the body.

11. Replace the remaining parts. If the cartridge has either a tab or a flat surface, make sure it faces forward.

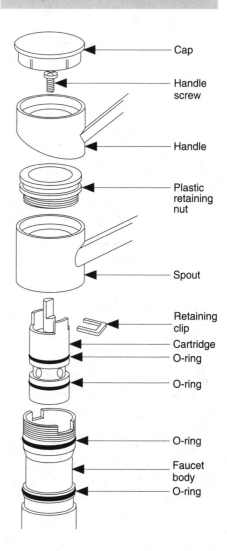

Cap

Handle screw

Handle

Plastic retaining nut

Spout

Retaining clip

Cartridge

O-ring

O-ring

O-ring

Faucet body

O-ring

REPAIRING A DISK FAUCET

The cylinder in a disk faucet rarely wears out. Try cleaning the rubber seals and the inlet holes or replacing the seals before purchasing the very expensive replacement cylinder. Also, remember to move the handle to the *ON* position before turning the water supply back on to avoid damaging the cylinder.

MATERIALS
- **Replacement rubber seals**
- **Replacement cylinder**

TOOLS
Allen wrench • Screwdriver

1. Turn off the water supply valves under the sink.

2. Locate the setscrew in the handle and find either an Allen wrench or a screwdriver that will fit it. Loosen the setscrew and remove both the handle and the escutcheon cap.

3. Remove the screws in the top of the cylinder, then lift the cylinder straight up and out.

4. Take the cylinder to a hardware store and purchase replacements for the three tiny rubber seals in the bottom of the cylinder.

5. Using a small screwdriver, remove the old seals, clean out the holes they were seated in, and install the new seals.

6. Line up the new seals with the holes in the faucet body, and reinstall the cylinder.

7. Replace the cap and handle. Move the handle to the *ON* position.

8. Turn on the water supply valves. As soon as the water runs steadily, move the handle to the *OFF* position.

9. If the faucet still leaks, purchase and install a new cylinder following these steps but replacing the cylinder instead of just the rubber seals.

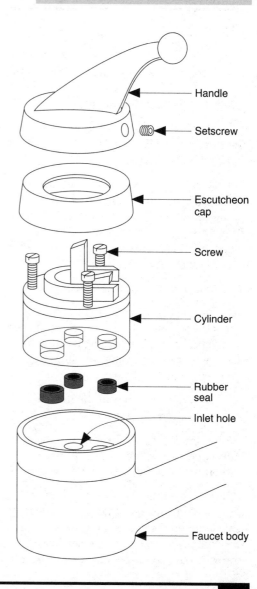

Handle

Setscrew

Escutcheon cap

Screw

Cylinder

Rubber seal

Inlet hole

Faucet body

REPAIRING A COMPRESSION FAUCET

Replacing the washer in a compression faucet is the classic home repair. There are many different washer sizes, so to make the job simple, take the threaded spindle with you to the hardware store to make sure the replacement O-ring, stem washer, and stem screw are all of exactly the right size.

MATERIALS

- Replacement O-ring, stem washer, and stem screw
- Packing string

TOOLS

Screwdriver • Adjustable wrench
• Adjustable pliers

1. Turn off the water supply valves under the sink.

2. If the handle has a cap, pry it off with a small screwdriver. Remove the handle screw. Lift the handle straight up and off.

3. Using an adjustable wrench, remove the stem assembly by turning the packing nut counterclockwise.

4. Separate the stem from the packing nut. Take the stem to a hardware store or home center and buy an identical O-ring, stem washer, and stem screw. Buy packing string if the packing nut contains packing instead of an O-ring.

5. Install the new washer and screw.

6. Put the new O-ring on the stem and screw the stem into the packing nut. If the stem has packing instead, dig it out and wind new packing around the stem inside the packing nut until nearly full.

7. Turn the stem to pull the threaded spindle up into the packing nut.

8. Insert the stem assembly into the faucet body. Using adjustable pliers, tighten the packing nut.

9. Turn on the water supply valves and turn off the faucet. If the faucet still leaks, tighten the packing nut further. Or see "Replacing a Worn Valve Seat" on the opposite page to install a new valve seat.

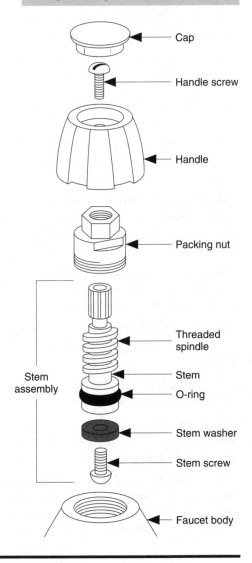

Cap

Handle screw

Handle

Packing nut

Stem assembly

Threaded spindle

Stem

O-ring

Stem washer

Stem screw

Faucet body

REPLACING A WORN VALVE SEAT

If your faucet eats washers more than one per year, it may have a damaged or corroded valve seat. Fortunately, the seat is replaceable. You can tell if the seat is damaged by inserting and twisting your forefinger in the faucet body. If the surface of the seat feels rough, replace it.

MATERIALS
Replacement valve seat

TOOLS
Screwdriver • Adjustable wrench • Allen wrench or valve-seat wrench

1. Turn off the water supply valves under the sink.

2. If the handle has a cap, pry it off with a small screwdriver.

3. Remove the handle screw. Lift the handle straight up and off (Figure A).

4. Using an adjustable wrench, remove the stem assembly by turning the packing nut counterclockwise.

5. Find a large Allen wrench that will fit snugly in the hexagonal hole in the valve seat. Or you can use a valve-seat wrench if you have one. Turn either wrench counterclockwise and remove the valve seat (Figure B).

6. Take the valve seat to the hardware store or home center and purchase a replacement.

7. Install the new valve seat with the same wrench.

8. Turn the stem counterclockwise to retract the stem washer.

9. Insert the stem assembly into the faucet body and tighten the packing nut with the adjustable wrench.

10. Turn on the water supply valves and turn off the faucet. If the faucet still leaks, tighten the packing nut further.

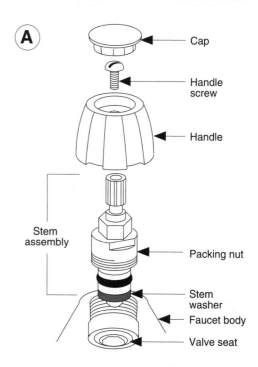

A — Cap, Handle screw, Handle, Stem assembly, Packing nut, Stem washer, Faucet body, Valve seat

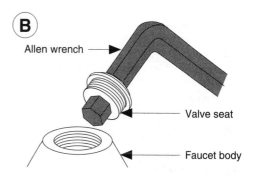

B — Allen wrench, Valve seat, Faucet body

REPLACING A WATER FILTER CARTRIDGE

Water filter cartridges are inexpensive and marvelous at removing sediment and bad taste from drinking water. Eventually, however, they become totally clogged by impurities. If you have one, you should replace the filter cartridge every few months even though the water still flows easily because it can become a breeding ground for bacteria.

MATERIALS
- **Replacement water filter cartridge**
- **Chlorine bleach**
- **Petroleum jelly**

TOOLS
Bucket • Oil-filter wrench • Sponge

1. Place a bucket under the filter, which should be near your main water shutoff valve or under your kitchen sink.

2. Turn off the water supply valve to the filter (Figure A). On some models the valve is built into the filter. If you can not find a water supply valve, turn off the main water shutoff valve.

3. If there is a pressure-release button on the filter cap, press it.

4. Take hold of the filter housing in both hands and unscrew it. If the housing will not turn, use an automotive oil-filter wrench to loosen it.

5. Remove the cartridge from the housing (Figure B) and take it to a hardware store to buy a replacement.

6. Wipe out the housing with a sponge and chlorine bleach.

7. If the replacement cartridge package contains an O-ring, coat it lightly with petroleum jelly and replace the old O-ring.

8. Place the new cartridge in the housing —either end up—and screw the housing clockwise onto the cap. Tighten the housing only hand-tight.

9. Turn on the water supply valve and check for leaks. Tighten the housing further, if necessary.

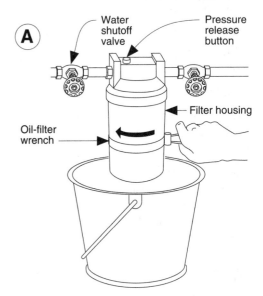

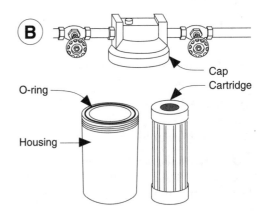

REPAIRING A FREEZE-PROOF EXTERIOR FAUCET

A freeze-proof exterior faucet, known as a sill cock, is similar to a common exterior faucet, known as a hose bib, except that it has an extra long stem reaching back about 12 inches inside the house. Like any other faucet, it requires periodic replacement of the stem washer to stop leaks.

MATERIALS
Replacement O-rings and stem washer

TOOLS
Screwdriver • Adjustable wrench

1. Turn off the water supply valve to the sill cock inside the house (Figure A). If you cannot find the shutoff, turn off the main water shutoff valve, which should be next to the water meter.

2. Remove the handle screw. Lift the handle straight up and off (Figure B).

3. Using an adjustable wrench, remove the hexagonal retaining nut by turning it counterclockwise.

4. Turn the stem counterclockwise and pull it all the way out.

5. Take the retaining nut and the stem to a hardware store and purchase replacement O-rings and a stem washer.

6. Replace the O-rings and washer.

7. Insert the stem into the sill-cock body and turn it clockwise as far as it will go.

8. Screw the hexagonal nut back on the stem with the adjustable wrench.

9. Replace the handle and secure it with the handle screw.

10. Turn the water supply valve back on and check for leaks. Tighten the retaining nut further, if necessary.

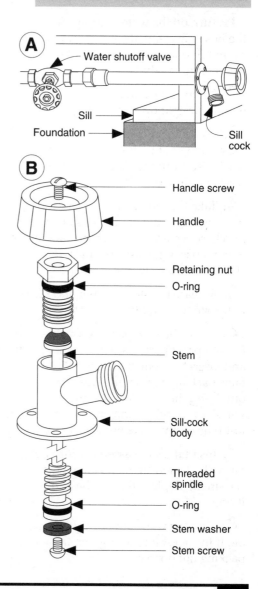

A — Water shutoff valve
Sill
Foundation
Sill cock

B
Handle screw
Handle
Retaining nut
O-ring
Stem
Sill-cock body
Threaded spindle
O-ring
Stem washer
Stem screw

REPAIRING AN EXTERIOR-TYPE FAUCET

An exterior-type faucet, known as a hose bib, has a threaded spout for connecting garden hoses outdoors and for connecting appliances such as clothes washers indoors. If the bib is leaking from the handle, try tightening the packing nut before replacing the washers.

MATERIALS
- Replacement packing washer or packing string
- Replacement stem washer
- Replacement stem screw

TOOLS
Screwdriver • Adjustable wrench

1. Turn off the water supply valve to the hose bib inside the house. If you cannot find the valve, turn off the main water shutoff valve.

2. Remove the handle screw. Lift the handle straight up and off (Figure A).

3. Using an adjustable wrench, remove the packing nut by turning it counterclockwise. Turn the stem counterclockwise and lift it out.

4. Take the stem assembly and the packing nut to the hardware store and purchase replacements for the packing—either a packing washer or packing string—and the stem washer and screw.

5. Replace the stem washer and screw in the stem assembly.

6. Insert the new packing washer and the old packing ring into the packing nut and insert the stem. If the packing nut contains packing instead of a washer, dig it out, insert the stem into the nut, and wind new packing string around the stem until the cavity in the nut is nearly full.

7. Insert the stem assembly into the faucet body and tighten the packing nut (Figure B). Replace the handle and turn it off.

8. Turn the water supply valve back on. If the bib still leaks, tighten the packing nut further.

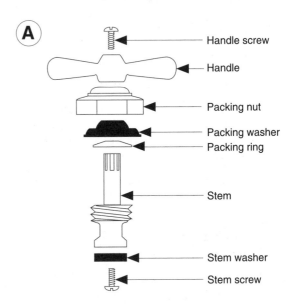

A

- Handle screw
- Handle
- Packing nut
- Packing washer
- Packing ring
- Stem
- Stem washer
- Stem screw

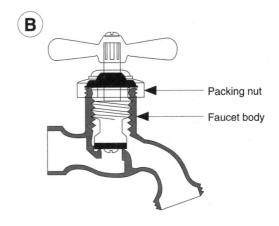

B

- Packing nut
- Faucet body

REPAIRING A SHOWERHEAD

A leaking or clogged showerhead is annoying and can waste water. Fortunately, removing and cleaning or replacing your showerhead is one of the easiest plumbing fix-ups you'll ever need to tackle.

MATERIALS

- **Masking tape**
- **Paper clip**
- **Vinegar**
- **Replacement O-ring**
- **Pipe-joint sealant**
- **Replacement showerhead**

TOOLS

Adjustable wrench • Groove-joint pliers

1. Place masking tape over the jaws of an adjustable wrench and remove the showerhead assembly by turning the swivel-ball nut counterclockwise.

2. Using groove-joint pliers wrapped in masking tape, remove the collar nut.

3. Clean out both inlet and outlet holes with a straightened paper clip. If there is a buildup of mineral deposits, soak the showerhead in vinegar overnight. Remove any loosened material with the straightened paper clip. Rinse.

4. If the O-ring is worn, remove it and take it to a hardware store or home center to purchase a replacement.

5. Reassemble the showerhead.

6. Apply pipe-joint sealant to the threads of the shower arm and screw on the showerhead assembly.

7. Turn the shower on and check the flow. If the showerhead leaks at the swivel, tighten the collar nut; if it leaks at the arm, tighten the swivel-ball nut.

8. If it still leaks or has an erratic spray, replace the showerhead assembly with a new water-saving showerhead with a shutoff button.

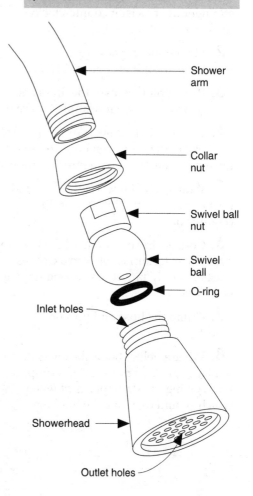

Shower arm

Collar nut

Swivel ball nut

Swivel ball

O-ring

Inlet holes

Showerhead

Outlet holes

UNCLOGGING A SHOWER DRAIN

Do you find yourself standing in a puddle every time you shower? If so, your shower drain is becoming clogged. You can forestall trouble by using drain cleaner before the drain becomes completely blocked. But if it does, here are two simple ways to clear the blockage.

MATERIALS
None

TOOLS
Long-nose pliers • Plunger • Garden hose • Small towel

1. Spread the prongs of a pair of long-nose pliers, insert them into the holes of the shower strainer, and either flip the strainer out or twist it counterclockwise to unscrew it (Figure A).

2. Fill the shower base to a depth of about 1 inch—if it isn't already!

3. Place a plunger over the drain and plunge up and down forcefully (Figure B).

4. If that didn't clear the drain, remove the nozzle from a garden hose and insert the hose as far as you can into the drain.

5. Wrap a small towel tightly around the hose and stuff it into the drain (Figure C).

6. Connect the other end of the hose to either an exterior faucet or to a clothes washer supply faucet. Use a long hose, if necessary.

7. Crimp the hose and turn on the faucet.

8. While a helper holds the towel firmly in place, quickly crimp and uncrimp the hose, giving the drain blasts of water, which should dislodge the blockage.

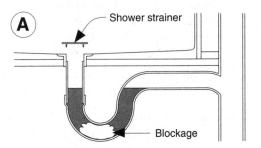

A — Shower strainer — Blockage

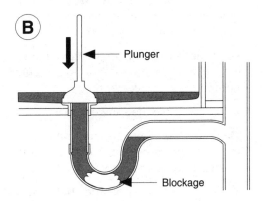

B — Plunger — Blockage

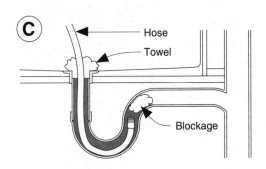

C — Hose — Towel — Blockage

CLEANING A POP-UP TUB DRAIN

Because we shampoo in our tubs, a lot of hair gets flushed down the drain, and hair is notorious for clogging drains. Unfortunately, the mechanism of a pop-up tub drain is especially good at attracting and catching hair. Fortunately, a pop-up drain is simple to pull out and clean.

MATERIALS
Vinegar

TOOLS
Screwdriver • Toothbrush • Hand auger • Adjustable wrench

1. Flip the drain lever up to pop up the drain stopper, and pull the drain stopper out of the tub drain (Figure A).

2. Remove the screws from the overflow cover plate, and pull the drain assembly out of the overflow hole (Figure B).

3. Remove the accumulated hair and other material and scrub the parts with a toothbrush and vinegar.

4. If the tub still drains slowly with the drain assembly removed, feed a hand auger into the overflow hole and down through the drain.

5. When resistance is met, start turning the auger clockwise and slowly withdraw it. With luck the clogging material will be hooked on the auger. Repeat Steps 4 and 5 until the tub drains normally.

6. Insert the drain assembly through the overflow hole and replace the cover plate.

7. Flip the drain lever up and insert the drain stopper into the drain.

8. If the tub now either drains slowly or will not hold water, take out the drain assembly again. Using an adjustable wrench, adjust the position of the threaded rod and nut at the top of the linkage: Turn the threaded rod up into the nut to speed draining; turn it out further to stop leaking (Figure B).

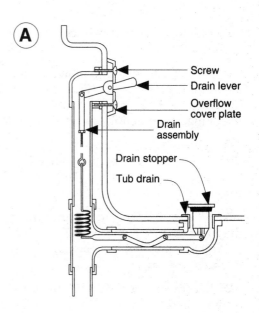

A — Screw, Drain lever, Overflow cover plate, Drain assembly, Drain stopper, Tub drain

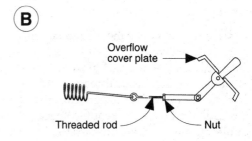

B — Overflow cover plate, Threaded rod, Nut

CLEANING A PLUNGER-TYPE TUB DRAIN

A pop-up drain often clogs with hair so that the water drains slowly or not at all. A plunger-type tub drain has the opposite problem—hair may prevent it from fully closing so that it does not hold water. Fortunately, it is simple to disassemble and clean.

MATERIALS
- Vinegar
- Petroleum jelly

TOOLS
Screwdriver • Toothbrush
• Hand auger • Adjustable wrench

1. Remove the screws holding the overflow cover plate (Figure A).

2. Pull the entire drain assembly out of the overflow hole.

3. Clean the linkage and plunger with a toothbrush and vinegar (Figure B). Then dry the drain assembly and smear the plunger with petroleum jelly.

4. If the tub drains slowly with the drain assembly removed, feed a hand auger into the overflow hole and down through the drain.

5. When resistance is met, start turning the auger clockwise, and slowly withdraw it. With luck the clogging material will be hooked on the auger.

6. Repeat Steps 4 and 5 until the tub drains normally.

7. Insert the drain assembly through the overflow hole and replace the overflow cover plate.

8. If the tub now either drains slowly or will not hold water, take out the drain assembly. Using an adjustable wrench, adjust the position of the threaded rod and nut at the top of the linkage: Turn the threaded rod up into the nut to speed draining; turn it out further to stop leaking (Figure B).

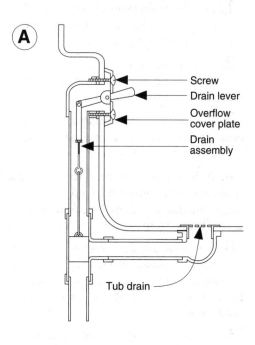

A

- Screw
- Drain lever
- Overflow cover plate
- Drain assembly
- Tub drain

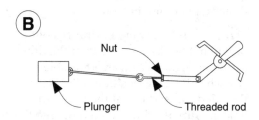

B

- Nut
- Plunger
- Threaded rod

ADJUSTING A TOILET HANDLE

If your toilet doesn't flush easily and completely when you trip the handle, chances are the handle or the lifting wire or chain attached to the handle needs tightening. This is the simplest of toilet repairs, requiring no new materials or parts.

MATERIALS
None

TOOLS
Adjustable wrench

If the toilet handle seems floppy, tighten the nut inside the tank by turning it counterclockwise with an adjustable wrench. Note that the direction is opposite to that of the usual nut (Figure A).

If the toilet trip lever connects to a lift chain and you have to hold the handle down to make the toilet flush completely, shorten the chain by moving the hook to a link further down (Figure A). The chain should have 1/2 inch of slack when the stopper is in its normal, closed position.

If the trip lever connects to a lift wire and you have to hold the handle down for a complete flush, bend the upper, right-angled lift wire up to lift the stopper further (Figure B).

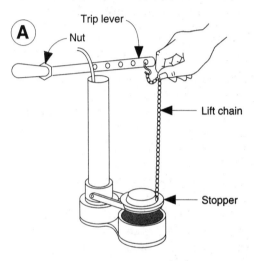

A   Trip lever — Nut — Lift chain — Stopper

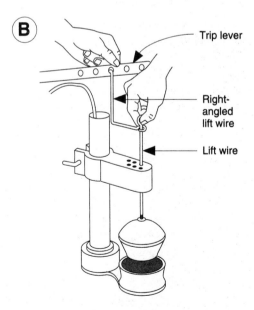

B   Trip lever — Right-angled lift wire — Lift wire

ADJUSTING TOILET TANK WATER LEVEL

If your toilet runs continuously and the water spills over into the top of the overflow tube, lower the tank level by adjusting the fill valve. The goal is to stop the toilet from running while retaining enough water in the tank for a complete flush. If you cannot adjust the water level enough to stop the runover, the entire fill valve should be replaced. (See "Replacing a Toilet Fill Valve" on the opposite page.)

MATERIALS
None

TOOLS
Screwdriver

If the fill valve in your toilet tank resembles Figure A, you can adjust the water level in the tank by bending the float arm with your hands: Bend it up for a higher water level, down for a lower water level.

If the fill valve in your toilet tank resembles Figure B, you can adjust the water level by squeezing the spring clip with your fingers and sliding the float: Slide it up for a higher water level, down for a lower water level.

If the fill valve in your toilet tank resembles Figure C, you can adjust the water level by turning the adjusting screw with a screwdriver: Turn it clockwise for a higher water level, counterclockwise for a lower water level.

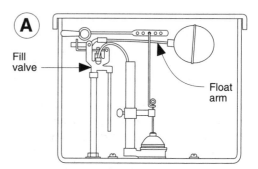

A

Fill valve

Float arm

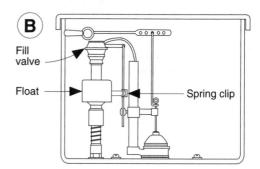

B

Fill valve

Float

Spring clip

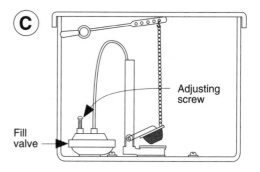

C

Adjusting screw

Fill valve

REPLACING A TOILET FILL VALVE

If your toilet runs continuously and water runs over the top of the overflow tube, lower the tank level. (See "Adjusting Toilet Tank Water Level" on the opposite page.) If the water still runs into the overflow tube, replace the toilet's old plunger-type fill valve with a modern float-cup fill valve.

MATERIALS
Replacement float-cup fill valve

TOOLS
Sponge • Adjustable wrench

1. Turn off the water supply valve under the toilet tank, flush the tank, and sponge the tank dry.

2. Using an adjustable wrench, remove the top supply slip nut underneath the toilet tank (Figure A).

3. Holding the fill valve with one hand, remove the fill valve locknut from under the tank with the adjustable wrench.

4. Unclip the refill tube from the overflow tube and lift the fill valve straight out (Figure B).

5. Purchase a float-cup fill valve at a hardware store or home center. Adjust the height of the new fill valve to fit in the tank by twisting its base (Figure C).

6. Insert the threaded base of the fill valve through the hole in the bottom of the tank and secure it with the locknut.

7. Clip the refill tube to the overflow tube.

8. Reconnect the top supply slip nut. Turn on the water supply valve and let the tank fill.

9. Flush the tank and adjust the float. (See "Adjusting Toilet Tank Water Level" on the opposite page.)

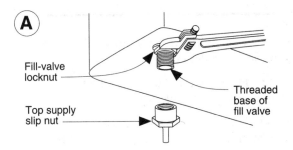

A

Fill-valve locknut

Threaded base of fill valve

Top supply slip nut

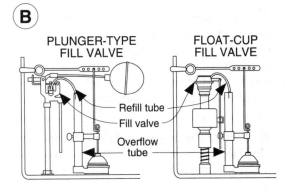

B

PLUNGER-TYPE FILL VALVE

FLOAT-CUP FILL VALVE

Refill tube
Fill valve
Overflow tube

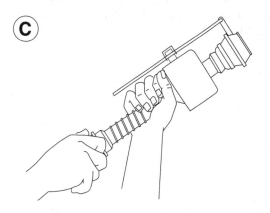

C

ADJUSTING A TOILET STOPPER

If your toilet runs continuously but the water never reaches the top of the overflow tube, the stopper may be misaligned with the flush valve seat. You can quickly fix this problem by adjusting the stopper guide arm. If the toilet still runs after this, the stopper may be worn or cracked. (See "Replacing a Toilet Stopper" on the opposite page.)

MATERIALS
None

TOOLS
Sponge • Slip-joint pliers
• Scrub pad

1. Turn off the water supply valve under the toilet tank.

2. Flush the toilet to empty the tank and sponge the tank dry.

3. Look at the lift wire to see if it is bent. If it is, bend it straight again with your hands (Figure A).

4. Using slip joint pliers, loosen the guide arm adjustment screw (Figure B). Adjust the guide arm back and forth as necessary so that it guides the stopper directly into the flush valve outlet. Retighten the guide arm adjustment screw.

5. Pull up the stopper and clean the inside of the flush valve outlet by scouring it with a scrub pad.

6. Drop the stopper into position and turn on the water supply valve under the toilet tank.

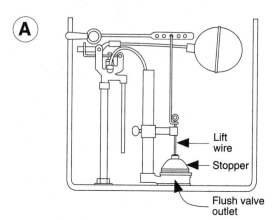

A

Lift wire

Stopper

Flush valve outlet

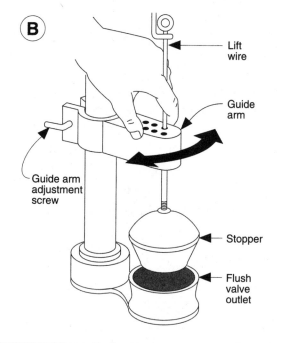

B

Lift wire

Guide arm

Guide arm adjustment screw

Stopper

Flush valve outlet

REPLACING A TOILET STOPPER

If your toilet runs continuously but the water never reaches the top of the overflow tube, the stopper guide arm may need adjusting. (See "Adjusting a Toilet Stopper" on the opposite page.) But if the toilet still runs after you have adjusted the stopper arm, the stopper may be worn or cracked. You can replace it quickly by following the steps below.

MATERIALS
Replacement toilet stopper

TOOLS
Sponge • Slip-joint pliers
• Scrub pad

1. Turn off the water supply valve under the toilet tank.

2. Flush the toilet to empty the tank and sponge the tank dry.

3. Unscrew the old stopper from the lift wire. If necessary, grip the top loop in the lift wire with slip-joint pliers to keep the lift wire from turning (Figure A) .

4. Take the old stopper to a hardware store or home center and purchase a replacement. Screw the new stopper onto the lift wire (Figure B).

5. Pull up the new stopper and clean the inside of the flush valve outlet by scouring it with a scrub pad.

6. Drop the stopper into position and turn on the water supply valve under the toilet tank.

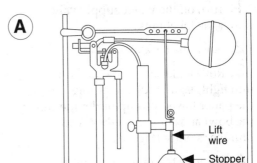

A

Lift wire

Stopper

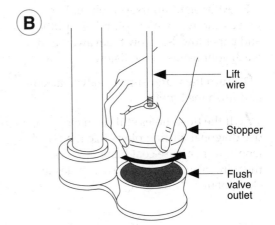

B

Lift wire

Stopper

Flush valve outlet

CLEANING TOILET RINSE HOLES

If your drinking glasses are cloudy or filmy, you probably live in an area with hard water, which contains dissolved minerals. The same mineral deposits you see on glasses build up on and will eventually clog the small rinse holes under the rim of a toilet bowl. Dissolving the deposits is a simple task.

1. Turn off the water supply valve under the toilet tank.

2. Flush the tank to empty it.

3. Roll single sheets of paper towel into tight, 1/2-inch-diameter rolls. Press the paper towel rolls up under the rim of the bowl and stick them there with plumber's putty (Figure A).

4. Remove the tank cover, lift the stopper by the lift wire or chain, and pour 16 ounces of commercial lime remover down the flush valve outlet in the tank (Figure B).

5. After eight hours, put on rubber gloves and remove the plumber's putty and paper towels, throw them away, and wash your hands immediately.

6. Turn the water supply valve back on and flush the toilet.

7. If the flush holes still seem clogged, use diagonal-cutting pliers to cut a 6-inch length from a wire coat hanger. Work the wire in and out of the rinse holes to clear them.

MATERIALS
- Paper towels
- Plumber's putty
- 16 oz. of commercial lime remover
- Wire coat hanger

TOOLS
Rubber gloves • Diagonal cutting pliers

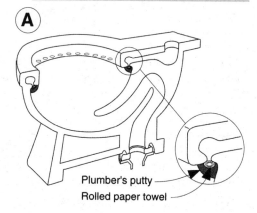

A

Plumber's putty
Rolled paper towel

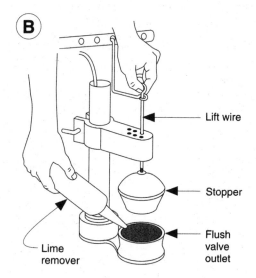

B

Lift wire

Stopper

Flush valve outlet

Lime remover

UNCLOGGING A TOILET

What lies beyond the flush hole in a toilet bowl is a great mystery to most homeowners. If you could see—as in the illustrations below—what was blocking the flow, freeing it would be simple. Here are two common tricks. Of course, the best rule is to never flush anything other than the waste the toilet was designed to handle.

MATERIALS
None

TOOLS
Rubber gloves • Funnel-cup plunger • Closet auger

1. Spread newspaper around the base of the toilet to catch any water that may splash out of the toilet bowl.

2. Put on rubber gloves, and place a funnel-cup plunger into the drain hole at the bottom of the toilet (Figure A).

3. Plunge up and down as hard as possible ten times. Remove the plunger and observe the results. If some of the standing water seems to flush away, the clog is gone.

4. If the toilet is still clogged, repeat Step 3.

5. If the toilet is still clogged, place the bend of a closet auger in the drain hole and feed the auger cable through the bend into the hole (Figure B).

6. When the cable meets an obstruction and you cannot push it any further, lock the handle with the thumbscrew and turn the handle clockwise.

7. Continue to turn the handle clockwise, slowly withdrawing the cable. With luck, the material clogging the toilet will be hooked on the end on the cable.

8. Repeat Steps 5 through 7 until the toilet flushes normally.

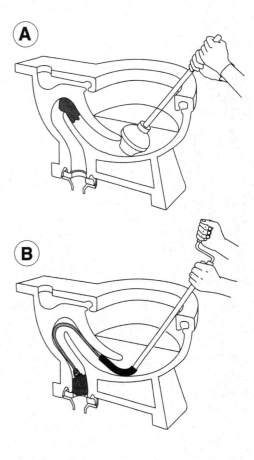

Troubleshooting Toilet Leaks

A toilet bowl or tank with a damp exterior doesn't necessarily indicate a leak. Depending on the temperature of the water in the toilet and the temperature of the air around it, your toilet can sweat up a storm. But whether your toilet is leaking or simply sweating, the resulting damage to the floor can be equally as bad.

MATERIALS
- **Toilet bowl cleaner**
- **Food coloring**
- **Paper towels**

TOOLS
Toilet brush • Teaspoon

1. Flush the toilet and clean it out with toilet bowl cleaner and a toilet brush. Flush the toilet again to rinse.

2. Pour a teaspoon of food coloring into the tank and mix it around with the toilet brush. Let the food coloring and water sit for one hour.

3. When the hour is up, wipe the base of the tank with a paper towel. If the water on the towel shows any sign of the food coloring, the toilet tank is leaking. (See "Fixing a Leaking Toilet Tank" on page 224.) If the food coloring doesn't show up on the towel, the moisture on the outside of the tank is caused by sweating. (See "Preventing Toilet Tank Sweating" on the opposite page.)

4. Flush the toilet so that the water and food coloring mixture drain into the bowl, and let it sit for another hour.

5. After the water and food coloring have been in the bowl for an hour, wipe around the base of the bowl with a fresh paper towel. If this towel shows any sign of food coloring, the toilet bowl base is leaking. (See "Fixing a Leaking Toilet Base" on page 226.) If the food coloring doesn't show up on the towel, the moisture around the toilet's base is just caused by sweating. (See "Preventing Toilet Tank Sweating" on the opposite page.)

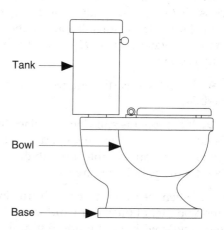

Tank →

Bowl →

Base →

PREVENTING TOILET TANK SWEATING

Condensation often forms on the outside of toilet tanks when air humidity is high. Occasional condensation is normal; continuous condensation may run down and rot the floor under the toilet. Preventing tank condensation requires insulating the inside of the tank. First, see "Troubleshooting Toilet Leaks" on the opposite page to be sure the toilet isn't leaking.

MATERIALS

- Kraft paper
- Common pins
- 1/2" molded polystyrene foam
- Waterproof mastic

TOOLS

Sponge • Scrub pad • Utility knife • Putty knife

1. Turn off the water supply valve under the toilet tank, and flush the toilet to empty the tank. Remove the remaining water with a sponge.

2. Scrub the inside walls of the tank with a scrub pad, rinse the tank, and let it dry completely overnight.

3. Using kraft paper, make patterns for the front and rear inside walls of the tank. Trim the paper to a close fit. Cut out around the tank handle.

4. Pin the paper patterns to 1/2-inch-thick molded polystyrene foam with common pins, and cut the foam to the shape of the paper with a utility knife. Split the front panel vertically as shown in the illustration to fit the panel behind the handle.

5. With a putty knife, apply waterproof mastic to the foam panels and press them against the inside walls of the tank.

6. Make patterns for the two side pieces, pin the patterns to foam, and cut the foam to shape.

7. After checking the fit, and making adjustments, apply mastic to the side pieces and press them into place.

8. Let the mastic dry overnight before turning the water supply valve back on.

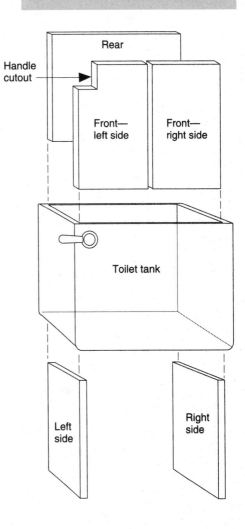

Rear

Handle cutout

Front— left side

Front— right side

Toilet tank

Left side

Right side

FIXING A LEAKING TOILET TANK

If you suspect that your toilet tank is leaking and you do not fix it quickly, the wood floor beneath the toilet could soak up the leaking water and eventually rot. Before removing the toilet, however, see "Troubleshooting Toilet Leaks" on page 222 to determine whether it is truly leaking or simply sweating.

First, determine whether the supply locknut, one of the tank bolts, or the flush valve outlet is leaking (Figure A). Lie down under the toilet and dry those areas with a paper towel. Using a flashlight, watch to see where the first drop of water develops. Turn off the water supply valve under the toilet, flush the toilet, and sponge the inside of the tank dry.

If the supply locknut is leaking, remove the fill valve and replace the gasket. (See "Replacing a Toilet Fill Valve" on page 217.)

If one or both of the tank bolts are leaking, follow these steps:

1. Using an adjustable wrench and screwdriver, remove one of the tank bolts and its gasket (Figure A).

2. Take the old gasket to a hardware store or home center and buy two replacement gaskets.

3. Reinstall the tank bolt with one of the new gaskets, and then replace the other tank bolt gasket.

4. Turn on the water supply valve and check for leaks. Tighten the tank bolts, if necessary.

MATERIALS

- Paper towel
- Ball-cock tailpiece gasket
- 2 toilet tank bolt gaskets
- Toilet tank spud washer

TOOLS

Flashlight • Sponge • Adjustable wrench • Screwdriver

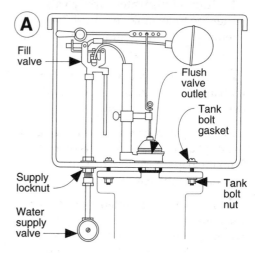

A

Fill valve

Flush valve outlet

Tank bolt gasket

Supply locknut

Water supply valve

Tank bolt nut

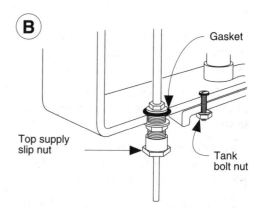

B

Gasket

Top supply slip nut

Tank bolt nut

If the flush valve outlet is leaking,
follow these steps:

1. Remove the top supply slip nut
(Figure B) and the two tank-bolt nuts
under the tank, and lift the tank
straight up.

2. Set the tank upside down on the
floor, and remove the spud washer by
hand (Figure C). Take it to a hardware
store or home center and purchase a
replacement.

3. Place the new spud washer over the
flush valve tailpiece.

4. With the new spud washer in place,
lower the tank onto the base so that
the tank bolts go through their holes in
the base. Attach the nuts and tighten
until just snug with the adjustable
wrench.

5. Reinstall the supply slip nut and
turn on the water supply valve. Check
for leaks. Tighten the tank bolts another
quarter turn, if necessary.

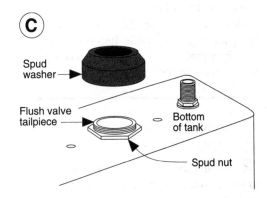

FIXING A LEAKING TOILET BASE

If a leaking toilet is not fixed quickly, the wood floor beneath it could soak up the leaking water and eventually rot. Needless to say, it is easier to fix a toilet's seal than to replace the entire floor. Before removing the toilet, however, see "Troubleshooting Toilet Leaks" on page 222 to determine whether it is truly leaking or whether it is simply sweating. Or if you find that your toilet is cracked, you can also follow these steps to replace it.

MATERIALS
- Wax ring
- Plumber's putty

TOOLS
Sponge • Adjustable wrench
• Screwdriver • Towel • Putty knife

1. Turn off the water supply valve under the toilet tank.

2. Flush the toilet. Using a sponge, remove all remaining water from the bowl and the tank.

3. Using an adjustable wrench, remove the supply slip nut holding the supply line under the tank by turning it counterclockwise (Figure A).

4. Pry off the closet bolt caps with a screwdriver.

5. Remove the closet bolt nuts and washer on each side of the toilet base with the adjustable wrench (Figure B).

6. Rock the toilet back and forth slightly until it seems loose.

7. Face the tank, straddle the toilet, and lift the toilet straight up (Figure C). Once it's free of the closet bolts, place it on its side on an old towel.

8. Using a putty knife, scrape the old wax ring from the closet flange and the base of the toilet (Figure D).

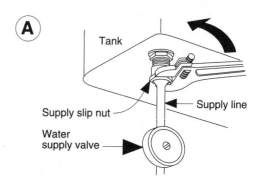

A

Tank

Supply slip nut

Supply line

Water supply valve

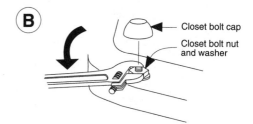

B

Closet bolt cap

Closet bolt nut and washer

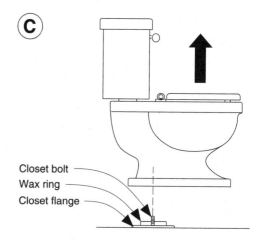

C

Closet bolt

Wax ring

Closet flange

9. Purchase a new wax ring at a hardware store or home center. Peel the paper from the wax ring and press it over the horn of the toilet base (Figure E).

10. Apply plumber's putty to the bottom edge of the toilet to help distribute the weight to the floor and to seal the base from water.

11. With a helper standing by, straddle the toilet again, pick it up, and hold it over the closet flange. Lower the toilet slowly while your helper guides the base onto the closet bolts.

12. Sit on the toilet seat to compress the plumber's putty and the wax ring.

13. Place the washers and nuts on the closet bolts and tighten the nuts with the adjustable wrench until just snug.

14. Repeat Steps 12 and 13 until the bolts no longer loosen under your weight. Do not tighten the bolts further or you may crack the toilet base. Replace the closet bolt caps.

15. Reconnect the supply line by replacing the slip nut.

16. Turn on the water supply valve, fill the tank, and flush the toilet. Check for leaks. Tighten the supply slip nut, if necessary.

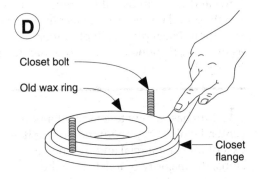

D

Closet bolt

Old wax ring

Closet flange

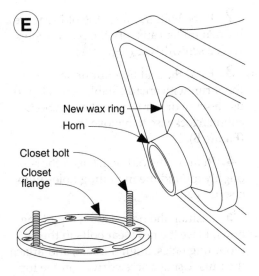

E

New wax ring

Horn

Closet bolt

Closet flange

REPLACING A TOILET SEAT

Does your toilet look old and tired? The porcelain bowl and tank can usually be refreshed by cleaning it with porcelain cleaner, but a chipped, stained seat should be replaced. Replacement seats can cost as little as $10; none require more than ten minutes to install.

MATERIALS
Replacement toilet seat

TOOLS
Screwdriver • Adjustable wrench • Scrub pad

1. Purchase a new toilet seat at a home center. Don't worry about measuring it—except for commercial and marine versions, the majority of toilets take the same size seat. Note if your toilet takes a round seat or an elongated one.

2. If the bolts securing the old seat are hidden under caps, pry the bolt caps up with a screwdriver (Figure A).

3. Hold the seat bolt nut under the toilet rim with an adjustable wrench and use a screwdriver to turn the seat bolts counterclockwise to remove them (Figure B).

4. Remove the old seat. Clean thoroughly around the mounting holes with a scrub pad.

5. Position the new seat on top of the bowl. Place the new seat bolts in the mounting holes, align the seat, and attach the nuts. Using a screwdriver on the top and the adjustable wrench on the bottom, tighten the seat bolts firmly.

6. Snap the bolt caps closed.

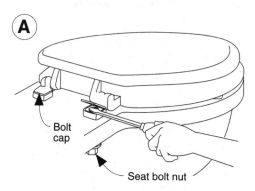

A

Bolt cap

Seat bolt nut

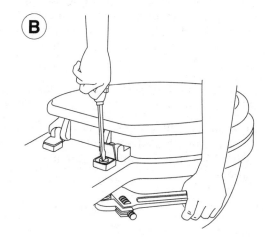

B

MAINTAINING A SEPTIC SYSTEM

If you are a homeowner whose household waste goes to a septic tank, you may have no idea where the access cover to your septic tank is. If so, find out—now! If the scum gets too thick, it can push through the access cover onto your lawn. If the tank totally fills up with sludge, the sludge will spill over and clog the drain field. Replacing the drain field can cost thousands of dollars.

MATERIALS
- 1 × 3 furring strip, 8' long
- Scrap of white sheet
- Staples

TOOLS
Tape measure • Staple gun
• Shovel • Garden hose

1. Locate your septic tank. If you do not know where it is, call the contractor who installed it or the previous owner of your home. If all else fails, you may have to ask a septic service to locate it.

2. Call a septic service to make an inspection. Find out the exact location of the access cover and guidelines for how deep the scum and sludge can get before the tank must be pumped out.

3. Using a tape measure, measure the distance from the access cover to two or more fixed locations on your property (Figure A). Sketch the distances (X and Y) on a map and store it with your deed.

4. Make a dipstick from an 8-foot length of 1 × 3 furring strip. Wrap the bottom 5 feet of the furring strip in a scrap of white sheet and staple the sheet in place.

5. Once a year, dig up the access cover and measure the depth of the sludge (Figure B). After measuring, spray the sludge off the stick with a garden hose.

6. In general, a family of three will have their tank pumped out every three years. To maximize the time between pump-outs, try composting your garbage rather than feeding it to the garbage disposal.

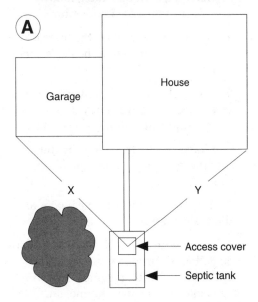

A

Garage

House

X   Y

Access cover

Septic tank

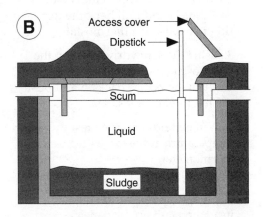

B

Access cover

Dipstick

Scum

Liquid

Sludge

ADJUSTING THE HOT WATER TEMPERATURE

You may wish to adjust the temperature of your hot water for one of several reasons. Lowering the temperature will lower your hot water heating cost. On the other hand, raising the temperature will increase the amount of heat in storage and allow longer showers. To protect against scalding, don't raise the temperature above 120°F.

MATERIALS
None

TOOLS
Candy thermometer • Screwdriver

If you have a gas water heater, follow these steps to adjust the temperature:

1. Change the setting on the thermostat control on the water heater's control box by 10 F° (Figure A).

2. After an hour, test the water temperature at the tap with a candy thermometer. Adjust the setting, as necessary.

If you have an electric water heater, follow these steps to adjust the temperature:

1. Turn off the power to the heater at the main panel.

2. Unless your water heater is less than 30 gallons, it probably has an upper and a lower heating element—each controlled by its own thermostat. Using a screwdriver, remove both access panels and pull back the insulation to expose the thermostats.

3. Using the screwdriver, adjust the thermostat controls by 10 F° (Figure B). Turn the power back on and push the red reset buttons.

4. Wait an hour and then test the water temperature at the tap with a candy thermometer.

5. Repeat Steps 3 and 4 until the water is the right temperature. Replace the insulation and access panels.

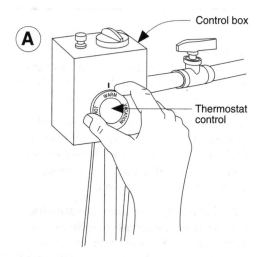

A — Control box / Thermostat control

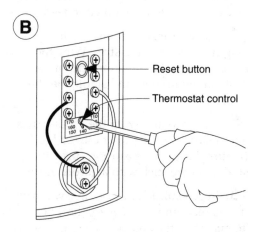

B — Reset button / Thermostat control

REPLACING A WATER HEATER ELEMENT

If you suddenly notice you have less hot water—and you haven't added a teenager to the household—you may have lost a heater element in your electric water heater. Heater elements can be easily replaced, so don't panic and install a new tank!

MATERIALS

- **Replacement water heater element and gasket**
- **Pipe-joint compound**

TOOLS

Garden hose • Screwdriver • Adjustable wrench

1. Determine which element needs replacing: Replace the top element if you get no hot water, the bottom element if you get less hot water than usual.

2. Turn off the water supply valve for the water heater (Figure A) and turn off the power at the main panel.

3. Connect a garden hose to the drain valve at the bottom of the tank and empty the tank into your basement drain. Close the valve and remove the hose.

4. Remove either the top or bottom access panel on the side of the tank and pull back the insulation. Loosen the terminal screws on the heating element. Remove the wires (Figure B).

5. Using an adjustable wrench, remove the element by turning it counterclockwise. If it is bolted in place, remove the bolts first. Purchase a replacement element of the same voltage, wattage, and length.

6. Coat both sides of the new gasket with pipe-joint compound, slide the gasket over the new element, and screw the element into the tank.

7. Turn on the water supply valve, then each of the hot-water faucets in the house until the water runs steadily.

8. Reconnect the wires to the terminals, restore the power, and press the red reset button on the thermostat. Replace the insulation and the access panel.

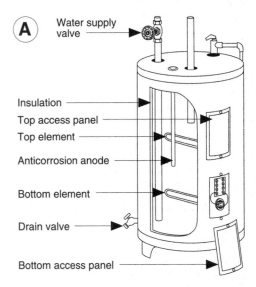

A — Water supply valve

Insulation
Top access panel
Top element
Anticorrosion anode
Bottom element
Drain valve
Bottom access panel

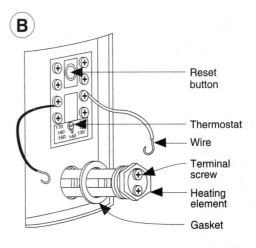

B

Reset button
Thermostat
Wire
Terminal screw
Heating element
Gasket

LIGHTING A GAS WATER HEATER PILOT

If your gas supply is ever totally shut off, the pilot light on your gas water heater will go out and stay out until you relight it. This pilot light is similar to and no more difficult to relight than the pilot light in a gas range. Note that many new gas water heaters have electronic ignitions with no pilot to light. Check your water heater manual.

MATERIALS
Wood match or barbecue lighter

TOOLS
Screwdriver • Flashlight

1. Remove the access panel at the bottom of the tank where the gas lines enter the tank (Figure A).

2. Smell the opening. If you detect a strong odor of gas, call the gas company immediately and go no further.

3. Turn the control knob on the top of the control box to *PILOT* (Figure B).

4. Look into the access opening with a flashlight and identify the pilot light orifice (Figure C).

5. Light a long wood match or barbecue lighter. Holding its flame up to the pilot light orifice, press the reset button on the top of the control box. Hold the reset button down for a full minute after the pilot ignites. If the pilot does stay lit, go to Step 6. If the pilot doesn't stay lit after you release the reset button, call the gas company.

6. Replace the access panel and turn the control knob to *ON*. The main burner should ignite. You can tell if you hear it go "whoosh"; if not, look to see if it ignited. If it doesn't, turn the control knob to *OFF* and call the gas company.

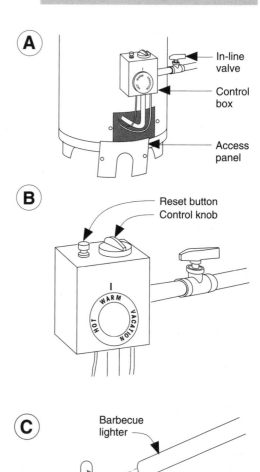

A
- In-line valve
- Control box
- Access panel

B
- Reset button
- Control knob
- WARM
- VACATION
- HOT

C
- Barbecue lighter
- Pilot light orifice

FIXING NOISY WATER PIPES

When a water valve closes too quickly, it can cause the pipes to bang—a condition called water hammer. The valves on clothes washers are the most common causes. The hammering can be prevented either by providing an air cushion inside the pipe or placing a foam-rubber cushion between the pipe and the object the pipe is striking.

MATERIALS
• 2 water hammer shock absorbers
• Foam pipe insulation

TOOLS
Slip-joint pliers • Utility knife

If the pipes bang only when the clothes washer runs, follow these steps:

1. Turn off both water supply valves to the washer.

2. Using slip-joint pliers, remove the supply hose couplings from the valves.

3. Screw a water hammer shock absorber on each of the supply valves, then attach the hoses to the shock absorbers (Figure A).

If the pipes bang even when the clothes washer is off, follow these steps:

1. On the chance that you have air chambers that have lost their air cushions, turn off the main water shutoff valve, which should be next to the water meter. Open all of your faucets until they stop running, then turn off the faucets, and turn the main valve back on.

2. Have a helper turn faucets on and off quickly while you see which pipes, if any, are still banging.

3. If you find an accessible pipe that is banging into a joist, a stud, or another pipe, cut a short length of foam pipe insulation with a utility knife, and slip it over the pipe to cushion the hammering effect (Figure B).

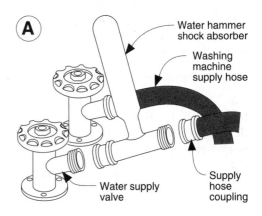

A — Water hammer shock absorber — Washing machine supply hose — Water supply valve — Supply hose coupling

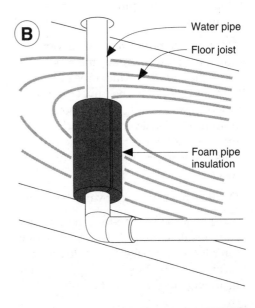

B — Water pipe — Floor joist — Foam pipe insulation

DEFROSTING A FROZEN PIPE

Many homeowners in northern states have experienced frozen pipes. The key to successful recovery is melting the frozen water but not turning it into explosive steam. Work from the open faucet toward the frozen section, and never let the pipe get too hot to touch.

MATERIALS
Duct tape or string

TOOLS
Hair dryer • Bath towel
• Saucepan or teakettle

1. Turn off the main water shutoff valve, which should be next to the water meter (Figure A).

2. Locate the section of frozen pipe.

3. Open the faucet nearest to the frozen section so that any steam you accidentally generate will have an exit and not burst the pipe.

4. Starting at the open faucet, heat the pipe with a hair dryer (Figure B). Hold it 6 inches from the pipe and move it back and forth as if you were spray painting. It is all right to use high heat as long as the pipe remains cool enough to touch. Advance along the pipe at about 1 foot per minute.

5. If you do not have a hair dryer, wrap a bath towel around the pipe and secure the ends with duct tape or string. Pour hot water over the towel (Figure C). As soon as the towel cools to room temperature, slide it several feet and repeat with more hot water until all the ice melts and water runs freely out of the faucet.

6. Turn the main water valve back on.

7. If it looks like pipe-freezing weather again, insulate the pipe (see "Insulating Water Pipes" on page 161) or leave the faucet served by this pipe slightly open. The moving water will not freeze.

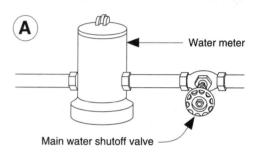

(A) Water meter — Main water shutoff valve

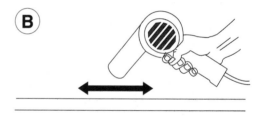

(B)

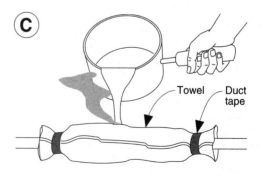

(C) Towel — Duct tape

PATCHING A LEAKING PIPE

The ultimate cure for a leaking pipe is replacement. If replacement is inconvenient at the time, pipes can be patched as if they were bicycle tubes. A good temporary patch may actually last for years.

MATERIALS
- $1/16$"-thick sheet of neoprene or bicycle tube patch
- Sleeve clamp or hose clamp

TOOLS
Tape measure • Flat mill file
• Scissors • Screwdriver

1. Turn off the water supply valve that supplies the pipe or the main water shutoff valve, which should be next to the water meter.

2. Determine whether the leak is through a split or through a pin hole (Figure A). Splits are due to the expansion of freezing water. Pinholes are due to corrosion inside the pipe.

3. Measure the diameter of the pipe. Most pipes will be one of these standard sizes—$3/8$ inch, $1/2$ inch, or $3/4$ inch.

4. Purchase a sheet of $1/16$-inch-thick neoprene or a bicycle tube patch depending on the size of the split or hole. Also, purchase either a sleeve clamp or hose clamp slightly larger than the diameter of the pipe. You may need to use more than one hose clamp on large splits.

5. If the split or hole has a rough edge, file it smooth with a flat mill file.

6. Using scissors, cut a rubber patch about 1 inch square for a pinhole or 1 inch wider and longer than a split.

7. Center the patch over the hole and install the clamp (Figure B). Tighten the clamp as tight as you can.

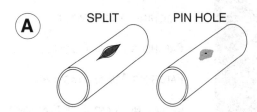

(A) SPLIT   PIN HOLE

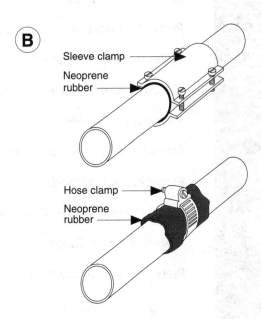

(B) Sleeve clamp
Neoprene rubber

Hose clamp
Neoprene rubber

FINDING A LEAK IN A PITCHED ROOF

By discovering the origin of a leak, you have accomplished the most difficult part of a roof repair. If you have any doubt about going up onto your roof, however, don't! If the roof slope is greater than 30 degrees, get a professional to find the leak.

MATERIALS

- 6d common nail
- String
- Chalk

TOOLS

Flashlight • Permanent marker • Tape measure • Hammer • Bucket • Ladder

1. While it is raining, inspect the entire underside of the attic roof with a powerful flashlight. Look for wetness, particularly at all of the edges—ridge, rakes, and eaves— and around roof penetrations— chimneys, vents, and skylights (Figure A).

2. If you find wetness, trace it as far up slope as you can and then mark the highest point with a permanent marker.

3. Using a tape measure and a helper, measure the horizontal distance, X, and vertical distance, Y, from the mark to the nearest exterior references—chimney, vent, ridge, or eave (Figure A). Make a sketch of the distances and references.

4. In the meantime, intercept the leaking water by driving a 6d common nail partway into the underside of the roof in the path of the water (Figure B). If the nail is placed correctly, the water should run down it and drip to the attic floor. Tie a string to the nail to guide the water into a bucket placed below it.

5. On a dry day, climb to the roof on a sturdy ladder with your sketch and tape measure and mark the location of the leak with chalk.

6. Inspect the roof above the mark. Look for cracked or missing shingles and damaged flashing on either side of the mark to the ridge. Carry out the needed repair, referring to the appropriate project in this chapter.

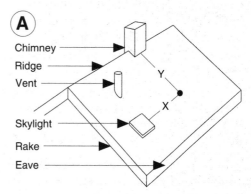

A

Chimney
Ridge
Vent
Y
X
Skylight
Rake
Eave

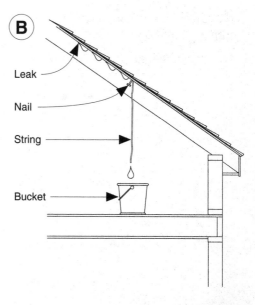

B

Leak
Nail
String
Bucket

REPAIRING AN ASPHALT SHINGLE

Asphalt shingles may come unstuck or torn after years of harsh weather, but they can be easily repaired. Make sure you have a sturdy ladder, and do not work near power lines. If the roof slope is greater than 30 degrees, get a professional to do the job. Great strength and agility are not required; caution, wisdom, and proper tools are.

MATERIALS
- Roofing cement
- Galvanized roofing nails
- Mayonnaise
- Rag

TOOLS
Ladder • Putty knife • Hammer

1. Wait until the sun warms the shingle so that it is very pliable. If the shingle breaks off, you will have to replace it—a more difficult job. (See "Replacing an Asphalt Shingle" on the opposite page.)

2. Carefully and slowly, lift the shingle and apply a layer of roofing cement to the underside with a putty knife (Figure A). If the shingle is torn, apply roofing cement to it on both sides of the tear.

3. Secure the shingle with a single galvanized roofing nail. Then drive three pairs of nails along the tear (Figure B).

4. Cover all the nails and tears with roofing cement (Figure C).

5. Clean the tools with mayonnaise and a rag.

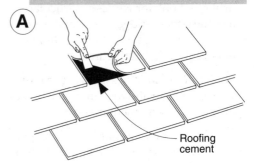

Roofing cement

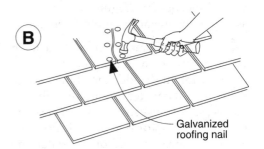

Galvanized roofing nail

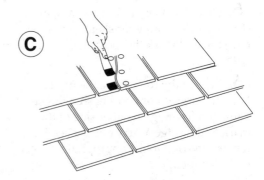

REPLACING AN ASPHALT SHINGLE

After years of wind, rain, and snow, asphalt shingles can become loose or cracked. If only a few of the shingles on your roof are damaged, they can be replaced individually, saving the cost of replacing the whole roof. Replacing asphalt shingles is simple; working on a steep roof is not. Make sure you have a sturdy ladder, and do not work near power lines. If the roof slope is greater than 30 degrees, get a professional to do the job.

MATERIALS
- **Piece of aluminum flashing**
- **Replacement asphalt shingle**
- **Galvanized roofing nails**

TOOLS
Ladder •Pry bar • Long-nose pliers • Utility knife • Hammer

1. If you can, wait for a warm day. Warm asphalt shingles can be bent without cracking. If you need a temporary fix until the weather warms, you can slide a piece of aluminum flashing under the damaged shingle as a temporary fix.

2. Asphalt shingles are fastened with four galvanized roofing nails—one at each end and one above each cutout slot. To access the nails, carefully raise the shingle above the damaged one. Then, using a pry bar, pry the nail out of the damaged shingle (Figure A).

3. After all four nails have been removed, you should be able to slide the shingle out. If not, it is because the top inch of the shingle is caught by the next row of nails. Do not try to remove these nails, but tear out as much of the shingle as you can reach with long-nose pliers.

4. Using a utility knife, cut the top inch and corners off a new shingle (Figure B).

5. Slide the new shingle into place and fasten it with four galvanized roofing nails (Figure B). If the shingle above is stiff and threatens to break, place the pry bar under the shingle and over the nail, and hammer the pry bar to drive the nail home. (Figure C).

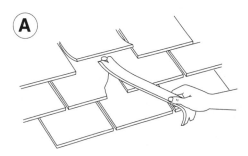

A

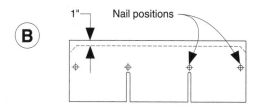

B

1"   Nail positions

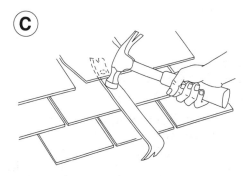

C

REPLACING A WOOD SHINGLE

Wood shingles, whether used as roofing or as siding, are durable and will last for years, but wind and weather will take their toll and cause the wood to split and pit. Luckily, wood shingles are easy to replace. If replacing one on the roof, make sure you have a sturdy ladder, and do not work near power lines. If the roof slope is greater than 30 degrees, get a professional to do the job.

MATERIALS
- Replacement wood shingle
- Galvanized shingle nails

TOOLS
Ladder • Wood chisel • Hammer • Pry bar • Utility knife • Block of wood • Nail set

1. Pull the damaged shingle out from under those above it. If it will not come easily, carefully split it with a wood chisel and a hammer and try again. Keep splitting and pulling until the entire shingle has been removed.

2. Place the flat end of a pry bar over the damaged shingle's nails, which are hidden under the shingle above, and strike the bar with the hammer to drive the old nails flush (Figure A).

3. If you don't have any spares, buy a bundle of matching replacement shingles at a home center. Using a utility knife, cut a new shingle ¼ inch narrower than the gap left by the old shingle.

4. Using a block of wood and the hammer, tap the new shingle into the gap until it protrudes ¼ inch below its row of shingles.

5. Using a nail set and the hammer, drive two nails into the new shingle at a 45-degree angle as close to the butt of the shingle above it as possible (Figure B). Drive the nails flush.

6. Using the block of wood and hammer, drive the butt of the new shingle in until it lines up with its row and the nails disappear under the shingle above (Figure C).

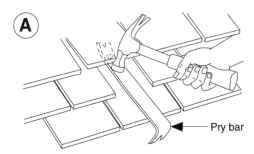

A

Pry bar

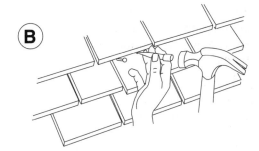

B

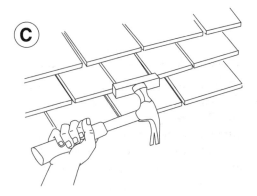

C

PATCHING A FLAT ROOF

Flat roofs are notorious for developing leaks. Fortunately, a flat roof is easy to work on, but wait for a mild day. If the weather is too hot, you may damage the softened roof surface. If it is too cold, you may need to warm the asphalt in a bucket of hot water to make it flow.

MATERIALS
- Roll roofing
- Roofing cement
- Galvanized roofing nails
- Mayonnaise
- Rag

TOOLS
Ladder • Carpenter's square
• Utility knife • Putty knife • Pry bar
• Hammer

1. Using a carpenter's square and a utility knife, cut a rectangular patch of roll roofing large enough to cover the damaged area. Cut on the side without granules to avoid dulling the knife.

2. Lay the patch over the damaged area and use it as a template as you cut through the top layer of damaged roofing (Figure A). Cut carefully; remove only the first 1/8 inch of roofing.

3. Using a putty knife or the flat end of a pry bar, pry up the damaged layer.

4. Using the putty knife, apply a thin layer of roofing cement to the stripped area and 2 inches beyond its perimeter.

5. Press the patch onto the cement.

6. Nail the patch down with galvanized roofing nails every 2 inches along a line 1 inch in from the perimeter (Figure B).

7. Cut a second patch 4 inches wider and longer than the first patch, apply roofing cement to its backside, and press it into place over the first patch.

8. Nail the second patch every 2 inches along a line 1 inch in from the perimeter. Smear roofing cement over each nail head (Figure C).

9. Clean the tools with mayonnaise and a rag.

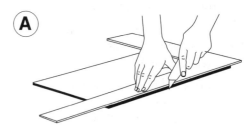

A

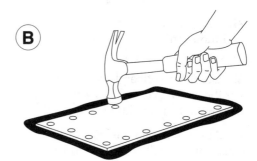

B

C

PATCHING METAL ROOFING

If your metal roof has just a few holes, you can patch it for another five years of life. Patching a metal roof is generally easier than patching either asphalt or wood shingled roofs. Make sure you have a sturdy ladder, and do not work near power lines. If the roof slope is greater than 30 degrees, get a professional to do the job. If you have any doubt about going onto the roof surface, don't!

MATERIALS
- Fiberglass cloth
- Roofing cement
- Mayonnaise
- Rag

TOOLS
Ladder • Hammer • Wire brush • Scissors • Wide putty knife

1. Hammer flat any rough edges in and around the damaged area.

2. Using a wire brush, clean and abrade the surface for 4 inches around the damaged area (Figure A).

3. Purchase fiberglass cloth at an auto-parts store. Using scissors, cut two patches of fiberglass cloth, each large enough to cover the abraded area.

4. Using a wide putty knife, apply a continuous, thin coat of roofing cement to the abraded area (Figure B).

5. Lay the first fiberglass cloth patch over the roofing cement and smooth the patch with the putty knife.

6. Apply a second thin coat of roofing cement over the fiberglass (Figure C).

7. Apply and smooth a second fiberglass cloth patch.

8. Apply a 1/8-inch coat of roofing cement over the second fiberglass cloth patch. Make sure the patch is completely covered.

9. Clean the putty knife with mayonnaise and a rag.

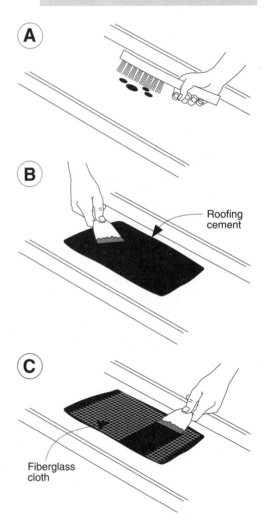

A

B

Roofing cement

C

Fiberglass cloth

PATCHING METAL FLASHING

Aluminum or galvanized steel flashing is used where the roof meets chimneys, vents, skylights, or walls, and where roof sections come together to form valleys. Leaks from these areas may indicate that the flashing has been damaged. If patching the flashing requires going onto the roof, make sure you have a sturdy ladder, and do not work near power lines. If the roof slope is greater than 30 degrees, get a professional to do the job.

1. Sand the flashing clean for several inches around the damaged area using 100-grit sandpaper wrapped around a block of wood (Figure A). Sand just enough to make the flashing bright. If the flashing is made from aluminum and it appears to be corroded, it may be because of a chemical reaction between aluminum flashing and galvanized roofing nails. Using a pry bar, pull the nails, then drive aluminum roofing nails next to each corroded nail hole before sanding.

2. Using metal snips, cut a patch of flashing large enough to extend 2 inches all around the damaged area. Make sure the patch is of the same metal—aluminum or galvanized steel—as the original flashing.

3. Bend the flashing patch to conform to the shape of the original flashing.

4. Using a putty knife, apply a 1/8-inch-thick coating of roofing cement to the damaged flashing.

5. Press the patch onto the cement and apply a top coat of roofing cement over the patch. Smooth it with the putty knife (Figure B).

6. Clean the putty knife with mayonnaise and a rag.

MATERIALS

- 100-grit sandpaper
- Roofing nails of same material as flashing
- Flashing to match original
- 100-grit sandpaper
- Roofing cement
- Mayonnaise
- Rag

TOOLS

Ladder • Block of wood • Hammer • Pry bar • Metal snips • Putty knife

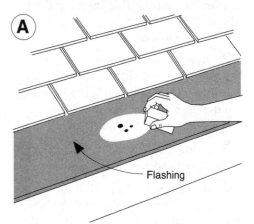

Flashing

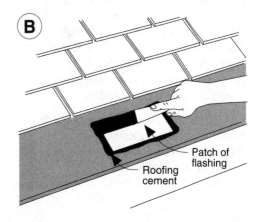

Patch of flashing

Roofing cement

REPLACING VENT-PIPE FLASHING

In the old days, vent-pipe flashings consisted of sheet lead pounded down around the pipe opening. Modern flashings incorporate a neoprene boot that stretches over the pipe and accommodates a wide range of pipe sizes and roof slopes. Make sure you have a sturdy ladder, and do not work near power lines. If the roof slope is greater than 30 degrees, get a professional to do the job.

MATERIALS

- Neoprene and aluminum vent flashing
- Aluminum roofing nails
- Roofing cement
- Mayonnaise
- Rag

TOOLS

Ladder • Pry bar • Hammer • Putty knife

1. Using a pry bar, carefully pry up the shingle tabs covering the top and sides of the old flashing to expose the nails securing the flashing (Figure A). If the tabs are stuck with adhesive, use a putty knife to pry them loose.

2. To pull the nails that hold the flashing, hammer the flat end of the pry bar under the flashing (Figure B) and pry up the flashing and the nails together. Then pull the old flashing out.

3. Using the putty knife and hammer, chip any old adhesive off the vent pipe.

4. Buy neoprene and aluminum vent flashing at a home center. Pull the new flashing part way down over the vent pipe. Bend the shingles back and slide the flashing under their tabs, one side at a time (Figure C). If the side shingles are narrow or damaged, remove and replace them. (See "Replacing an Asphalt Shingle" on page 239 or "Replacing a Wood Shingle" on page 240.)

5. When the flashing is in place, bend back the side shingles and secure the flashing with one aluminum roofing nail 1 inch in from each edge (Figure D).

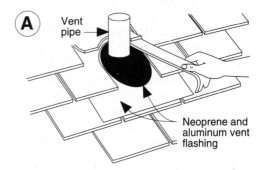

A   Vent pipe

Neoprene and aluminum vent flashing

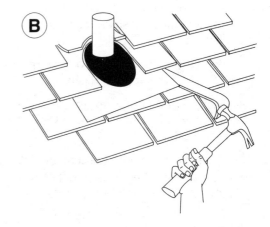

B

6. Press the shingles down and mark the edges on the flashing with a pencil.

7. Using the putty knife, apply ⅛ inch of roofing cement to the flashing behind the pencil lines (Figure E). Press the shingles into the cement.

8. Clean the tools with mayonnaise and a rag.

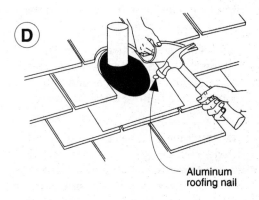

Aluminum
roofing nail

SEALING A GUTTER JOINT

Leaky gutter joints defeat the whole purpose of gutters, which is to control the path that rainwater takes to the ground around your house. Sealing gutter joints is easy using modern silicone sealants. Silicone sealants are truly amazing, and the manufacturers' claims really are true—they do last 20 years! The key to success is preparing the surface.

MATERIALS
- Window cleaner
- Tube of clear silicone sealant

TOOLS
Ladder • Bucket • Toothbrush
• Utility knife • Screwdriver or nail

1. From the roof or a sturdy ladder, pour a bucket of water into the gutter at its highest point. Watch the gutter joints from below for dripping water to determine which joints are leaking.

2. Clean away the debris from the leaking joint, then scrub the joint inside and out with window cleaner and a toothbrush to remove dirt and grease (Figure A).

3. After the joint has thoroughly dried—including on the inside—cut the tip of a tube of clear silicone sealant to an inside diameter of $1/8$ inch, using a utility knife. Using the tip of a screwdriver or a long nail, puncture the inner seal, if there is one.

4. Squeeze sealant into the joint between the gutter sections and the gutter connector. Apply sealant both inside and outside the gutter (Figure B).

5. Smooth the sealant with a wet forefinger.

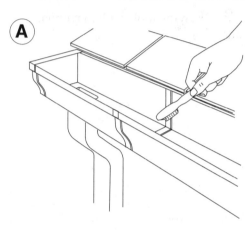

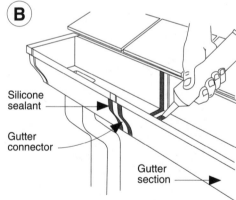

Silicone sealant

Gutter connector

Gutter section

PATCHING A HOLE IN A METAL GUTTER

Metal gutters always seem to develop holes in the most inconvenient spots, and they often keep dripping long after the rain has stopped. By patching a few annoying holes, you can probably put off replacing the whole gutter for a good five years.

MATERIALS

- 100-grit sandpaper
- Roofing cement
- Compatible metal flashing
- Mayonnaise
- Rag

TOOLS

Ladder • Bucket • Garden hose
• Stiff brush • Putty knife
• Metal snips

1. From the roof or a sturdy ladder, pour a bucket of water into the gutter at its highest point. Look from below for water dripping from holes.

2. To repair a hole, first use water from a garden hose and a stiff brush to clean trapped debris from the gutter.

3. Using 100-grit sandpaper, scour the inside of the gutter around the hole.

4. If the hole is no larger than a nail hole, simply dab roofing cement over the hole and smooth the cement with a putty knife (Figure A). But, if the hole is larger than a nail hole, cut a patch of metal flashing 4 inches longer and wider than the hole using metal snips. Cut the patch of the same type of metal.

5. Bend the patch to match the shape of the gutter. If the gutter has a rounded bottom, find a bottle that approximately matches the radius of the gutter and bend the flashing around it (Figure B).

6. Using a putty knife, apply a ⅛-inch coating of roofing cement to the underside of the patch and press it into place (Figure C). Smooth the cement that squeezes out with your finger.

7. Clean the putty knife with mayonnaise and a rag.

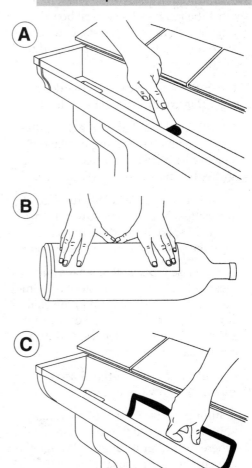

FIXING A SAGGING GUTTER

If you notice water dripping from a gutter hours after the rain has stopped, chances are good that the leak is from water that is gathering at a low spot. The low point can be easily eliminated by leveling the gutter and adding one or more supports to it. This repair is ten times easier with a helper on a second ladder than going it alone.

Determine the type of hanger by which your gutter is attached. Then, using two ladders and a helper, snap a chalk line against the fascia—the vertical board against which the gutter rests. Extend the line from the gutter's downspout end to its highest end (Figure A).

If the gutter has a sleeve-and-spike-type hanger (Figure B), follow these steps:

1. Pull out the spikes where the gutter is sagging by hammering the flat end of a pry bar between the fascia and the gutter behind the sleeve (Figure C).

2. Drill a new spike hole in the face of the gutter about 2 inches away from each old spike hole. Make the new hole the same diameter as the old ones.

3. Purchase replacement spikes and sleeves from a hardware store or home center. Hold the gutter up to the chalk line and drive the new spikes through the spike holes and sleeves, and into the fascia with the hammer.

If the gutter has a strap-type hanger (Figure D), follow these steps:

1. Lift up the front edge of the house shingles to expose the strap hangers where the gutter is sagging. Wedge the flat end of the pry bar under each strap hanger and pry out the nails.

MATERIALS

- **Replacement spikes and sleeves**
- **Galvanized roofing nails**
- **6d galvanized common nails**
- **Picture-hanging wire**
- **Replacement brackets and bracket clamps**

TOOLS

Ladders • Chalk line • Hammer • Pry bar • Drill and bit

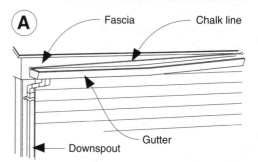

(A) Fascia — Chalk line — Downspout — Gutter

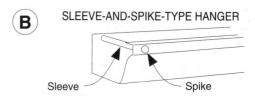

(B) SLEEVE-AND-SPIKE-TYPE HANGER — Sleeve — Spike

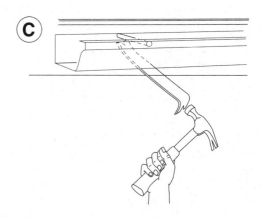

(C)

2. Have your helper hold the gutter even with the chalk line as you pull the straps tight and refasten them with new galvanized roofing nails (Figure E).

If the gutter has a bracket-type hanger (Figure F), follow these steps:

1. Compress each bracket and remove the bracket clamps.

2. Drive a 6d galvanized common nail partway into the fascia just below each bracket. Tie the end of a 3-foot length of picture-hanging wire to each nail.

3. Lift the gutter out of the brackets and suspend it by looping the picture hanging wire around the gutter and tying the loose end to the nail.

4. Pry the old brackets off the fascia with a pry bar (Figure G).

5. Purchase replacement brackets and clamps at a home center, and align them with the chalk line. Fasten the new brackets with 6d galvanized nails.

6. Untie the picture hanging wire that is suspending the gutter, and insert the gutter into the new brackets. Compress each bracket slightly and attach the bracket clamps.

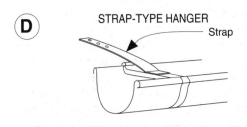

D STRAP-TYPE HANGER
Strap

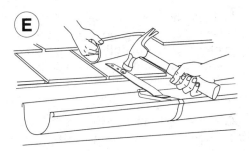

E

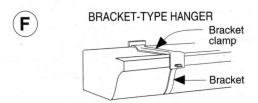

F BRACKET-TYPE HANGER
Bracket clamp
Bracket

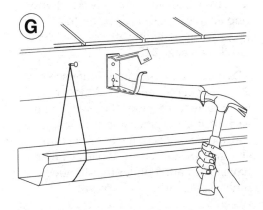

G

CLEANING AND COVERING GUTTERS

Gutters are designed to collect and dispose of water from the roof before it can run down the wall or splash dirt against the base of the wall. But a gutter clogged with leaves is worse than no gutter at all. Clean out your gutters yearly or cover them with gutter screens. Gutter screens, which snap into place over the gutter, eliminate the annual chore of cleaning out rotted leaves.

MATERIALS
Aluminum gutter screens

TOOLS
Ladder • Hand brush • Stiff brush • Plastic spatula • Garden hose • Metal snips

1. From the roof or a sturdy ladder, use a hand brush to remove the leaves and other debris out of the gutter, then use a stiff brush and a plastic spatula to loosen and remove the heavier deposits (Figure A).

2. Using a garden hose, wash down the inside of the gutter (Figure B).

3. If the downspout is clogged, turn the nozzle to create a forceful jet and feed the nozzle end down the spout until the water runs clean out of the bottom. For stubborn clogs, it may be necessary to have a helper shake the downspout or bang on it with a broom as you run water through it to loosen the debris.

4. After the gutter is completely clean, look from beneath for any leaks. If you find any, see "Sealing a Gutter Joint" on page 246 or "Patching a Hole in a Metal Gutter" on page 247.

5. Purchase aluminum gutter screens at a home center and install them over all open sections of gutter (Figure C). Slide each section of screen about 1 inch under the bottom edges of the bottom course of shingles. (Some screens have tabs that have to be nailed under the shingles; other screens are merely trapped between the gutter edge and the first course of shingles.)

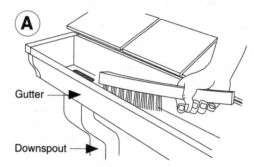

A

Gutter →

Downspout →

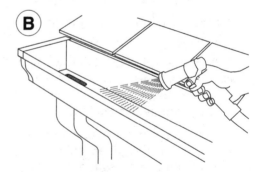

B

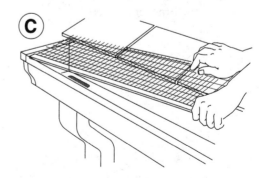

C

REPLACING A DOWNSPOUT

Gutter and downspout parts are readily available in several styles at home centers. When replacing a damaged downspout, make sure the gutter parts and the fasteners are compatible.

MATERIALS
- **Replacement gutter parts**
- **#4 × ¹/₄" self-tapping aluminum screws**

TOOLS
Ladder • Drill and pilot bit • Screwdriver • Tape measure • Metal snips • Hacksaw

1. From a sturdy ladder, slip the first elbow over the drop leader. Then, drill two ¹/₁₆-inch pilot holes through the joint. Attach the #4 × ¹/₄-inch self-tapping aluminum screws.

2. Hold the second elbow against the wall, moving it until it aligns with the first elbow. Measure the distance between the two and add 3 inches. Using metal snips for a metal gutter or a hacksaw for a plastic gutter, cut the leader to that length.

3. From the ladder, place the leader over the first elbow and place the second elbow over the leader. Adjust the fit, then mark the joints with a pencil.

4. Unscrew the first elbow from the drop leader. On the ground, attach the elbows to the leader. Drill two ¹/₁₆-inch pilot holes per joint. Screw the joints together.

5. From the ladder, fasten the assembly to the drop leader with the two screws and strap the second elbow to the wall.

6. Fit together the bottom elbow and downspout, drill pilot holes, and screw them together.

7. Shim the bottom elbow up so it is just above the splash block, hold the downspout against the second elbow and mark the downspout 1¹/₂ inches above the bottom of the second elbow.

8. Cut the downspout, drill pilot holes, and screw it to the second elbow with two screws. Fasten it to the wall with straps.

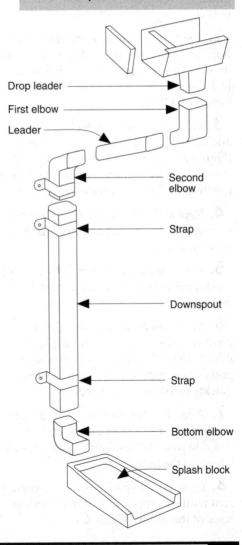

Drop leader

First elbow

Leader

Second elbow

Strap

Downspout

Strap

Bottom elbow

Splash block

REPAIRING A DENT IN ALUMINUM SIDING

Aluminum siding may eliminate the seemingly endless chore of house painting, but it is vulnerable to denting. If you live near a ball field or golf course, you need to know how to fill dents. Who knows? With practice, this may lead to a career in auto-body work!

MATERIALS
- #6 self-tapping screw
- 120-grit sandpaper
- 2-part auto-body filler
- Color-matched enamel paint

TOOLS
Drill with 1/8" bit • Screwdriver
- Locking pliers • Carpenter's square
- Wide putty knife • Block of wood
- Paint pad

1. Sighting along the siding at a low, grazing angle, outline the dent with a pencil.

2. Using a drill and 1/8-inch bit, drill a hole at the deepest point of the dent, and drive a #6 self-tapping screw halfway into the hole but not into the wood behind the siding.

3. Grip the screw with locking pliers and carefully pull the dent toward you (Figure A). Do not pull the dent beyond the plane of the undamaged siding. Check it with the edge of a carpenter's square.

4. Repeat Steps 2 and 3 as necessary to pull the dent approximately flush, then remove the screw.

5. Sand the damaged area with 120-grit sandpaper until the bare aluminum is exposed.

6. Mix two-part auto-body filler according to the directions, and apply the filler to the area of the dent with a wide putty knife (Figure B). Smooth the area quickly before the filler hardens.

7. After the filler hardens, use 120-grit sandpaper wrapped around a block of wood to smooth the edges and any irregularities in the filler.

8. Using a paint pad, paint the repaired area with enamel paint that matches the color of the siding (Figure C).

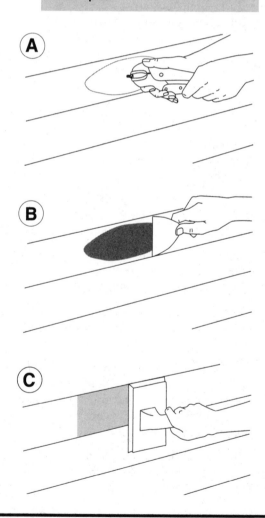

REPLACING ALUMINUM SIDING

Don't panic! I don't mean replacing all of your siding or even a whole strip—just an itty-bitty piece. You can easily make a patch to replace punctured or torn aluminum siding. Think of the operation as cutting and pasting paper. With a new blade in your utility knife, cutting aluminum siding is not much more difficult than cutting paper.

MATERIALS
- Matching piece of siding
- Household cleaner
- Tube of clear silicone sealant
- Masking tape

TOOLS
Utility knife • Carpenter's square • Stiff brush • Screwdriver or nail

1. Using a sharp utility knife, cut a rectangle around the damaged area, guiding the utility knife against the edge of a carpenter's square as you cut (Figure A). Bend the damaged section down and finish cutting the bottom edge.

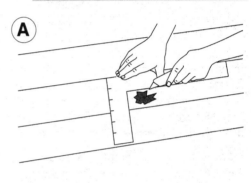

A

2. If you haven't saved a piece of siding from the original installation, buy a replacement section at a home center. Use the carpenter's square and utility knife to cut a patch from a matching piece of siding. The patch should be 3 inches longer than the cutout in the siding. Cut off the nailing strip from the top edge of the patch (Figure B).

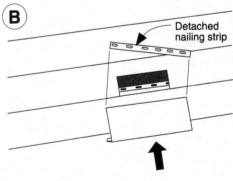

B

Detached nailing strip

3. Scrub the area around the cutout and the back side of the patch with a stiff brush and household cleaner. Let the siding dry.

4. Using the utility knife, cut the tip of a tube of clear silicone sealant to an inside diameter of 1/8 inch. Puncture the inner seal, if there is one, with a screwdriver or long nail. Apply a bead of the sealant around the perimeter of the back side of the patch and press it into place with its top edge under the siding above and its bottom edge locked onto the bottom of the siding on either side of the cutout.

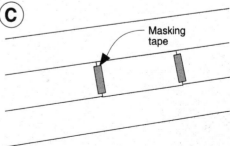

C

Masking tape

5. Tape the side edges of the patch with masking tape for one hour while the sealant cures (Figure C).

FIXING POPPED NAILS IN CLAPBOARD SIDING

Nails pop up from clapboard siding when the substrate—either framing or sheathing—dries and shrinks away from the nail head. Other than making sure the framing and sheathing is perfectly dry before nailing, the cure is to drive new, longer nails into the old holes and touch up the paint.

MATERIALS
- Galvanized siding nails
- Wood putty
- White shellac primer
- Matching house paint

TOOLS
Pry bar • Hammer • Nail set
• Putty knife • 1-inch paintbrush

1. Pull out the popped nails with the hooked end of a pry bar (Figure A).

2. Using a hammer, drive new galvanized siding nails that are $1/2$ inch longer than the originals into the same nail holes. If the original nails were set below the surface of the siding and puttied over, set the new nails with a nail set (Figure B) and fill the holes with wood putty. If not, just drive the nail heads flush with the siding.

3. Using a 1-inch paintbrush, paint over the new nails with white shellac primer (Figure C).

4. When the primer dries, paint over the primed spots with matching house paint.

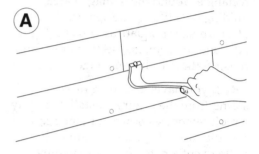

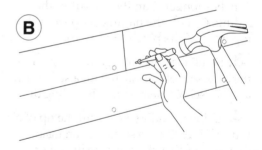

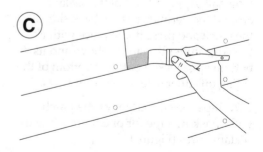

REPAIRING A SPLIT CLAPBOARD

Most old houses with clapboard siding have a few split ends. Using a truly waterproof glue and a little care, a split can be made invisible to the casual observer. To make the split even less visible, smooth it with acrylic latex caulk before painting. Do not use a silicone sealant or caulk because most silicones do not hold paint well.

MATERIALS

- Waterproof glue
- 6d galvanized nails
- Clean rag
- Cartridge of acrylic latex caulk
- Matching house paint

TOOLS

Screwdriver • Plastic gluing syringe • Hammer • Utility knife • Screwdriver or nail • Caulking gun • Paintbrush

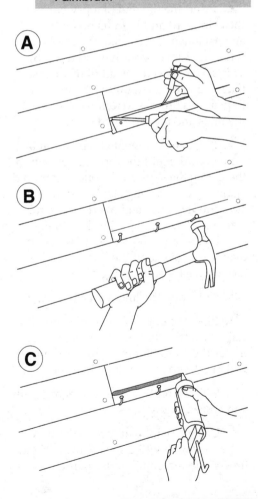

1. Insert a small screwdriver into the open end of the crack and twist to open the crack to about ⅛ inch.

2. With the crack wedged open, use a plastic gluing syringe to squeeze waterproof glue deep into the crack as far along as the glue will penetrate (Figure A).

3. Remove the screwdriver, and push the crack together. Using a hammer, nail 6d galvanized nails every 6 inches as tight against the bottom of the clapboard as possible.

4. Tap and bend the nail ends upward so that they hold the crack tightly closed (Figure B). Wipe up the excess glue immediately with a clean rag.

5. After 24 hours, remove the nails with the claw end of the hammer.

6. Using a utility knife, cut the tip off a cartridge of acrylic latex caulk to an inside diameter of ⅛ inch. Puncture the inner seal, if there is one, with a screwdriver or long nail. Load the caulk into a caulking gun. (See "Caulking Building Cracks" on page 159.) Squeeze out a ⅛-inch bead of caulk along the crack (Figure C), and spread and smooth it with a moistened forefinger.

7. After 24 hours, paint the crack to match the siding.

REPLACING A CLAPBOARD

A damaged clapboard can be replaced easily but before doing so, make sure it doesn't simply need renailing (see "Fixing Popped Nails in Clapboard Siding" on page 254) or gluing (see "Repairing a Split Clapboard" on page 255).

MATERIALS

- Replacement clapboard
- Galvanized siding nails
- White shellac primer
- Matching house paint

TOOLS

Screwdriver • Pry bar • Hammer • Try square • Backsaw • Paint pad

1. Insert a large screwdriver under the damaged clapboard and next to each nail, and pry the edge of the clapboard up ¼ inch (Figure A).

2. Insert the flat end of a pry bar under the clapboard and hold its notch hard against a nail. Then strike the clapboard with the palm of your hand (Figure B). This should pop the head of the nail so that it can be pulled out with the pry bar. Repeat this process to remove the rest of the nails and the damaged clapboard.

3. Buy a replacement clapboard at a lumberyard. Hold the replacement up to the gap in the siding with one end butted against the bordering clapboard at one side and the other end overlapping the clapboard on the opposite side. Make a pencil line on the replacement where it overlaps and extend the line across its face with a try square (Figure C).

4. Cut along the line with a backsaw.

5. Push the edge of the replacement clapboard (the thin edge if it is beveled) under the bottom of the clapboard above, and tap it into place with a hammer.

6. Nail the replacement clapboard with galvanized siding nails.

7. Using a paint pad, prime the new clapboard with white shellac primer and finish with matching house paint.

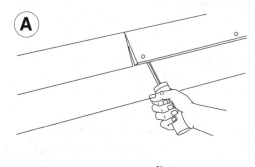

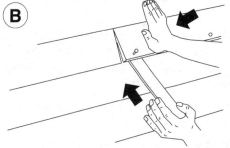

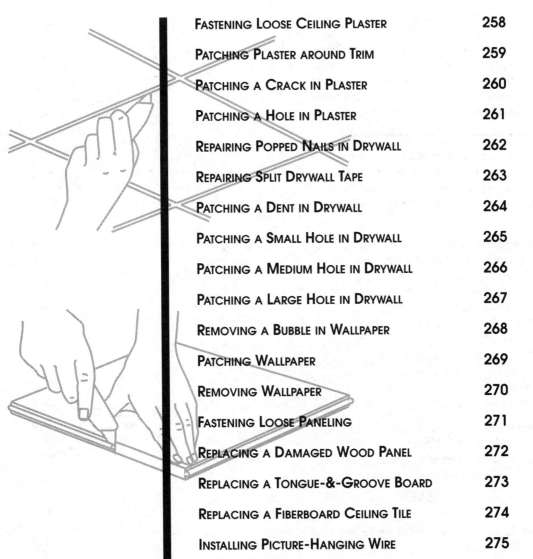

FASTENING LOOSE CEILING PLASTER

Older homes often suffer from drooping plaster ceilings. If the entire ceiling looks like it might come down, let it! Then have a new drywall ceiling installed in its place. If the plaster is sagging in just a small area, however, you can save major inconvenience and money by tucking it up with plaster buttons, available at the hardware store.

1. Using a crosscut saw, cut one 2-foot length and one 4-foot length from a 2 × 4. Nail the two pieces together with a single 10d common nail to form a T that swivels (Figure A).

2. Starting at the perimeter of the ceiling and working toward the area of maximum sag, have a helper press the T up against the loose plaster, while you screw plaster buttons up against the ceiling (Figure B). Install a plaster button every 4 inches in a grid pattern within the area of the sag. If a screw misses the lath above, move it 1/2 inch and try again. The screws should be tight enough to just draw the buttons flush with the ceiling.

3. When the entire loose area has been secured, sand loose paint from the ceiling with 150-grit sandpaper wrapped around a block of wood, and apply drywall joint compound over each button with a wide putty knife.

4. After the first coat of compound has dried, sand it to remove bumps or ridges.

5. Apply a thin finish coat of joint compound over the entire area with a 10-inch drywall knife (Figure C).

6. After 24 hours, lightly sand the finish coat of joint compound smooth and paint the ceiling. (See "Painting a Ceiling" on page 277.)

MATERIALS

- 2 × 4
- 10d common nail
- Plaster buttons
- Drywall screws
- Drywall joint compound
- 150-grit sandpaper

TOOLS

Crosscut saw • Hammer • Screwdriver • Wide putty knife • Block of wood • 10" drywall knife

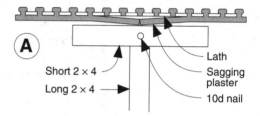

A — Short 2 × 4, Long 2 × 4, Lath, Sagging plaster, 10d nail

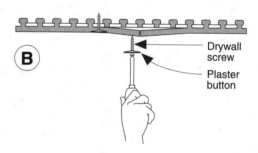

B — Drywall screw, Plaster button

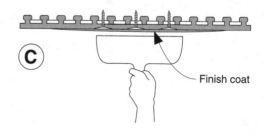

C — Finish coat

PATCHING PLASTER AROUND TRIM

As houses settle, the plaster around doors and windows often cracks. If your house is old, chances are good that there is at least one door or window with cracked plaster around its trim. You should repair any cracks before repainting.

1. Using a cold chisel and a hammer, carefully chip away all the cracked plaster up to the door or window casing. Try to not loosen any plaster that is still sound.

2. Using a utility knife, undercut the edge of the plaster beneath the inside casing and at the edge of the sound plaster (Figure A). Dampen the exposed plaster lath—whether wood, metal, or gypsum—with a wet sponge.

3. Mix patching plaster in a bucket to the consistency of soft ice cream, and apply it to the lath with a putty knife (Figure B). Work the plaster under the casing and the undercut plaster. The surface of this layer should be 1/4 inch below the finished surface of the wall.

4. As the plaster hardens, scratch its surface with a dinner fork.

5. After 24 hours, dampen the first coat of plaster. Mix a second batch of plaster and apply a second coat so that it comes to just below the finished surface. Again, make scratches in the wet plaster.

6. After another 24 hours, apply drywall joint compound with a 10-inch drywall knife and smooth it into the surrounding wall (Figure C).

7. After 24 hours, sand it smooth with 150-grit sandpaper wrapped around a block of wood. Paint the wall. (See "Painting an Interior Wall" on page 276.)

MATERIALS

- Patching plaster
- Drywall joint compound
- 150-grit sandpaper

TOOLS

Cold chisel • Hammer • Utility knife • Sponge • Bucket • Putty knife • Dinner fork • 10" drywall knife • Block of wood

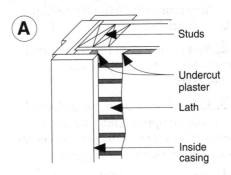

(A) Studs — Undercut plaster — Lath — Inside casing

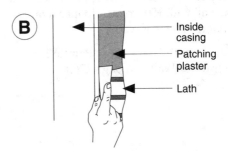

(B) Inside casing — Patching plaster — Lath

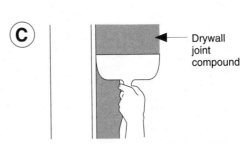

(C) Drywall joint compound

PATCHING A CRACK IN PLASTER

I'd like to tell you that this repair is permanent, but it probably isn't. Cracks in plaster walls are usually a sign that the building is settling. The settling will probably continue, and so will the cracking. Luckily, patching a crack is simple. It should be done before you paint the wall.

MATERIALS
- Drywall joint compound
- 150-grit sandpaper

TOOLS
Utility knife • Artist's brush
• Wide putty knife • Block of wood

1. Use a utility knife to remove any loose plaster from the crack. Undercut the edges of the crack slightly (Figure A). The undercut edges will help hold the plaster patch in place when it dries.

2. Wet the inside of the crack with an artist's brush that has been dipped in water (Figure B).

3. Using a wide putty knife, force dry-wall joint compound into the crack. Remove the excess with long, sweeping passes of the putty knife (Figure C).

4. After 24 hours, lightly sand the joint compound smooth and blend its edges into the wall with 150-grit sandpaper wrapped around a block of wood.

5. Paint the wall. (See "Painting an Interior Wall" on page 276.)

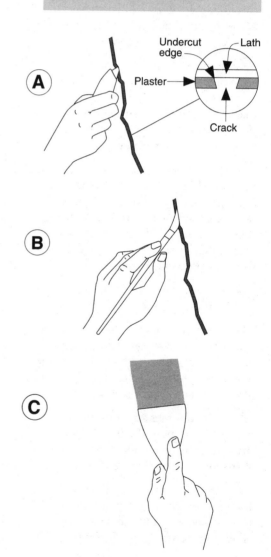

A — Undercut edge — Lath — Plaster — Crack

B

C

PATCHING A HOLE IN PLASTER

I won't ask how you got a hole in your plaster wall, but I will tell you how to fix it so that no one will ever know. Don't start this repair if you're leaving town tomorrow. The procedure involves several small steps spaced over a three-day period.

1. Using a cold chisel and a hammer, carefully chip away any loose plaster.

2. Using a utility knife, undercut the perimeter of the hole (Figure A).

3. Dampen the lath—whether wood, metal, or gypsum—with a wet sponge.

4. Mix patching plaster in a bucket. Using a wide putty knife, apply the patching plaster to within 1/4 inch of the finished wall surface (Figure B). As the plaster hardens, scratch its surface lightly with a dinner fork.

5. After 24 hours, mix a second batch of patching plaster.

6. Dampen the first coat of plaster. Apply a second coat of plaster with the wide putty knife, then level the plaster with the edge of a carpenter's square (Figure C).

7. After another 24 hours, sand down any plaster sticking to the adjacent wall, then spread a finish coat of drywall compound over the patch with a 10-inch drywall knife. Smooth the edges of the compound onto the surrounding wall.

8. After 24 hours, smooth the compound with 150-grit sandpaper wrapped around a block of wood, and paint the patch to match the wall.

MATERIALS
- **Patching plaster**
- **Drywall joint compound**
- **150-grit sandpaper**
- **Matching wall paint**

TOOLS
Cold chisel • Hammer • Utility knife • Sponge • Bucket • Wide putty knife • Dinner fork • Carpenter's square • 10" drywall knife • Block of wood • Paintbrush

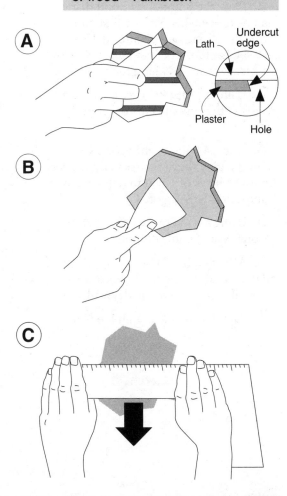

Ⓐ Lath / Undercut edge / Plaster / Hole

Ⓑ

Ⓒ

REPAIRING POPPED NAILS IN DRYWALL

Popped nails are common in new homes. If a builder uses unseasoned studs or furring strips behind drywall, the wood can shrink away from the nail as it dries, causing the nail head to pop out. The cure is simply to wait for the wood to dry, re-nail, and then cover the nail heads with drywall joint compound.

MATERIALS
- Drywall nails
- Drywall joint compound
- 150-grit sandpaper
- Matching wall paint

TOOLS
Hammer • Nail set • Putty knife
• Block of wood • Wide putty knife
• Paintbrush

1. Tap the popped nail flush with the drywall surface with a hammer.

2. Place the point of a second drywall nail next to the head of the first nail and drive the second nail (Figure A). Using a nail set, hammer both nails just below the surface without breaking the paper.

3. Using a putty knife, cover the nail heads with drywall joint compound (Figure B).

4. After 24 hours, lightly sand the compound with 150-grit sandpaper wrapped around a block of wood to remove any bumps or ridges (Figure C).

5. Using a wide putty knife, apply a second coat of joint compound.

6. After another 24 hours, lightly sand again. Avoid raising the fibers of the drywall paper face of the drywall.

7. Paint the area to match the wall.

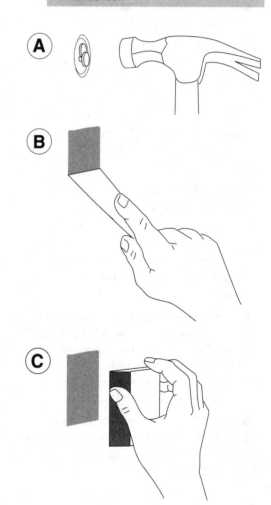

(A)

(B)

(C)

REPAIRING SPLIT DRYWALL TAPE

Drywall tape that has become wet due to a water leak will often shrink and split upon drying. The shrinking tape can cause the drywall joint compound over it to crack. First find and fix the source of the leak that caused the trouble, and then repair the split tape and cracked joint compound as shown below. Always fix the leak first, or you'll be repairing the wall over and over again.

MATERIALS
- Drywall joint compound
- Paper drywall tape
- 150-grit sandpaper
- Matching wall paint

TOOLS
Utility knife • Wide putty knife
- Block of wood • 6" drywall knife
- 10" drywall knife • Paintbrush

1. Using a sharp utility knife, carefully remove all of the loose tape around the split (Figure A). Do not remove tape that is attached soundly or you may damage the paper surface of the drywall.

2. With a wide putty knife, apply a thin, 4-inch-wide layer of drywall joint compound over the crack, extending 2 inches above and below it.

3. Lay 2-inch-wide paper drywall tape into the joint compound and force it into the compound by pulling the wide putty knife over it (Figure B). Remove the excess compound that squeezes out with the putty knife.

4. After 24 hours, lightly sand the compound using 150-grit sandpaper wrapped around a block of wood. Be careful not to raise the fibers of the paper tape.

5. Using a 6-inch drywall knife, apply a second coat of compound.

6. After another 24 hours, lightly sand again, then apply a final coat of joint compound with a 10-inch drywall knife.

7. After 24 hours, lightly sand the compound a final time, and paint the area to match the wall.

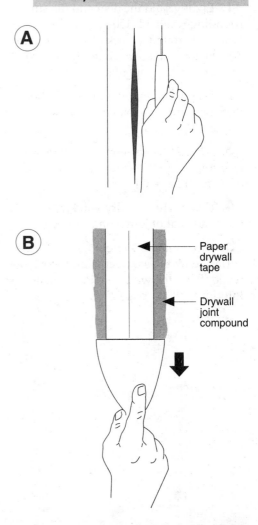

A

B

Paper drywall tape

Drywall joint compound

PATCHING A DENT IN DRYWALL

Paint can never hide dents in drywall and, since repairing dents is easy, there is no excuse not to do it before repainting the wall. An hour's worth of patching will save you from looking at imperfections in your wall year after year. If the dent is due to a door handle striking the wall, install a door stop on the door or on the wall to prevent further damage.

MATERIALS

- 150-grit sandpaper
- Drywall joint compound

TOOLS

Block of wood • Wide putty knife
• 10" drywall knife

1. Lightly sand the dent and the surrounding wall with 150-grit sandpaper wrapped around a block of wood (Figure A). Do not sand so much that you raise the fibers of the paper face on the drywall.

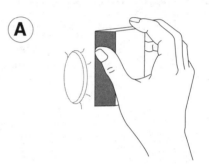

(A)

2. Using a wide putty knife, fill the dent with drywall joint compound (Figure B).

3. After 24 hours, remove any ridges or bumps with the sandpaper and block of wood (Figure C).

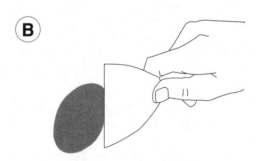

(B)

4. Using a 10-inch drywall knife, apply a second coat of joint compound.

5. After another 24 hours, smooth the surface with the sandpaper and block of wood. Paint the wall (see "Painting an Interior Wall" on page 276).

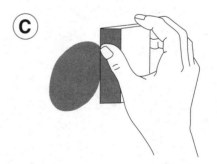

(C)

PATCHING A SMALL HOLE IN DRYWALL

To patch a small hole that penetrates all the way through drywall, you need to give the drywall joint compound support in the form of fiberglass drywall tape. The tape is buried in the compound and prevents it from cracking. You can also use perforated paper drywall tape, if you wish. If the drywall is simply dented, see "Patching a Dent in Drywall" on the opposite page.

MATERIALS
- Fiberglass drywall tape
- Drywall joint compound
- 150-grit sandpaper
- Matching wall paint

TOOLS
Utility knife • Wide putty knife
• Block of wood • 6" drywall knife
• 10" drywall knife • Paintbrush

1. Using a utility knife, trim away any torn paper edges that stick out of the hole.

2. Cut two 4-inch lengths of fiberglass drywall tape with the utility knife, and apply the tape over the hole in a criss-cross fashion (Figure A).

3. Apply a thin coat of drywall joint compound to the tape and to the surrounding wall with a wide putty knife (Figure B). The tape may show through the compound on this first pass.

4. After 24 hours, sand away any ridges or bumps—but not the fiberglass tape—with 150-grit sandpaper wrapped around a block of wood. Apply a second coat of compound with a 6-inch drywall knife.

5. After another 24 hours, sand the compound until it is smooth, and apply a final coat of compound with a 10-inch drywall knife (Figure C). Make sure the fiberglass tape is covered, and smooth the compound's edges to make the wall appear to be flat.

6. After 24 hours, lightly sand the compound a final time and paint the patch to match the wall.

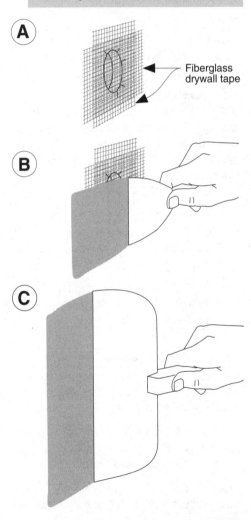

(A) Fiberglass drywall tape

(B)

(C)

PATCHING A MEDIUM HOLE IN DRYWALL

If the hole in drywall is larger than a half dollar, the simplest repair is to install a drywall plug of the same thickness. The plug reduces the gap the patching compound is required to bridge and reduces the likelihood of subsequent cracking.

1. Using a pencil and a carpenter's square, draw a rectangle around the hole, and drill ½-inch holes in each corner. Using a keyhole saw, cut out the rectangle (Figure A).

2. Cut two lengths of a 1 × 3 furring strip, each 3 inches longer than the width of the hole, with the keyhole saw.

3. Insert the furring strip through the hole and, while holding it in place, drive drywall screws through the drywall and into the furring strip (Figure B). The screw heads should lie flush with the drywall but shouldn't break through the paper. Do the same with the second strip.

4. Using a utility knife, cut a drywall patch to fit the hole, and secure the patch with a single drywall screw into each furring strip (Figure B).

5. Apply fiberglass drywall tape over the patch, then apply joint compound over the tape and surrounding wall with a wide putty knife (Figure C).

6. After 24 hours, smooth the patch with 150-grit sandpaper wrapped around a block of wood, and apply a second coat of compound with a 6-inch drywall knife.

7. After another 24 hours, sand again and apply a final coat of joint compound with a 10-inch drywall knife.

8. After 24 hours, lightly sand a final time and paint the patch to match the wall.

MATERIALS

- 1 × 3 furring strip
- Drywall screws
- Scrap of wallboard
- Fiberglass drywall tape
- Drywall joint compound
- 150-grit sandpaper
- Matching wall paint

TOOLS

Carpenter's square • Drill with ½" bit • Keyhole saw • Screwdriver • Block of wood • Utility knife • Wide putty knife • 6" drywall knife • 10" drywall knife • Paintbrush

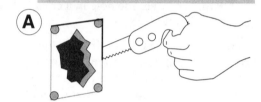

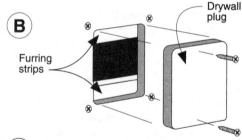

Drywall plug

Furring strips

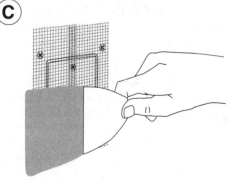

PATCHING A LARGE HOLE IN DRYWALL

Repairing a large hole in drywall involves installing new drywall, as if you were building a new wall. If you must have a perfect wall, consider hiring a professional "mudder" to apply a skim coat of drywall joint compound to the entire wall.

1. Using a keyhole saw, make horizontal cuts in the drywall that extend from the hole to the wall studs (Figure A).

2. When you have located the studs, mark a rectangle, from stud to stud, around the damaged area using a carpenter's square and pencil. Cut out the rectangle with the keyhole saw.

3. Cut two 1 × 3 furring strips, each 2 inches longer than the height of the rectangle. Drill 1/8-inch pilot holes 2 inches from each end of the strips. Hold the strips against the back of the drywall and attach them to the studs by driving drywall screws through the pilot holes (Figure B).

4. Using a utility knife, cut a patch of drywall to fit the hole and screw it to the furring strips with drywall screws spaced every 4 inches along the edges.

5. Put fiberglass drywall tape over the joints, then apply joint compound to the tape and the surrounding wall with a wide putty knife (Figure C).

6. After 24 hours, sand with 150-grit sandpaper wrapped around a block of wood, and apply a second coat of compound with a 6-inch drywall knife.

7. After a second 24 hours, sand the joints smooth and apply a final coat of compound using a 10-inch drywall knife.

8. After 24 hours, lightly sand the joints. Paint the patch to match the wall.

MATERIALS

- 1 × 3 furring strips
- Drywall screws
- Scrap wallboard
- Fiberglass drywall tape
- Drywall joint compound
- 150-grit sandpaper
- Matching wall paint

TOOLS

Keyhole saw • Carpenter's square • Drill with 1/8" bit • Screwdriver • Utility knife • Wide putty knife • Block of wood • 6" drywall knife • 10" drywall knife • Paintbrush

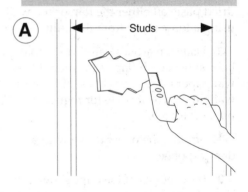

A Studs

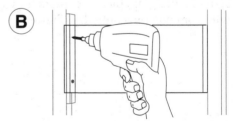

B

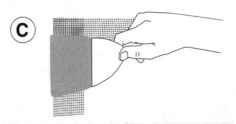

C

REMOVING A BUBBLE IN WALLPAPER

As wallpaper dries, small air pockets sometimes form causing the paper to bubble out. Luckily, with a sharp knife in hand, you can easily fix an unsightly bubble, and no one will ever notice the repair. If all of the wallpaper is blistered and coming away from the wall, it should be removed (see "Removing Wallpaper" on page 270) and the surface prepared correctly before papering again.

MATERIALS
• Wallpaper paste
• Common pins

TOOLS
Utility knife • Artist's paintbrush
• Sponge

1. Using a utility knife with a new blade, slit the bubble in a big cross pattern from edge to edge (Figure A).

2. Peel each flap back and scrape the dried paste off either the flap or the wall, using a loose blade from the utility knife.

3. Using an artist's paintbrush, coat the back side of each flap with compatible wallpaper paste—vinyl paste for vinyl wallpaper, wheat paste for regular wallpaper (Figure B).

4. Smooth the paper down with a damp sponge.

5. If the points of the flaps show any sign of curling up, pin the corners down with common pins until dry (Figure C).

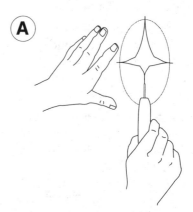

A

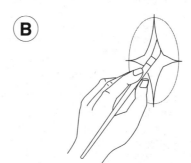

B

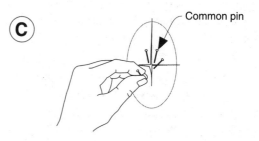

C

Common pin

PATCHING WALLPAPER

Unsightly spots or holes in wallpaper are common, especially if you have children or pets. Many people shy away from this repair because they are afraid they won't be able to match the pattern of the patch to that of the wallpaper. The key to a perfect match is cutting through the patch and the original wallpaper at the same time.

MATERIALS
- Scrap of matching wallpaper patch
- Masking tape
- Wallpaper paste

TOOLS
Carpenter's square • Scissors
• Utility knife • Putty knife • Paintbrush
• Sponge • Seam roller

1. Using a pencil and a carpenter's square, lightly draw a rectangle around the damage, and extend each line 6 inches beyond the corners (Figure A).

2. Using scissors, cut a patch of matching wallpaper that is 2 inches higher and wider than the rectangle. Place the patch over the damaged area and align its pattern with the pattern of the original wallpaper.

3. Tape the edges of the scrap to the wall with masking tape (Figure B).

4. Using the pencil and carpenter's square, connect the extension lines drawn in Step 1 to create the same rectangle on the patch.

5. Guide a utility knife against the carpenter's square to cut the rectangle through both the patch and the original wallpaper.

6. Remove the top rectangle and put it aside. Carefully strip the bottom rectangle from the wall with a putty knife and throw it away (Figure C).

7. Using a small paintbrush, apply wallpaper paste to the back of the patch—vinyl for vinyl wallpaper, wheat for regular wallpaper. Smooth the patch into place with a damp sponge. Roll the edges of the patch with a seam roller.

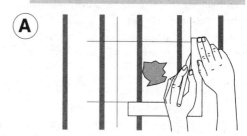

A

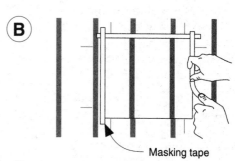

B

Masking tape

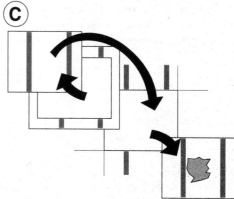

C

REMOVING WALLPAPER

This is the low-cost way to remove wallpaper. If the wallpaper proves to be stuck too tight, if you have several rooms to do, or if you have money to burn, you can rent a wallpaper steamer from a tool rental store or a paint and wallpaper store. Have a helper on hand to remove the wallpaper before the paste dries out again.

MATERIALS
- Wallpaper remover
- Trisodium phosphate

TOOLS
Utility knife • Bucket • Sponge mop • 6" drywall knife • Putty knife

1. Using a sharp utility knife, slit the wallpaper every 6 inches, both vertically and horizontally (Figure A). Change knife blades often if the wall is plaster. The sand in plaster dulls knife blades quickly.

2. Buy wallpaper remover from a paint and wallpaper store. Mix it in a bucket and apply it with a sponge mop on a handle (Figure B). Apply it to about 50 square feet at a time. If the wallpaper comes off easily, you can increase the area of application, and conversely, if it doesn't come off easily, you may want to decrease the area of application.

3. Using a 6-inch drywall knife, remove the wallpaper (Figure C). Switch to a regular putty knife if the wallpaper is difficult to remove.

4. After all of the wallpaper has been removed, wash the wall down with trisodium phosphate using the sponge mop.

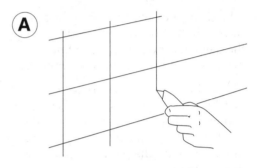

A

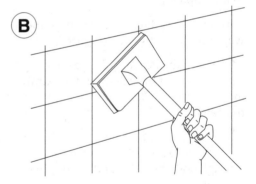

B

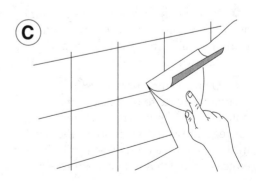

C

FASTENING LOOSE PANELING

Moisture will sometimes buckle paneling. The easy fix is to fasten it with more nails. A longer lasting fix is to pull the panel out and apply panel adhesive to the stud behind it before renailing. Nails can be purchased with heads in a variety of colors to match the paneling. Otherwise, cover the nail heads with a colored wax touch-up stick.

MATERIALS
- Cartridge of panel adhesive
- Nails
- Colored wax touch-up stick

TOOLS
Pry bar • Long-nose pliers
• Scraps of wood • Caulking gun
• Hammer • Nail set • Sponge

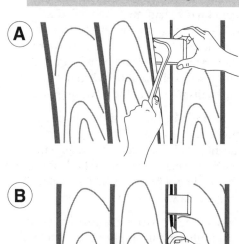

1. Slip the hooked end of a pry bar under an edge of the loose panel. Slip a scrap of wood between the pry bar and the sound paneling to protect the finish, and pry the loose panel out (Figure A). Loosen the edge, one nail at a time, until the entire edge is free.

2. Using long-nose pliers, remove all of the nails from the loose edge and save them for later use if they are not bent.

3. Wedge the entire edge of the panel out several inches with scraps of wood.

4. Using a cartridge of panel adhesive in a caulking gun, apply a bead of panel adhesive along the exposed studs or furring strips (Figure B). (To load a caulking gun, see "Caulking Building Cracks" on page 159.)

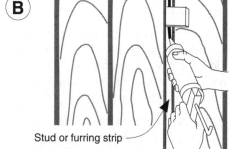

Stud or furring strip

5. Wait for the adhesive to set up as specified in the directions. Remove the wedges, and press the panel into place.

6. Buy new nails that match the old ones or reuse the old ones if they are not bent. Using a hammer and nail set, fasten the panel edge by driving nails through the old nail holes (Figure C). If necessary, cover the nail heads with a colored wax touch-up stick.

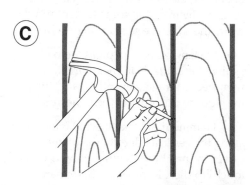

7. Wipe up any adhesive that has squeezed out using a wet sponge.

REPLACING A DAMAGED WOOD PANEL

The burden of replacing an entire panel is lightened by the fun you will have punching holes in the old panel and ripping it off the studs. To get the full benefit, make sure you growl savagely when attacking the panel.

---

1. If there is a baseboard, remove it. (See "Replacing a Baseboard" on page 128.)

2. Punch holes through the damaged panel with a hammer, then insert gloved fingers through the holes and tear away the pieces of paneling. Use a pry bar to remove small pieces and nails (Figure A). Slip a scrap of wood between the pry bar and nails to protect the adjacent paneling.

3. Buy a replacement panel from a home center. Measure the height of the adjacent panel, mark that measurement on the new panel at the top on both sides, and draw a line between the marks. Using a crosscut saw, cut the panel to length.

4. Using a cartridge of panel adhesive in a caulking gun, apply a bead of panel adhesive to the faces of the exposed studs. (To load a caulking gun, see "Caulking Building Cracks" on page 159.)

5. Holding the top of the panel against the ceiling, drive panel nails through the panel into the top of the studs. Hold the panel away from the studs for ten minutes while the adhesive sets up (Figure B).

6. Starting at the top, press the panel against the studs. Hammer a brick wrapped in a rag against the panel over the studs to push it into the adhesive.

7. Hammer panel nails every 6 inches along the vertical edges of the panel. Cover the nail heads with a colored wax touch-up stick. Replace the baseboard.

MATERIALS
- Replacement wood panel
- Cartridge of panel adhesive
- Panel nails
- Colored wax touch-up stick

TOOLS
Hammer • Gloves • Pry bar • Tape measure • Chalk line • Crosscut saw • Caulking gun • Block of wood • Rag

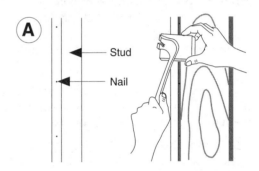

(A) Stud — Nail

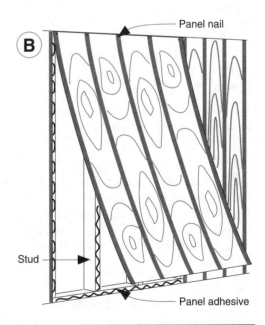

(B) Panel nail — Stud — Panel adhesive

REPLACING A TONGUE-&-GROOVE BOARD

Tongue-and-groove boards can be replaced without tearing out the whole wall. The only difficult part is matching the color of the new board to the old. Since unpainted wood changes color with age, it is nearly impossible to match the color today and have it still match in five years. Perhaps you can steal a board from an inconspicuous location.

1. If there is a baseboard, remove it. (See "Replacing a Baseboard" on page 128.)

2. Run a sharp utility knife down the tongued edge of the damaged board several times until the tongue is severed (Figure A).

3. Screw a drywall screw into the board near the edge you just cut. Grab the head of the screw with the claw end of a hammer, and pull the edge of the board out until you can insert the hooked end of a pry bar behind the edge. Pry out the damaged board and nails with the pry bar.

4. Lay the damaged board over the replacement board and mark its length. Using a crosscut saw, cut the replacement board to length.

5. Hold the board up to the wall and choose the best side to face out. Place the board's good side down, and slice off the groove cheek on the back of the board with the utility knife (Figure B).

6. Insert the tongue of the new board into the groove of the adjoining board and press the board into place (Figure C).

7. Fasten the groove side of the board to the wall with 6d finish nails. Countersink the nails with a nail set, and replace the baseboard. Cover the nail heads with a colored wax touch-up stick.

MATERIALS

- Drywall screw
- Replacement tongue-and-groove board
- 6d finish nails
- Colored wax touch-up stick

TOOLS

Utility knife • Screwdriver
• Hammer • Pry bar • Crosscut saw
• Nail set

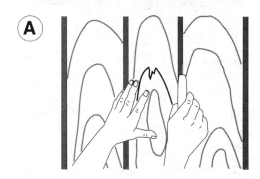

(A)

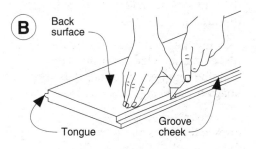

(B) Back surface

Tongue

Groove cheek

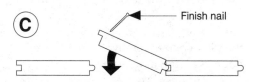

(C)

Finish nail

REPLACING A FIBERBOARD CEILING TILE

Tongue-and-groove fiberboard ceiling tiles are easy to damage—even a popped champagne cork can dent one. Luckily, they are also easy to replace. They come in standard 12 × 12-inch squares and since they can be painted, a quick coat of paint will hide any replacements.

1. Using a utility knife, cut along all four edges of the damaged tile (Figure A).

2. Jab a large screwdriver through the center of the tile, wedge the tip against the ceiling, and pull down on the tile. This will either dislodge the tile or break it.

3. If the tile is broken and still in place, use the hooked end of a pry bar to pry it down piece by piece.

4. Remove any staples with long-nose pliers. Scrape off any old adhesive with a wood chisel.

5. Buy a replacement tile at a home center, if you don't have one saved from the original installation. Cut off one of the two tongues with the utility knife (Figure B).

6. On the back side of the replacement tile, along the edge opposite to the remaining tongue, squeeze or dab fiberboard tile adhesive.

7. Insert the tongue of the tile into the groove that runs along one furring strip, then press the edge with adhesive up against the other furring strip (Figure C).

8. Drive 4d finish nails through the seam of the glued edge and partway into the furring strip. Bend the nails to hold the tile in place. Remove the nails after 24 hours with the long-nose pliers.

MATERIALS
- Replacement fiberboard ceiling tile
- Fiberboard tile adhesive
- 4d finish nails

TOOLS
Utility knife • Screwdriver • Pry bar • Long-nose pliers • Wood chisel

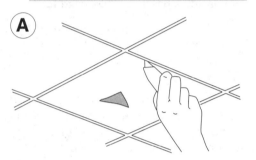

A

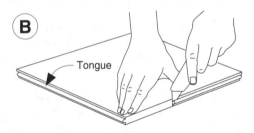

B

Tongue

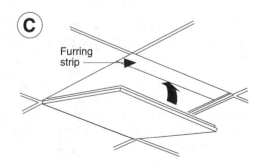

C

Furring strip

INSTALLING PICTURE-HANGING WIRE

Everyone has hung a picture on the wall, but not everyone has done it right The correct materials and techniques will keep your pictures from falling off the wall, and you won't have to straighten them every time your children or grandchildren run through the house.

MATERIALS
- Two screw eyes
- Picture-hanging wire

TOOLS

Drill and pilot bit • Screwdriver
• Diagonal-cutting pliers

1. On the back of the sides of the picture frame, mark screw eye locations. The screw eyes should be one third of the way down from the top of the frame and centered on the width of the side pieces (Figure A).

2. Buy screw eyes with shank lengths equal to half the thickness of your frame. Drill pilot holes of a diameter equal to the diameter of the screw eye to a depth that equals half the frame thickness.

3. Using a small screwdriver inserted through the screw eyes, turn them until the eyes just touch the frame.

4. For a small picture, use a single hanger (Figure B). Using diagonal-cutting pliers, cut a length of picture-hanging wire that is 1¹/₂ times the width of the frame. Feed one end through an eye, around the base of the eye, and then around itself four times. Pull the second end through the second eye until the wire between the eyes can be pulled halfway to the top of the frame, then loop it around itself four times.

5. For a heavy picture, use a double hanger (Figure C). Cut a length of wire three times the frame width. Feed one end through both eyes. Cross the ends at the top of the frame. Loop them around each other, then back around themselves four times. Pull each half of the wire up over the hangers on the wall to hang the picture.

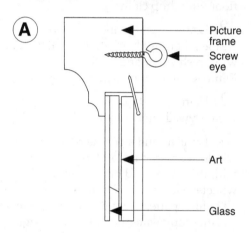

Figure A — Picture frame, Screw eye, Art, Glass

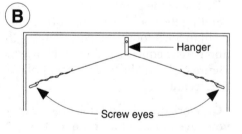

Figure B — Hanger, Screw eyes

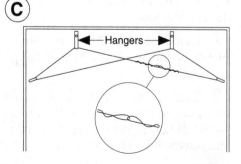

Figure C — Hangers

PAINTING AN INTERIOR WALL

The use of paint rollers and pads has vastly simplified and speeded the painting of interior walls and ceilings. The professional tips below will speed the process further and produce seamless surfaces.

1. Move all furniture and rugs well away from the wall and cover the bare floor with drop cloths.

2. Using a sponge and household cleaner, thoroughly wash the wall. Rinse with fresh water and let the wall dry. Remove outlet and switch covers.

3. Using a putty knife, repair nail holes with drywall joint compound.

4. Paint around all of the edges—doors, windows, baseboard, and intersections with the ceiling and other walls—with a wheeled edger pad (Figure A). Clean up all spills, spatters, and the edger pad in warm, soapy water before proceeding.

5. Using the paint roller and tray, start painting the wall from a top corner and paint in 3 × 3-foot sections, following the numbered sequence shown in Figure B. Figure C shows the basic roller application technique.

6. Work quickly and don't pause until you have finished the entire wall or reached a major vertical break, such as a door or window.

7. Wait until the wall has dried completely before deciding whether to apply a second coat.

8. Clean the roller and tray with warm, soapy water. If you plan to use the roller within 24 hours, wrap it in plastic wrap, and put the lid on the paint can.

MATERIALS
- Drop cloths
- Household cleaner
- Drywall compound
- Latex interior paint
- Plastic wrap

TOOLS
Sponge • Screwdriver • Putty knife • Wheeled edger pad • Paint roller and tray

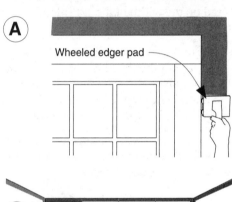

Wheeled edger pad

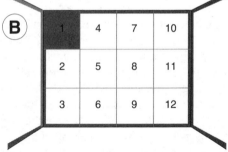

1	4	7	10
2	5	8	11
3	6	9	12

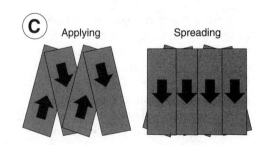

Applying   Spreading

PAINTING A CEILING

Painting a ceiling need not be any more difficult than painting a wall. You still need to worry about drips and spatters, but using a roller on a long handle eliminates dripping on your head and the need for a stepladder.

MATERIALS
- **Drop cloths**
- **Household cleaner**
- **Flat latex ceiling paint**
- **Plastic wrap**

TOOLS
Sponge • Screwdriver • Wheeled edger pad • Paint roller with extension handle and tray

1. Remove all easily moved furniture and rugs from the room. Cover the remaining furniture and the floor with drop cloths.

2. If the ceiling is dirty or greasy—as is likely in a kitchen or bath—wash it with a sponge and warm household cleaner. Rinse with fresh water and let the ceiling dry.

3. Remove the cover of any ceiling fixture to allow painting under it.

4. Paint the edges—where the ceiling meets the wall—with a wheeled edger pad (Figure A). Clean up spills, spatters, drips, and the edger pad in warm, soapy water before proceeding.

5. Using the paint roller with the extension handle and tray, paint the ceiling in 3 × 3-foot sections, following the numbered sequence shown in Figure B. Figure C shows the basic roller application technique.

6. Work quickly and don't stop until the entire ceiling is covered.

7. Wait until the ceiling has dried completely before deciding whether to apply a second coat.

8. Clean the roller and tray with warm, soapy water. If you plan to use the roller within 24 hours, seal it in plastic wrap, and put the lid on the paint can.

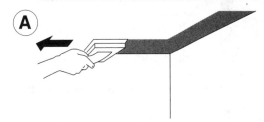

A

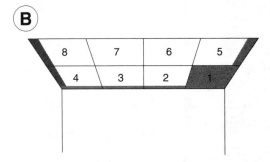

B

| 8 | 7 | 6 | 5 |
| 4 | 3 | 2 | 1 |

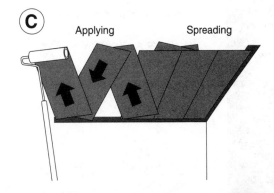

C

Applying   Spreading

REPLACING A WINDOW CRANK

Casement window cranks are simple to replace once you have found the correct replacement unit. In large cities there are companies that do nothing but sell replacement window hardware. Look in the Yellow Pages under "Windows." If you live in the country, ask your local lumberyard for help.

MATERIALS
Replacement casement crank

TOOLS
Screwdriver

1. Crank the window open at least halfway.

2. Remove the screws that fasten the crank to the windowsill or the bottom of the window casing (Figure A).

3. Run your fingers along the underside of the track at the bottom of the window sash until you feel a gap in the track. Slide or crank the outer end of the arm to the gap and pull the arm down and out of the track (Figure B).

4. Remove the entire crank assembly by pulling the arm through the slot at the bottom of the window (Figure C).

5. Take the crank to a lumberyard or a store that specializes in windows and purchase a replacement casement crank.

6. Install the new crank in the reverse order, as follows:

    1. Insert the arm through the slot at the bottom of the window.

    2. Insert the end of the arm into the gap in the bottom of the track.

    3. Screw the crank to the windowsill or window casing.

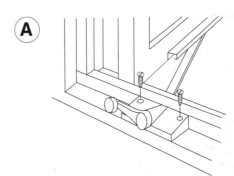

(A)

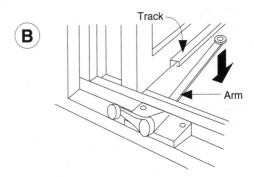

(B)

Track

Arm

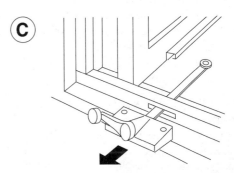

(C)

ADJUSTING A SASH LOCK

Old-fashioned clamshell sash locks are designed to bring the rails of double-hung window sashes together tightly to prevent infiltration of cold air. The lock tolerates a fair amount of misalignment, but the window frame may ultimately shift enough to prevent locking. When that time comes, either half of the lock can be shimmed, as shown below.

1. Close the window firmly, but do not attempt to lock the sash.

2. Using the end of a tape measure, measure the vertical distance, T, by which the upper and lower sashes misalign (Figure A).

3. Purchase a 1-foot length of flat wood molding of thickness T and at least 1 inch wide to use as a shim. If you can not find a suitable piece of molding, use an old wood ruler or yardstick.

4. Unscrew and remove the half of the lock that must be shimmed.

5. Using a sharp pencil, trace both the lock outline and its screw holes onto the molding (Figure B).

6. Clamp the molding in a vise with pieces of cardboard between the wood and the vise jaws.

7. Cut the molding to shape with a coping saw. Clean up any ragged edges with a sharp utility knife and 100-grit sandpaper. Using a drill and a bit of the diameter of the screws, drill screw holes in the new shim.

8. Place the lock back on the window with the shim under it. Screw the lock down with brass wood screws of the same diameter but ¼ inch longer than the original screws (Figure C).

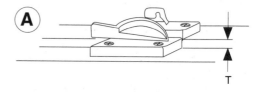

A

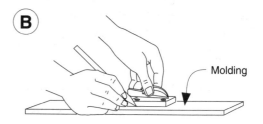

B

Molding

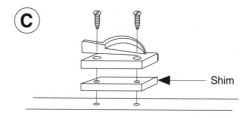

C

Shim

Installing a Sash Lock

If you have installed a new window and wish to match its lock to the clamshell sash locks on your existing windows, you can still purchase these locks at home centers. You can install a new clamshell lock in 15 minutes.

1. Close the window.

2. Place the clamshell sash lock at the midpoint of the sash rails where they meet when the sash is closed. The latch goes on the lower sash and the catch goes on the upper sash.

3. With a sharp pencil, trace the outlines of the lock and screw holes onto the tops of the adjoining sash rails (Figure A).

4. Drill $^1/_{16}$-inch pilot holes $^1/_4$ inch deep for the sash-lock screws (Figure B).

5. Fasten the latch and the catch to the sashes with the brass screws (Figure C).

MATERIALS

• Clamshell sash lock
• 4 brass screws to match lock

TOOLS

Drill and $^1/_{16}$" bit • Screwdriver

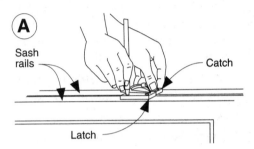

A

Sash rails

Catch

Latch

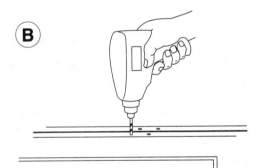

B

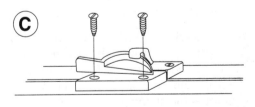

C

REPLACING A SASH CORD

Sash cords wear over time and may eventually break. But you can replace them easily as long as there's access to the weight pockets. If you don't find access plates in the jambs, your only alternative may be to install friction channels. (See "Installing Friction Sash Channels" on page 286.)

MATERIALS

- **Replacement sash cord**
- **4d finish nail**

TOOLS

Utility knife • Pry bar • Screwdriver • Slip-joint pliers

1. Using a utility knife, cut through the paint film between the inside stops and casing, then pry the stops off with a pry bar (Figure A). Remove the sash.

2. Cut the sash cords with the utility knife and let the weights drop inside.

3. Unscrew and remove the access plate in the jamb covering the weight pocket at the side of the window (Figure B).

4. Note how the cord is tied to the weight, then untie and remove the weight.

5. Pull out the old sash cord. Purchase matching sash cord at a hardware store or home center. Feed the new sash cord down through the empty pulley and tie the end to the weight. If you forget how to tie the knot, look at the weight on the other side.

6. Pull the cord until the weight is at the top and push a 4d finish nail through the cord to hold it (Figure C).

7. Holding the sash on the windowsill, feed the cord through the channel and the knot hole (Figure D). Cut the cord to length with the utility knife and tie a figure-8 knot in the end (Figure E).

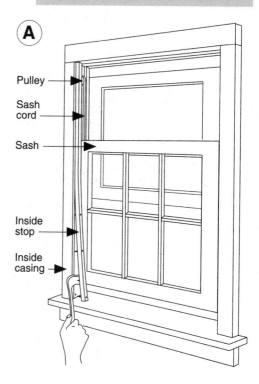

A

Pulley

Sash cord

Sash

Inside stop

Inside casing

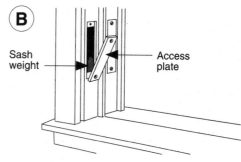

B

Sash weight

Access plate

8. Pull the finish nail out of the cord and carefully lower the weight.

9. Replace the weight access plate, install the sash in its channel, and replace the inside window stops.

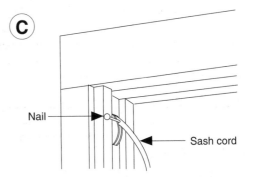

Nail

Sash cord

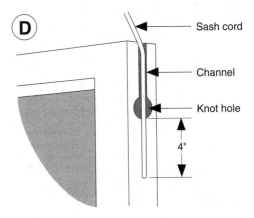

Sash cord

Channel

Knot hole

4"

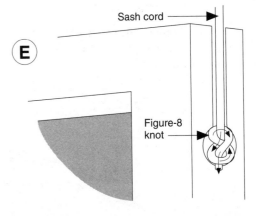

Sash cord

Figure-8 knot

ADJUSTING A TUBE BALANCE

A tube balance contains a spring that exerts force to balance the weight of a window sash. If the sash will not stay up, the spring needs adjusting. If tightening or loosening the spring has no effect, the whole balance should be replaced. (See "Replacing a Tube Balance" on the opposite page.)

MATERIALS
None

TOOLS
Screwdriver

1. Lower the sash, exposing the top of the tube balance.

2. Grip the tube with one hand and loosen the screw at the top of the tube (Figure A).

3. Pull the tube away from the frame, and using the screw for leverage, twist the tube (Figure B). Looking down at the top of the tube, try one of these options:

• To increase the upward spring pressure on the sash, which makes the window easier to raise, twist the tube clockwise two turns.

• To decrease the upward spring pressure on the sash, which makes the window harder to raise, twist the tube counterclockwise two turns.

4. Refasten the tube at the top of the frame with the screw.

5. Repeat Steps 2 through 4 to adjust the tube balance on the other side of the window frame.

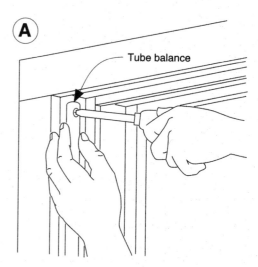

A · Tube balance

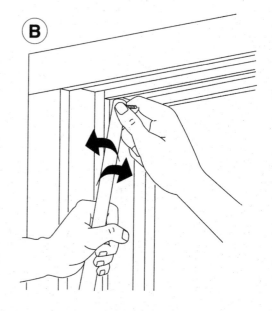

B

REPLACING A TUBE BALANCE

If the sash in a window with tube balances just won't stay up, the spring in the tube balance may be broken. But, before replacing the tube balance, try simply adjusting the tension on the spring. (See "Adjusting a Tube Balance" on the opposite page.)

MATERIALS
Replacement tube balance

TOOLS
Screwdriver • Pry bar

1. Lower the sash, exposing the top of the tube balance to be replaced.

2. Remove the screw at the top of the tube balance (Figure A).

3. If the sash is held in by a wood stop, pry the stop off with a pry bar. If the sash slides in an aluminum channel, bend the channel back with your fingers. Pull the edge of the sash out of the frame. Use the pry bar between the sash and the channel, if necessary.

4. While a helper holds the sash, remove the bracket at the bottom of the sash with a screwdriver (Figure B).

5. Take the old tube balance and bracket to a hardware store or home center and buy a replacement.

6. Install the new bottom bracket and lay the new tube in the groove in the side of the sash.

7. Slide the sash back into place in the window frame.

8. Pull the top of the tube up and screw it in place.

9. Replace the wood stop—or bend back the aluminum channel—to hold the sash in place. Adjust the tension of the new balance. (See "Adjusting a Tube Balance" on the opposite page.)

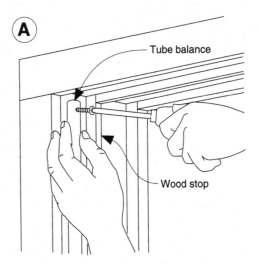

A — Tube balance / Wood stop

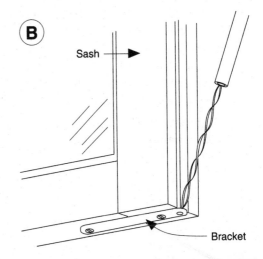

B — Sash / Bracket

INSTALLING FRICTION SASH CHANNELS

Friction sash channels replace old-fashioned sash cords and weights and also help seal the sides of the window sashes like weather stripping. They can pay for themselves in just a few years in energy savings alone. With a helper, you can upgrade all of the windows in an average home in a weekend.

MATERIALS
- **Set of friction sash channels**
- **Duct tape**
- **4d finish nails**

TOOLS
Utility knife • Pry bar • Screwdriver • Metal snips • Nail set

1. Using a utility knife, cut through the paint film between the inside stops and the jambs, then carefully pry the stops off with a pry bar (Figure A). Remove the bottom sash.

2. Cut the sash cords with the utility knife and let the weights drop.

3. With a screwdriver, remove the pulleys and tape the holes with duct tape.

4. Pry out the parting strips that separate the sashes and remove the upper sash.

5. Buy a set of friction sash channels at a home center. Hold one of the old parting strips against the parting strips of the new friction channels, and mark the lengths. Draw cut lines, angled at the slope of the sill. Cut the friction channels along the cut lines with metal snips.

6. Put the upper and lower sashes between the friction channels with the upper sash lowered, and bind them together with duct tape (Figure B).

7. Place the bottoms of the channels in the window frame, then swing the top into place against the outside stop (Figure B). Cut and remove the duct tape.

8. Reinstall the inside stops with 4d finish nails and a nail set.

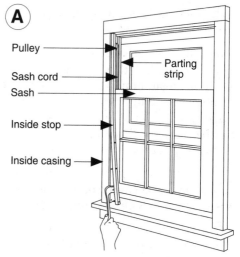

A

Pulley

Sash cord

Sash

Inside stop

Inside casing

Parting strip

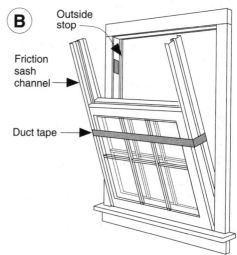

B

Outside stop

Friction sash channel

Duct tape

REPLACING A SCREEN IN A METAL SASH

Replacing the screen in a metal sash is nearly as simple as zipping up your coat, provided you have a spline roller—a tool specially developed for the purpose. In fact, the spline roller and special aluminum frame extrusions available in home centers allow you to make new screen frames as well.

MATERIALS

- **Screening material**
- **Tubular screen spline**

TOOLS

Screwdriver • Utility knife
- **Screen spline roller**

1. Remove the screen from the window.

2. Pry up the end of the tubular screen spline with a screwdriver, then pull it out of the channel all around the frame (Figure A). Remove the old screening.

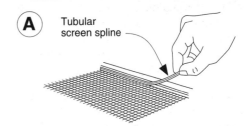

A   Tubular screen spline

3. Take the old screening and spline to a hardware store or home center, and purchase replacements.

4. Using a utility knife, cut the new screening at least 2 inches wider and longer than the old screen. Lay it over the opening.

5. Press the screening into the channel at one end of the frame using the convex wheel of a screen spline roller (Figure B).

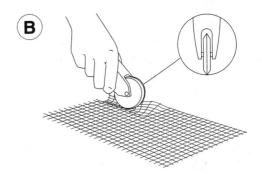

B

6. Place the spline over the screen that you just pressed into the channel, and force the spline into the channel using the concave wheel of the spline roller (Figure C). Pull the screen tight, and as you insert the spline, it will automatically stretch the screening the right amount. Be careful not to press too hard or the screen may break.

7. Repeat Steps 5 and 6 for the opposite side of the frame and then for the two remaining sides.

8. Trim the excess screening by running a sharp utility knife along the outside edge of the spline.

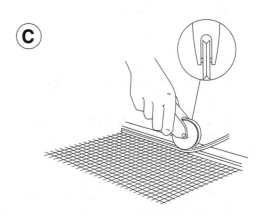

C

REPLACING A SCREEN IN A WOOD SASH

You can easily replace a screen in a wood sash by following the directions below, but if the sash is rotted from years of weather exposure, you may be better off making or buying aluminum replacement screens.

1. Using a wood chisel, carefully pry up all the wood molding around the screen. Find the brads and wedge the chisel as close to them as possible to pry up the molding. If the molding breaks, take a sample to a lumberyard to replace it.

2. Using long-nose pliers, remove the old screening and any brads that pulled through the molding. Buy replacement screening at a hardware store.

3. Place the sash on a table or the floor with a 2 × 4 under each end. Place a third 2 × 4 across the middle of the frame, and weight it down to bow the frame (Figure A).

4. Using a utility knife, cut the new screening 2 inches larger than the opening. Then, using ¼-inch staples and a staple gun, staple the screening to one end of the frame placing the staples in the sequence shown in Figure B. Pull the screen tight, and staple the screening to the opposite end.

5. Unbow the sash and staple the screening to the sides, working from the center to both ends.

6. Using ½-inch brads and a tack hammer, fasten the screen molding. Use a hacksaw to cut new molding, if necessary.

7. Trim the excess screening by running the utility knife along the outside of the molding (Figure C).

MATERIALS
- Wood molding (if original is damaged)
- Screening
- Three 2 × 4s
- ¼" staples
- ½" brads

TOOLS
Wood chisel • Long-nose pliers • Weight • Utility knife • Staple gun • Tack hammer • Hacksaw

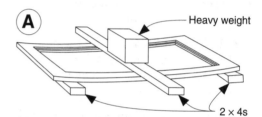

Ⓐ   Heavy weight   2 × 4s

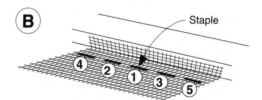

Ⓑ   Staple

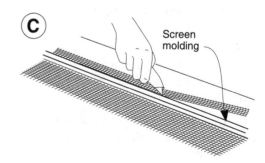

Ⓒ   Screen molding

ADJUSTING A ROLLER SHADE

There is no need to live with shades that refuse to catch or roll up all the way. And all you need to perform this repair is your toothbrush! Purchase a new one for hygenic purposes, however.

MATERIALS
Spray can of silicone lock lubricant

TOOLS
Toothbrush

If the shade refuses to catch even when you release it slowly, the latching mechanism is either dirty or needs lubrication. Follow these steps:

1. Remove the shade.

2. Brush away any dust on the ratchet and pawl with a toothbrush.

3. Spray silicone lock lubricant on the ratchet and pawl and reinstall the shade.

If the shade will not fully rewind, the spring tension needs to be increased. Follow these steps:

1. Pull the shade down 2 feet and let the ratchet catch in the pawl.

2. Remove the shade.

3. Roll the shade up 1 foot manually and reinstall it.

If the shade winds up too fast, the spring tension needs to be reduced. Follow these steps:

1. Pull the shade down 2 feet and let it catch.

2. Remove the shade.

3. Unroll the shade at least 1 foot and reinstall it.

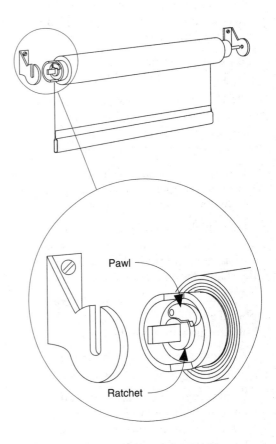

Pawl

Ratchet

REPLACING GLASS IN A METAL SASH

Replacing glass in a metal sash is actually simpler than the equivalent operation on a wood sash because you cannot gouge the metal sash. The trickiest part of the operation is measuring the size of the glass. If possible, take the sash to a glass store and let them do the measuring.

MATERIALS

- Masking tape
- Metal primer
- Replacement glass
- Glazing compound
- Exterior paint

TOOLS

Gloves • Goggles • Hammer • Long-nose pliers • Wood chisel • Wire brush • Sash brush • Tape measure • Putty knife

1. Tape the broken glass with masking tape to prevent fragments from flying. Then, wearing gloves and goggles, break the glass with a hammer.

2. Using long-nose pliers, remove small pieces of glass and the spring clips.

3. Using a wood chisel, remove the old glazing compound (Figure A) and then wire brush the frame. If the frame is rusted, paint it with a metal primer.

4. Measure the size of the opening, and purchase glass 1/8 inch smaller in height and width at a glass store.

5. Roll glazing compound between your palms to form a rope about 1/4 inch in diameter, and press the compound into the channel with a putty knife.

6. Press the new glass into the compound and install the spring clips that hold the glass in place (Figure B).

7. Press a second 1/4-inch rope of glazing compound over the glass.

8. Starting at a corner, smooth the compound with a single, continuous stroke of the putty knife until you reach the opposite corner (Figure C). Trim away excess compound with the putty knife.

9. Paint the glazing compound with exterior paint, sealing it to the glass.

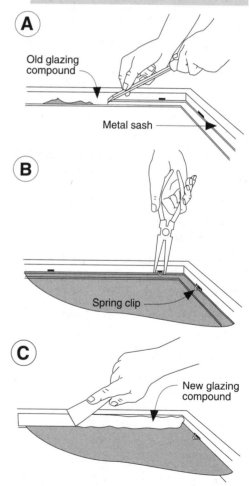

A Old glazing compound

Metal sash

B Spring clip

C New glazing compound

REPLACING GLASS IN A WOOD SASH

Did you tape the cracks in a few window panes years ago, thinking you would get around to replacing them the next spring? If so, it's time to get to work. Replace all your broken windows at the same time. Then, you can purchase all the glass and clean up the glazing compound just once.

MATERIALS

- Masking tape
- White shellac primer
- Replacement glass
- Glazing compound
- Glazier's points
- Exterior paint

TOOLS

Gloves • Goggles • Hammer
• Slip-joint pliers • Wood chisel
• Sash brush • Tape measure
• Putty knife

1. Tape the broken glass with masking tape to prevent fragments from flying. Then, wearing gloves and goggles, break the glass with a hammer. Using slip-joint pliers, remove the small pieces of glass and old glazier's points.

2. Using a wood chisel, remove the old glazing compound (Figure A). Using a sash brush, paint the bare wood in the channel with white shellac primer.

3. Measure the size of the opening and purchase glass 1/8 inch smaller in height and width at a glass store.

4. Roll glazing compound between your palms to form a rope about 1/4 inch in diameter, and press the compound into the primed channel with a putty knife.

5. Press the new glass into the compound, then push glazier's points against the glass and into the sash sides with the putty knife (Figure B). Use two per side.

6. Press a second 1/4-inch rope of glazing compound over the glass.

7. Starting at a corner, smooth the compound with a single, continuous stroke of the putty knife until you reach the opposite corner (Figure C). Trim away the excess compound with the putty knife.

8. Paint the glazing compound with exterior paint, sealing it to the glass.

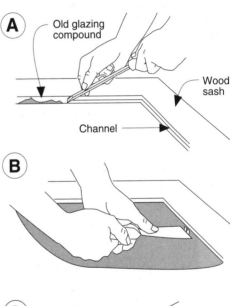

(A) Old glazing compound

Wood sash

Channel

(B)

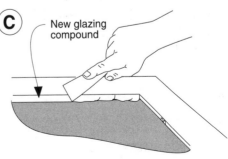

(C) New glazing compound

REPLACING GLASS IN A STORM WINDOW

Replacing glass in a storm window is as simple as replacing the screen in a metal frame. As with replacing the glass in a metal sash, however, the dimensions of the glass are crucial. Take the storm window frame to the glass store to make sure the new glass will fit. There are few things more aggravating than discovering that replacement glass is $1/16$" too large after you're home.

MATERIALS
- Masking tape
- Replacement glass
- Replacement gasket

TOOLS
Gloves • Blanket or towel
• Screwdriver • Slip-joint pliers
• Tape measure • Utility knife

1. Tape the broken glass with masking tape to prevent it from breaking further. Wearing gloves, remove the storm window and lay it on a table covered with an old blanket or large towel.

2. Using a screwdriver, pry one end of the gasket away from the frame. Grip the end of the gasket with slip-joint pliers and pull it out of the frame (Figure A).

3. Repeat Step 2 for the other three sides of the frame.

4. Carefully lift the old glass out of the frame and lay it on the table.

5. Take the old gasket and the frame to a glass store and purchase new glass to fit and a new gasket of the same type and length.

6. Lay the new glass in the frame.

7. Using a utility knife, cut the gasket material into lengths and press it between the glass and the frame with your thumb (Figure B).

A

Gasket

Storm window frame

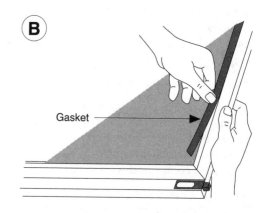

B

Gasket

RESTORING A WOOD SASH

Have you priced new windows lately? They aren't cheap and you'll never find any that match your house as well as the old wood originals do. So, consider refurbishing your old windows by strengthening the sashes, as shown below.

MATERIALS

- Two 1" × 2" × 4' wood strips
- Sheet of plywood
- 3d wire nails
- Masking tape
- $5/16$" dowel
- 100-grit sandpaper
- Carpenter's glue

TOOLS

Hammer • Pair of C-clamps
• Drill and $5/16$" bit • Hacksaw
• Sponge

1. Make a window-squaring jig by nailing two 4-foot-long wood strips along the adjoining edges of an uncut sheet of plywood with 3d wire nails (Figure A). Leave a 1-inch gap between the ends of the wood strips and the corner, and make sure the edges of the wood strips and the plywood line up perfectly.

Wood strip
Plywood

2. Push one corner of the window sash firmly into the corner of the jig so that the joint is tight and square. Clamp the sash in place with C-clamps.

3. Put a piece of masking tape on a $5/16$-inch bit to mark the depth of the wood sash. Drill through the center of the corner joint with a drill and the bit until the tape meets the sash (Figure B).

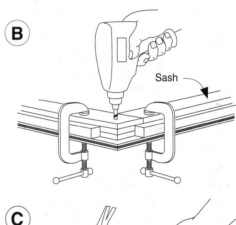
Sash

4. Using a hacksaw, cut a $5/16$-inch dowel to the thickness of the sash. Round one end of the dowel slightly with 100-grit sandpaper.

5. Dip the dowel halfway into carpenter's glue, and drive the dowel rounded end first into the hole until it bottoms on the plywood (Figure C). Wipe away excess glue with a damp sponge.

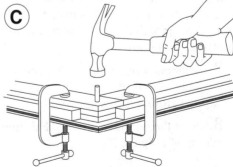

6. Repeat Steps 2 through 5 for the other three corners of the sash.

7. Sand and repaint the sash. (See "Painting a Window" on page 296.)

REPAIRING A WINDOWSILL

Replacing a rotted windowsill is a major job requiring the services of a carpenter. Luckily, most mildly rotted sills can be repaired instead. Visit any boatyard and you will see rotted boat planking being restored by injecting epoxy resin. You can do the same for your windowsill. If you can not find the epoxy at a hardware store, visit a marine supply store or boatyard.

MATERIALS
- Epoxy wood restorer
- Epoxy auto-body filler
- 100-grit sandpaper

TOOLS
Wood chisel • Hammer • Drill and ⅛" bit • Utility knife • Plastic gluing syringe • Putty knife • Wide putty knife • Block of wood

1. Let the damaged area dry thoroughly. If necessary, cover the sill with plastic at night and during rainy periods.

2. Using a wood chisel and hammer, cut away any soft, spongy areas in the windowsill (Figure A).

3. Drill ⅛-inch-diameter holes every ½ inch throughout the cut-away area. Do not drill all the way through the sill.

4. Using a utility knife, cut the tip of a plastic gluing syringe (available at a hardware store) back until the tip just fits into the drilled holes.

5. Mix epoxy wood restorer and use the syringe to fill each hole to the top (Figure B).

6. After 24 hours, mix a batch of epoxy auto-body filler and, using a putty knife, fill the chiseled-out area. Work quickly because the epoxy hardens in just a few minutes. Smooth the epoxy with a wide putty knife (Figure C).

7. After one hour, sand the hardened filler smooth with 100-grit sandpaper wrapped around a block of wood.

8. Paint the windowsill. (See "Painting a Window" on page 296.)

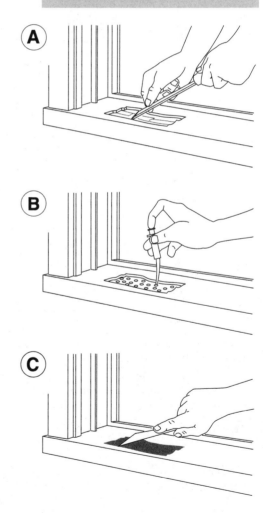

A

B

C

FREEING A STUCK SASH

When a window sash refuses to open, it is usually because someone—probably you— has painted the joint between the sash and the stop. Following the steps below, you should be able to correct the problem. But be on the lookout for evidence that some misguided, security-minded person has nailed the sash shut!

MATERIALS

- 4d finish nails
- Spray furniture wax

TOOLS

Utility knife • Wide putty knife
• Hammer • Pry bar

1. If the window has been painted shut, you may see a visible paint film connecting the window stop and the sash. Carefully cut through it with repeated passes of a utility knife (Figure A).

2. If the sash still will not budge, force a wide putty knife into the crack between the stop and the sash by tapping it with a hammer (Figure B). Repeat along the entire length of the sash on both sides.

3. If the sash still will not move, hammer the flat end of a pry bar under one corner of the sash and push down on the end of the pry bar (Figure C). As soon as the corner lifts $1/8$ inch, move the pry bar to the opposite corner. Alternate prying at the corners until you can raise the sash by hand. If the window opens, go to Step 5.

4. If the window sash is still difficult to open, pry off the inside stops with the pry bar, and remove the old nails with the claw end of the hammer. Move the stops out $1/16$ inch and reinstall them with 4d finish nails.

5. Open the sash all the way and spray furniture wax on the meeting surfaces of the stops and the parting strips, which are between the sashes.

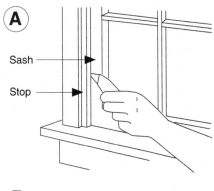

A

Sash

Stop

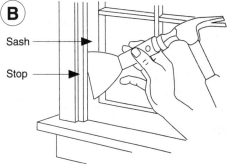

B

Sash

Stop

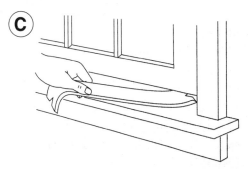

C

PAINTING A WINDOW

Painting a window, with all of its overlapping surfaces and multiple panes, can take forever, or it can be a pleasant, well-planned one-hour job. Here is the right way to do it.

1. Wash all of the painted surfaces with a sponge and household cleaner. Rinse with fresh water and let dry. Lightly sand with 180-grit sandpaper if the existing finish has a high gloss.

2. Remove any easily removed hardware, such as sash locks.

3. Raise the lower sash nearly all the way, and lower the upper sash nearly to the sill (Figure A).

4. Using a 2-inch paintbrush, paint all of the lower sash and the bottom half of the upper sash. Using a 1-inch sash brush, paint the muntins, letting the brush drag paint 1/16 inch onto the glass (Figure B). Extra paint can be removed later with the blade from a utility knife (Figure C).

5. Reverse the positions of the sashes and finish painting the upper sash.

6. Paint the casings and then the sill. Use a paint guard to protect the wall.

7. After the sashes are dry, push both sashes down and paint the upper halves of the jambs. Do not paint the weather strips or metal channels!

8. After the paint dries, push both sashes up and paint the lower halves of the jambs.

9. After all of the paint has dried, spray the jambs with furniture wax to make operating the sashes easier.

MATERIALS
- Household cleaner
- 180-grit sandpaper
- Interior latex paint
- Spray furniture wax

TOOLS
Sponge • Screwdriver
- 2" paintbrush • 1" sash brush
- Utility knife blade • Paint guard

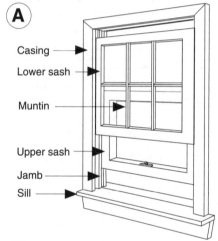

A

Casing
Lower sash
Muntin
Upper sash
Jamb
Sill

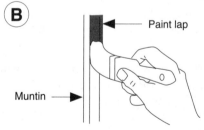

B

Paint lap
Muntin

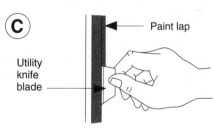

C

Paint lap
Utility knife blade

SEALING KNOTS

If the trim around your windows and doors is knotty pine, you've probably seen the resin bleed from knots through the paint. No matter how many times you paint the wood, the knots eventually prevail. Stop the bleeding now by sealing the knots with shellac, then paint them for the last time.

MATERIALS
- Clean rags
- Denatured alcohol
- Steel wool pad
- White shellac primer
- Matching finish paint

TOOLS
Paint scraper • 1" paintbrush

1. Remove any hardened resin deposits from the knot with a paint scraper (Figure A).

2. Alternately, wet the stained area with a clean rag dipped in denatured alcohol and scrub it with a steel wool pad until the resin is removed (Figure B). Wipe the final time with a clean rag dipped in the alcohol.

3. Using a 1-inch paintbrush, apply white shellac primer to the area of the knot (Figure C).

4. Let the primer dry for five minutes and apply a second coat.

5. Clean the paintbrush in denatured alcohol and then in warm, soapy water.

6. After one hour, apply a finish coat of paint to match the surrounding area.

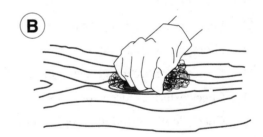

SEASONAL CHECKLISTS

SPRING
Time for cleaning and renewing

- ☐ Clean clogged clothes washer inlet screens
- ☐ Clean lint from clothes dryer vent
- ☐ Vacuum refrigerator and freezer coils
- ☐ Fix sagging screen doors
- ☐ Adjust storm-door closers
- ☐ Repair holes in screens
- ☐ Replace forced air furnace filters
- ☐ Clean central air conditioner coils
- ☐ Clean window air conditioner coils
- ☐ Clean window air conditioner filters
- ☐ Check garden hoses for leaks
- ☐ Fix rotted or broken deck boards
- ☐ Fix or replace rotted porch posts
- ☐ Shore up sagging fences
- ☐ Fix rotted or broken garden tool handles
- ☐ Check exterior faucets for leaks
- ☐ Check depth of sludge in septic tank
- ☐ Check roof for loose or missing shingles
- ☐ Clean winter debris from gutters
- ☐ Fix leaking gutters
- ☐ Fix sagging gutters
- ☐ Mend or replace broken downspouts

SUMMER
Time for fixing and enjoying

- ☐ Fix binding door edges
- ☐ Fix squeaky or loose hinges
- ☐ Fix balky patio doors
- ☐ Adjust balky garage doors
- ☐ Adjust doors that won't latch
- ☐ Replace dirty oil furnace filters
- ☐ Sweep soot buildup from chimney
- ☐ Fix cracks and holes in sidewalks
- ☐ Fix chipped concrete steps
- ☐ Fix loose railings
- ☐ Repair damaged stucco
- ☐ Fix cracks and holes in blacktop
- ☐ Fix crumbling mortar joints
- ☐ Check drains and traps for leaks
- ☐ Clean deposits from faucet aerators
- ☐ Check for dripping faucets
- ☐ Clean clogged showerheads
- ☐ Check for toilet leaks or sweating
- ☐ Adjust hot water temperature
- ☐ Fix dented aluminum siding
- ☐ Fix popped nails in clapboard siding
- ☐ Fix cracks in clapboard siding
- ☐ Replace damaged clapboard siding
- ☐ Repair broken vinyl siding
- ☐ Replace broken window glass

FALL
Time for tightening the defenses

- ☐ Touch up appliance scratches
- ☐ Replace nonfunctioning locks
- ☐ Bleed hot water radiators
- ☐ Replace forced-air furnace filters
- ☐ Seal leaks in forced-air ducts
- ☐ Replace worn weather strips
- ☐ Replace loose or missing caulk
- ☐ Eliminate cold air infiltration at sills
- ☐ Renew deteriorated deck finish
- ☐ Find and repair roof leaks
- ☐ Replace broken or missing roof shingles
- ☐ Repair holes in metal flashing
- ☐ Clean gutters and downspouts
- ☐ Repair or replace leaking gutters
- ☐ Repair sagging gutters
- ☐ Replace broken downspouts
- ☐ Repair or replace broken sash lifts
- ☐ Replace loose or missing window putty
- ☐ Free stuck window sashes
- ☐ Lubricate balky windows

WINTER
Time for working indoors

- ☐ Check for leaks around sink rims
- ☐ Replace leaking tub/tile sealant
- ☐ Remove mildew around tub or shower
- ☐ Replace ceramic tile grout
- ☐ Replace loose or broken ceramic tiles
- ☐ Refasten loose towel racks
- ☐ Replace frayed lamp cords
- ☐ Replace defective switches
- ☐ Replace defective receptacles
- ☐ Test and replace faulty GFCIs
- ☐ Replace smoke detector batteries
- ☐ Refasten raised vinyl tile
- ☐ Refasten loose carpet edge
- ☐ Eliminate floor and stair tread squeaks
- ☐ Tighten loose hand rails or balusters
- ☐ Even legs of wobbly chairs
- ☐ Reglue loose chair rungs
- ☐ Replace broken chair rungs
- ☐ Unstick balky drawers
- ☐ Repair loose plaster
- ☐ Fix cracks and holes in plaster
- ☐ Repair popped drywall nails
- ☐ Patch dents and holes in drywall
- ☐ Reglue peeling wallpaper
- ☐ Refasten loose ceiling tiles

INDEX

stopping midcycle, 31
timers, replacing, 31
vents, cleaning, 30
Clothes washers
inlet screens, clogged, 24
inlet valves, replacing,
26–27
jumping, 22
leveling, 22
level switches, replacing, 25
noisy, 23, 26–27
not filling, 26–27
overflowing, 25
slow-filling, 24
snubbers, replacing, 23
winterizing, 28
Cold chisel, 6
Combination square, 3
Compression faucets, repairing,
206
Concrete
chipped steps, 184
cracked, 181
floors, repairing, 181, 182–83
holes in, 182–83
patching, 181, 182–83, 184
railings in, refastening, 185
sidewalk slabs, replacing,
186–87
Coping saw, 5
Countertops
replacing, 42–43
sealing to wall, 44
Crawl-space walls, insulating,
160
Crosscut saw, 4

D

Deadbolts. *See* Locks
Decks
boards, replacing, 171
refinishing, 172

springy, 170
stiffening, 170
swaying, 170
Diagonal-cutting pliers, 15
Dishwashers
float switches, replacing, 21
inlet screens, clogged, 19
inlet valves, replacing, 20
noisy, 20
not filling, 20, 21
overflowing, 21
slow-filling, 19
Disk faucets, repairing, 205
Doorbells
chimes, replacing, 99
switches, replacing, 100
troubleshooting, 98
Doors. *See also* Hinges; Locks;
Thresholds
binding, 52–53, 54
bracing, 57
closet
bifold, adjusting, 58
sliding, adjusting, 59
garage
adjusting, 66
insulating, 156
hollow, patching, 60
insulating, 153, 155
not latching, 69, 70, 71
painting, 76
patio
hard to open and close,
61
latches, replacing, 62
rollers, adjusting, 61
weather strips, replac-
ing, 63
planing, 54
sagging, 56, 57, 58
screens
patching holes in, 73
replacing, in metal door

frames, 75
replacing, in wood door
frames, 74
sagging, 57
turnbuckles, 57
storm, adjusting closer, 72
troubleshooting binding,
52–53
weather-stripping, 155
Door sweeps, installing, 153
Downspouts, replacing, 251
Drains
clogged, 197, 212, 213
hair in, 213, 214
plunger-type, cleaning, 214
pop-up
adjusting, 195
cleaning, 213
shower, unclogging, 212
stopper, adjusting, 195
strainer, replacing, 196
trap, replacing, 198
tub, cleaning, 213, 214
Drawers, stuck, 135
Drill bits, 7
masonry, 7
spade, 7
twist, 7
Drills
electric, 7, 11
manual, 7
Driveways. *See* Blacktop
Dryers. *See* Clothes dryers
Drywall
dents in, 264
holes in, 265, 266, 267
installing new, 267
patching, 264, 265, 266, 267
plugging, 266
popped nails in, 262
split tape, repairing, 263
water damage, repairing,
263

clogged, 250
covering, 250
downspouts, replacing, 251
hanger types, 248–49
holes in, patching, 247
joints, sealing, 246
leaking, 246, 247, 248–49
leveling, 248–49
sagging, 248–49
Gutter screens, installing, 250

H

Hacksaw, 5
Hammers
claw, 8
handles, replacing, 178
mallet, 9
sledge, 9
tack, 8
Hand auger, 14
Handrails, loose
in concrete, 185
wood, 126, 127
Heating and cooling. See Air
conditioners; Ductwork;
Furnaces; Insulation;
Radiators
Hinges
adjusting, bifold door, 58
shimming, 56
tightening, 55
Hoses, leaky, 168–69
Hose bibs, repairing, 210

I

Insert tips, 11
Insulation
attics
access panels, 164
ductwork, 165
floors, 166
building cracks, 159

crawl-space walls, 160
doors, 153, 155, 156
fiberglass, 157, 160, 162, 165
floors, 157
garage doors, 156
sill plates/foundation joints,
158
soffit vents and, 166
water heaters, 162–63
water pipes, 161
windows, 154, 286

K

Keyhole saw, 4
Kitchens. See Countertops; Sinks;
Water filter cartridges, replac-
ing
Knives
putty, 13
utility, 6
Knotty pine, sealing, 297

L

Lamps
cords, replacing, 79
repairing, 80
troubleshooting, 80
Latches. See also Locks
patio door, replacing, 62
strike plates and, 69
Lawn and garden. See Decks;
Fences; Gates; Hoses, leaky;
Hose bibs, repairing; Porch
posts; Tools, garden
Level, carpenter's, 3
Light fixtures. See also Switches
fluorescent
ballasts, replacing, 86
bulbs, replacing, 84
starters, replacing, 85
troubleshooting, 82–83

replacing, 81
Locking pliers, 12
Locks
cylinder, replacing, 67
deadbolt, replacing, 68
mortises, replacing, 68
window sash
adjusting, 280
installing, 281
Long-nose pliers, 15

M

Mallet, 9
Masonry. See Blacktop; Bricks;
Concrete; Mortar joints,
repointing; Stucco
Masonry drill bits, 7
Metal files, 6
Metal flashing, patching, 243
Metal roofs, patching, 242
Metal snips, 6
Mildew, removing, 46
Mortar joints, repointing, 192
Multimeter, 15
Multitester, 15

N

Nails, popped
in clapboard siding, 254
in interior walls, 262
Nail sets, 8
Neon circuit tester, 15
Newel posts, tightening, 126
Notched spreader, 13
Nutdriver, 11

O

Offset screwdriver, 11
Oil furnaces, replacing fuel filter,
144

Outlets. *See* Receptacles
Oven elements, replacing, 35

P

Paintbrushes, 16
    foam, 16
Painting
    ceilings, 277
    doors, 76
    preparation for, 259, 260
    tools for, 16–17
    walls, 276
    windows, 296
Paint pads, 16
Paint rollers, 17
Paint scraper, 17
Paint tray, 17
Paneling
    buckled, 271
    knotty pine, sealing, 297
    loose, 271
    replacing, 272
    tongue and groove board,
      replacing, 273
Patio doors. *See* Doors
Phillips screwdrivers, 11
Phones. *See* Telephones
Picture-hanging wire, installing,
   275
Pipe wrench, 14
Plane, block, 6
Planing, doors, 54
Plaster
    cracked, 259, 260
    holes in, 261
    patching, 259, 260, 261
    sagging ceiling, 258
Pliers
    diagonal-cutting, 15
    groove-joint, 12
    locking, 12
    long-nose, 15

slip-joint, 12
Plugs
    polarized and nonpolarized,
      90
    three-prong, replacing, 91
    two-prong, replacing, 90
Plumbing. *See also* Drains;
   Faucets; Septic systems, main-
   taining; Sinks; Toilets
    tools for, 14
Plunger, 14
Pointing tool, 13
Porch posts
    repairing, 173
    replacing, 174
    rotted, 173
Pry bar, 9
Putty knives, 13

R

Radiators
    bleeding, 143
    cold, 143
Railings. *See* Banisters;
   Handrails, loose
Rake handles, replacing, 179
Ranges
    oven elements, replacing, 35
    surface elements, replacing,
      34
Receptacle tester, 15
Receptacles
    grounded, installing, 97
    Ground Fault Circuit
      Interrupter (GFCI),
      installing, 94–95
    replacing, 93, 96
    switched, replacing, 96
    testing, 92
Refrigerators
    coils, cleaning, 37
    defrost heaters, replacing,
      38

doors not closing, 36
frost-free failure, 38
laboring, 37
leveling, 36
Ripsaw, 4
Roller shades
    adjusting, 289
    rewind too fast, 289
    won't catch, 289
    won't rewind, 289
Roofs
    asphalt shingles
      cracked, 239
      loose, 238, 239
      repairing, 238
      replacing, 239
      torn, 238
    climbing on, 237, 238, 239,
      240, 242, 243, 244
    flashing
      metal, patching, 243
      vent-pipe, replacing,
        244–45
    flat, patching, 241
    leaks
      flashing and, 243
      flat roofs and, 241
      locating, 237
    metal, patching, 242
    pitched, locating leak in, 237
    wood shingles, replacing,
      240
Rotating-ball faucets, repairing,
   203

S

Saber saw, 5
Sash cords, replacing, 282–83
Sash locks
    adjusting, 280
    installing, 281
Sawing techniques, 4